BIBLICAL PASTORS WERE NOT AND ARE NOT CEOS.

✠

James D. Martin

authorHOUSE®

AuthorHouse™
1663 Liberty Drive
Bloomington, IN 47403
www.authorhouse.com
Phone: 1 (800) 839-8640

Published by AuthorHouse 06/01/2020

ISBN: 978-1-7283-6365-3 (sc)
ISBN: 978-1-7283-6364-6 (e)

Library of Congress Control Number: 2020910117

Print information available on the last page.

Preface

The emergence of the pastor Chief Executive Officer (CEO) position in churches today has become widely acceptable in Mega and Meta churches. Recent studies have not explored this issue. David Fisher acknowledges that in the 21st century, being a pastor presents major challenges because it leads to professional and personal identity crisis resulting from secular and ecclesial challenges. Studies have supported the idea that there is the need for church leaders to adopt the secular models of leadership and several noted authors have shown that churches today have become like other organizations that have to market their products. This is a problematic interpretation because leadership in modern churches has gone beyond the biblical and theological definitions of becoming shepherds of their flock and servants of God. In the search for an effective pastoral leadership role, this paper will explore the contemporary definition of pastoral leadership and compare it with what the scriptures say concerning the elders and servants of God assigned the duty of being shepherds of their flock.

This book will further define how pastoral duties are established according to the Biblical models of the Old and New Testament, and contrast those models against contemporary models. An extensive literature review will be presented that will guide us on how the leaders of churches today have attained their professions and how they have to act in contemporary churches. A comparative narrative will be presented to show areas where the church leaders have abandoned the initial intention of God and the foundation and their role as shepherds of the flock. Finally, I will suggest what the leaders in contemporary churches can do to carry out their tasks as servants and shepherds and to form the organic church, which God initially intended.

Acknowledgements

"How blessed is the man who does not walk in the counsel of the wicked, Nor stand in the path of sinners, Nor sit in the seat of scoffers! But his delight is in the law of the Lord, And in His law he meditates day and night. He will be like a tree firmly planted by the streams of water, Which yields its fruit in its season, And its leaf does not wither; And in whatever he does, he prospers." (Ps. 1:1–3, NAS)

I am grateful to God for blessing me with the strength and patience to complete this project. I am also thankful to my family and friends who have prayed for me, encouraged me, and had faith in me as I pursued my dream.

About the Author

James D. (J.D.) Martin believes that Jesus is the Son of God, gave His life for man's sin, rose on the third day, ascended back into heaven, and makes intercession for us at the right hand of the Father. "For God so loved the world that he gave his one and only Son, that whoever believes in him shall not perish but have eternal life." John 3:16, NIV. He holds a Doctorate of Philosophy Degree and a Master of Art Degree in Religious Studies. He is a licensed Minister at Grace Fellowship Church of Milwaukee where he regular preaches and teaches the Word of God. "It was he who gave some to be apostles, some to be prophets, some to be evangelists, and some to be pastors and teachers, to prepare God's people for works of service, so that the body of Christ may be built up until we all reach unity in the faith and in knowledge of the Son of God and become mature, attaining to the whole measure of the fullness of Christ " Ephesians 4:11-12, NIV J.D. loves God, the Church, and his family.

"For the love of money is a root of all kinds of evil. Some people, eager for money, have wandered from the faith and pierced themselves with many griefs." 1st Timothy 6:10, NIV

"He has shown you, O mortal, what is good. And what does the LORD require of you? To act justly and to love mercy and to walk humbly with your God." Micah 6:8, NIV

"Anyone, then, who knows the good he ought to do and doesn't do it, sins." James 4:17, NIV

Contents

Preface v

Acknowledgements.. vii

About the Author ix

Chapter 1: Introduction 1

Statement of the Problem 1

    The Influence of Money.. 2

    Control.. 3

The Seduction of Success (2 Chronicles 26) 7

    True Success Comes Only From the Lord 7

    Success is a great Danger if we do not Guard against

    Pride... 10

Background Information 13

    Pastor as CEO 13

    The Emergence of the Pastor as CEO 14

    Theoretical Basis for the Project....................................17

    The Ministry and Team Theory 20

Literature Review.. 25

    How the Position of Pastor CEO Came Into Being 28

    Secular Understanding of Leadership in Churches................. 29

    Pastoral Leadership of American Pastors between 1900 and

    1980 31

        History of Church Leadership 33

        Management vs. Leadership 34

        Transformational leadership in the Church 35

        The 20th Century Church................................ 39

A Secularization of Modern Day Churches...................... 41

Differentiation Theory and the Secularization 42

Review on Pastoral Leadership as Understood and Defined
Within the Mega Church and Church Growth Literature 46

The Pastor from a Shepherd to a Leader........................... 46

Peter Wagner on the Role of Growth in Churches........... 46

Leadership Development in Christian Literature Genre ... 48

Changing Image in the Ministry................................. 49

Fostering Institutional Change 51

Statement of Limitations... 52

Chapter 2: Survey On Leadership **53**

The Old Testament 53

New Testament.. 57

The Biblical Standard..61

The Body of Christ 61

Charismata 62

Corporate Personality 62

The Roles of Church Leadership 70

Elders 70

Boards 72

Congregational 73

The Role of the Pastor 74

Biblical Role 74

Presbyteros 75

Contemporary Role 81

Godly Leadership 86

A Godly Leader must portray a Servant Leadership
Behavior 87

A Godly Leaders must possess Transparent Integrity 88

A Godly Leaders should portray Godly Characteristics 89

A. Humility-as part of Godly Character.................. 89

B. Love, concern, and compassion-part of
Godly Character 90

C. Steadfastness in trials-part of Godly Character... 91

A Godly Leader is identified by his Faithful Biblical
Teaching..92

    A.   Faithful teaching involves not hiding or
           manipulating difficult/ harsh truth 92

    B.   Faithful teaching involves practically
           applying and helping people to grow in
           their faith. 93

    C.   Faithful biblical teachings must be
           provided both in informal as well as formal
           settings...93

    D.   Faithful biblical teaching requires
           reflecting seriousness about the everlasting
           truths. 94

    E.   Faithful biblical teaching must assert
           that faith and repentance are the core
           requirements for the people who want to
           be right with God. 94

Chapter 3: Cultural Influences On Church Leadership 96

The Contemporary State of the Church 96
The Influence of Culture on Church Leadership 99
    Business Principles...99
    Congregational 103
    Materialism 106
Decline of Religion Thesis.. 109
Evidence That Shows a Reduced Belief in Religion 110
McDonaldization Model and Growth of Churches.....................112
McDonaldization in Modern Day Mega Churches 112
History of Mega Churches..113
    The New Movement of Mega churches....................................114
        Comparisons in Numbers..114
        Target the Population 115
        Staging and Services Productions 116
Differences between Mega Churches of the Past and Present 118
    Mega Churches' Unique Culture 118

Poverty and Affluence 119
Staff Specialization and Finances 120
Denominational Ties 121
Architecture 122
Consequences of Size and the Church Decline 123
The Decline of Mainstream Federation Churches 124
Compromise with the World 125
Danger for Even the Most Godly of Believers 126
Subtlety 126
Wrong Relationships 127
Leads to Disastrous Results 130

Chapter 4: Return To The Scriptural Standard **132**

The Servant Shepherd 132
Offering Protection 133
Spiritually Alert 135
Courage 136
Feeding the Flock 136
Leading the Flock 137
Every Leader is a Servant and Follower 138
The Priesthood of All Believers 143
The Organic Church 146
Mega Churches as Businesses 149
Vision Statement 150
The Spiritual Shopping Center Mall 152
The Product 153
Variety of Worship Styles 153
Availability 24/7 154
Professional Worship Services 154
Competition 156
Competition with Government and Citizens 158
Advertising 160
The Pastor-CEO 161
Church Governance 161
Leadership 162

Characteristics of Quality-Oriented NCD 163
The Components of NCD 165
    Empowering Leadership 165
    Gift-Oriented Ministry 167
    Passionate Spirituality.. 168
    Functional Structures 169
    Inspiring Worship Services 170
    Holistic Small Groups 172
    Need Oriented Evangelism 172
    Loving Relationships 173

Chapter 5:   Conclusion **174**

The Biblical Model for Pastoral Leadership 176
    Old Testament-God referred as Shepherd 176
    Under-Shepherds described in the Old Testament................. 177
    Under-Shepherds described in the New Testament 178
    21st Century Shepherds 179
The Unbiblical Model of Pastoral Ministry 180
Jesus is the Role Model for all Shepherds in 21st Century 180
Primary Qualities of the 21st Century Pastors 183
    Pastoral Care 183
    Church Administration 185
    Preaching.. 186
        Impact and Use of Technology in 21st Century for
        Preaching Purposes 187
    Conclusion 188

List Of Figures..189
Bibliography..191
  Books..191
  Dissertations and Unpublished Works 210
  Articles 211
  Cassette Recordings 214
  Internet/Online..214

✣

Chapter 1

Introduction

Statement of the Problem

In the past several decades, many churches have abandoned the model of leadership practiced in the New Testament in exchange of a corporate-based and consumer structure. The impact of this approach means that most churches are being led by a board, comprised of elders or deacons, where the pastor ends up serving as Chief Executive Officer (CEO) instead of being under the direction of scripture[1] or the vision of God. These pastor CEOs often find themselves under control of forces with no interest in the maintenance of the status quo or the spiritual traditions to work as disciples of Jesus Christ and to fulfill His mission before all other things.[2]

Pastors, who serve as CEOs, through the use of their position, unwarranted elevated status, and by their example of trusting in worldly systems, are leading Christians and seekers of God away from God instead of guiding them to worship God according to the plan that Christ established to build His church. This contemporary worship style glorifies man and worldly methods. It is unscriptural[3] and has serious consequences. All the formulas, strategic planning, mission statements, leadership training, and visionary sermons are not making disciples. Instead, the flock is engaged in a routine of worldly religious activities that do not facilitate

---

[1] 1 Thess. 2:5–12, New Testament. New International Version (NIV)
[2] Matt. 6:19–34.
[3] 1Pet. 5:1–4.

change. After all the effort that is put into weekend services, Bible studies, small groups and outreach events, there is very little, if any, personal or spiritual transformation. As a result, this kind of worship, no matter how appealing to the masses, is devoid of the power of the Holy Spirit. It is not building the Church of God; instead, it is building the church of man. The church of man creates a barrier to the Church of God through its worldly infrastructure, customs and traditions. It is an institution held together by roles and hierarchy, rather than a relational community based on relationships of trust, and servant hood.

The Influence of Money

So, why are pastors deserting the biblical model[4] of pastoring in the shepherd servant model in favor of the CEO model?[5] This question is answered simply in one word—money. Even in the world of churches, the pastors are the owners of wealth and money, and they are the ones who control the congregation. In much the same way as the government that takes people's money and regulates their lives, pastors convince their followers to pay taxes in the form of tithes and offerings. Through this means, many pastors accumulate a lot of wealth as well as manipulate much of what their followers believe.

Why is it that the moneymen control and rule the lives of many people? What are the main reasons that make money and power go together? The issue is that power and money are corrupt entities. Today, there are some protestant churches that are seen as multibillion (dollar) entities with a lot of accumulated wealth, assets, and cash. These are the top leading organizations in society that control the lives, beliefs and thinking of millions of people around the globe. Some preachers in protestant churches earn millions of dollars every year. They have managed to exert great influence and are admired by many people who are convinced that through providing financial support to the church and to their celebrity pastors, they will receive God's blessings. These pastors have earned their celebrity status through media broadcasting that they pay for with the contributions from their church followers. This means that without such

---

[4] See Figure 1.
[5] See Figure 2.

contributions, these celebrity pastors could not afford to be on television or radio broadcasting. As a result of the endless flow of money, these pastors have managed to deceive God seekers and maintain their positions in neon lights. They delude people's thinking that Christ chooses celebrities and millionaires as His disciples; yet, in reality, Christ personally chose people of simple and low status in life to be His disciples. For example, He chose Peter, who was a fisherman, to help him spread the Gospel of God.

In light of this model, several churches have lost their way and have decided that millionaire and multimillionaire pastors are their shepherds and masters. Many believers have acquired various positions and roles in major church organizations with the belief that these massive churches have the true message from God. The churchgoers also believe that, through the doors of these churches, they will earn their salvation and a ticket to heaven. Other churchgoers are carried away by expensive church structures that are attractive to their eyes and will wish to establish their spiritual homes in these churches.

Control

Money is not only an attraction because of what it can buy but a strategy of putting others under control. Pastor CEOs preach to their congregation that pastors like themselves are entitled to their followers' bank accounts and pocketbooks. Many pastor CEOs use this psychological gimmickry to fill their private treasure chests with cash extracted from churchgoers and television viewers. The use of psychological methods has proven to be very effective given the significant number of Christians who are swayed by the convincing pastor CEOs in their pulpits. Because of the great return on investment of this method, these pastor CEOs continue to use this sales technique. The inverse observation of this technique is that if money were not involved, these massive church organizations would not be in existence.

We can infer that Christians would not be under the control and influence of these gigantic churches nor required to give their money to be blessed by the pulpit saleswomen and men. In simple terms, the money principle indicates that if churchgoers stop giving their hard earned money to religious salesmen, their lives would not be under the latter's control. Currently, the benefit of giving money to churches is one sided. The material benefit only goes to the pastor CEOs, who deceive God seekers that they are their human lords, ~~their~~ masters and teachers. These pastor CEO's manipulate their congregations' beliefs and loot their bank account all in the name of Jesus Christ. They convince churchgoers to send in their pledges on a monthly and weekly basis because God, who is the Creator of the universe, is in dire need of money and that the money belongs to God. To many churches, money has become an obsession, and many Christians have been brainwashed that there will be no church without their financial contributions. This approach supports the existence of "non-profit" Christian organizations, and Church Corporations exist that depend on monetary contributions. All pastors live partially or totally on church welfare with few exceptions. This methodology is not in accord with the command of Jesus, who commanded Peter to "feed my sheep." Given the current state of affairs of church leadership, it is apparent that pastor CEOs love the "ministry" because it is a source of free money.

Though most people contribute and make donations to the churches with good intentions, they are not fully informed about the biblical standard[6] for giving and are instead informed on what to believe and not to believe. They are informed that the pastor CEOs, or puppeteers, are experts in issues of spirituality and know God and the Truth. To various worshippers around the world, the church system is viewed to comprise of two classes of worshippers. This means that the pastor CEOs, bishops, pastors, and human priests are viewed as being in an elevated status and considered as "special" in God's eyes. The second class in the church system is the "laity," who is perceived to be the low clones, personal disciples, and lackeys of the "special." This perception is not spiritual because Jesus taught that we all are brethren.[7] In light of this teaching, it is wrong for the church to have class systems where some are viewed as celebrities and others are viewed as pawns of the celebrities. This brings to mind the question: what happened to the biblical command to test[8] all things that come our way? Given the corruption in Churches, this command does not appear to be taken seriously by churchgoers because they readily accept all things that

---

[6] 2 Cor. 9:7.
[7] Matt. 23:8.
[8] 1 John 4:1.

come their way from the pulpit without question. The Bible also teaches Christians to discern[9] spirits so that they know which spirit comes from God and which is from otherworldly forces. However, this teaching and practice is obviously missing from the lives of most churchgoers.

If Christians persist in being ruled over and controlled by professional clergy and continue to provide them financial support, these pastor CEOs will continue their unscriptural pastoral practices. On the other hand, if Christians need Jesus Christ to be their shepherd, counselor, lord, teacher, savior, way, master, truth and life, there is need for them to read His personal teachings in the four Gospels and follow Him. The fact is that God can never be bought. Why then should pastor CEOs deserve to be bought through the church followers' money? If the money is taken away from pastor CEOs, they will disappear. They will not be able to maintain their luxurious lifestyles, not be able to afford media coverage, or pay for other unnecessary programs in the church. Therefore, their actual motive in pastoring is money, control, and power.

In sum, just like any other worldly business enterprise, it is obvious that the protestant churches are under the control of professional clergymen who operate the church as a huge financial business. The scriptures are clear that Jesus Christ never handpicked professional clergy types but rather the uneducated and lowly to act as His representatives. Christ's disciples on earth were simple people such as fishermen and carpenters. Peter, one of Christ's disciples, was an ordinary man who never merchandised the gospel of God or preached with the goal of earning money or becoming a celebrity. The disciples of Jesus Christ never sold their sermons for tithes and offerings, and in the scripture, we do not find that Jesus Christ passed a bucket to take up a collection for ministering to the people.

The West Angeles Church of God is among the largest mega churches in the world. This church has a membership of over 25,000 people. The cathedral has an architectural masterpiece worth $65 million and 5,000 sitting spaces. Many celebrities such as Denzel and Paulette Washington, Samuel and LaTanya Jackson, Ervin "Magic" and Cookie Johnson, Courtney Vance, Angela Bassett, and Stevie Wonder, among others, attend this church. Bishop Charles Blake and his wife, Mae Lawrence, have led the church since 1969. Blake is among the most prominent and

---

[9] Rom. 12:2.

influential pastors in Los Angeles and the United States. His recognition is comparable to T.D. Jakes and Joel Osteen. The debate on whether super mega churches or mega churches are making use of their prestige and power for the goodness of the community or abusing their prestige and power for personal gains is ongoing. Blake opines[10] that he is in agreement with the Holy Scripture; he states that the mega church, when committed to the advancement and the good of the people as its main mandate, can provide and serve resources. These provisions are provided to the community through the mega church's strong organizational and structural strength that exerts influence on the political, social, and economic agendas in the community.

Unlike Blake, most of the mega church pastors' egos, much in the same way as their worldly counterparts, have grown large along with the growth of their congregations. During the 1980s, some of the super mega pastors found themselves in major trouble. Jimmy Swaggart, a prominent pastor, was excommunicated from the church after he committed adultery with prostitutes. Jim Baker, another popular pastor, was charged with twenty-four counts of conspiracy and fraud. He and his accomplice served a five-year jail term. His wife, Tammy Faye, was a prolific shopper and also misused church funds. In the recent past, similar cases about errant pastors have also arisen such as the case of Creflo Dollar, who he allegedly assaulted his daughter over a quarrel about her attending a party. He was charged for child cruelty, family violence, and simple battery.[11]

Another pastor, Eddie Long, also made headlines[12] for allegedly being involved in sexual relationships with men younger than him. Apart from these scandals, opponents who question their ability to manage

[10] Tanya Young Williams, "Bishop Charles Blake Reveals Mega Churches Political Impact and Social Responsibilities," *Huffington Post* (blog), September 4, 2012, accessed June 23, 2013, http://www.huffingtonpost.com/tanya-young-williams/bishop-charles-blake-shar_b_1852150.html.

[11] John Murgatroyd and John Blake, "Police Arrest Georgia Mega church Pastor After Disturbance at Home," *Belief Blog, CNN.com*, June 8, 2012, accessed February 15, 2013,http://religion.blogs.cnn.com/2012/06/08/mega church-pastor-arrested-for-battery/.

[12] Lawsuits: Atlanta pastor coerced males into sex, NBC News, Sept 22, 2010, accessed June 23, 2013Retrieved from http://www.nbcnews.com/id/39297257/ns/us_news-crime_and_courts/t/lawsuits-atlanta-pastor-coerced-males-sex/

multimillion-dollar corporations and their financial worth keenly watch the mega church pastors. Several of these mega church pastors earn annual incomes[13] that exceed $1 million. The problem and effect of modeling the corporate model, which is money, power, and control, is clearly what Jesus Christ warned about.

The Seduction of Success (2 Chronicles 26)

We all want to succeed in our family and personal lives, and we have all heard of successful people, athletes, musicians, movie stars, or businessmen, whose success opened them up to temptations that ruined or even killed them.

The life of King Uzziah illustrates this point. Uzziah succeeded admirably, but his success seduced him into pride; his pride led to a sin that in a few moments nullified years of achievements. Though he reigned for fifty-two years and had many outstanding accomplishments, he was remembered by the sad epitaph, "He is a leper" in 2 Chron. 26:23. Uzziah's life teaches us that the seductive danger of success is pride. His success is described in 2 Chron. 26:1–15; his downfall is described in 2 Chron. 26:16–23.

True Success Comes Only From the Lord

Uzziah was a hard-working, visionary king. However, 2 Chron. 26:5 shows that the source of his success was not his effort or genius, but the Lord: "And he continued to seek God in the days of Zechariah, who had understanding through the vision of God; and as long as he sought the Lord, God prospered him." Uzziah's success was due to seeking God and His Word. The Hebrew word "seek" means literally "to trample under foot." The idea being that when we frequent a place, we beat a path underfoot. To seek the Lord means going to Him for His wisdom and help so often that we wear a path to God.

---

[13] Jaweed Kaleem, "Best Paid Pastors Make Hundreds Of Thousands To Millions Of Dollars Annually," *Huffington Post*, January 19, 2012, accessed June 23, 2013, http://www.huffingtonpost.com/2012/01/19/best-paid-pastors_n_1214043.html.

Uzziah did just that. In Prov. 3:5–6, he followed Solomon's counsel, "Trust in the Lord with all your heart/ and do not lean on your own understanding/ in all your ways acknowledge Him/ and He will make your paths straight." Isaiah, whose calling to ministry began in the year King Uzziah died,[14] chided the people for consulting mediums and spiritists and said, rather, "should not a people consult their God?"[15] Uzziah consulted God.

The source of God's wisdom is His Word. In Uzziah's day, the Bible was not completed. He no doubt had at least the Law of Moses and perhaps Job, the Psalms, and a few other portions of the Old Testament. However, he also had a godly counselor, Zechariah, who had an understanding about the visions of God. Uzziah listened to the counsel of the prophet Zechariah who understood God's Word. So, through God's Word and prayer, Uzziah sought God and God prospered him.

This is the only formula for success and prosperity that matters when we live by seeking God and His wisdom through His Word and prayer. As Psalm 1:1–3 puts it:

> How blessed is the man who does not walk in the counsel of the wicked, nor stand in the path of sinners, nor sit in the seat of scoffers!/ But his delight is in the law of the Lord, and in His law he meditates day and night/ He will be like a tree firmly planted by streams of water, which yields its fruit in its season, and its leaf does not wither; and in whatever he does, he prospers.

Without question, some are successful in the eyes of the world, even the Christian world, but God does not share the same opinion. Others also may be considered insignificant by the world, even by the Christian world, but God considers them eminently successful. So, we must be careful to seek after true success that comes from seeking God through His Word and through prayer. Then, if God grants a measure of success, realize that success can be used for the benefit of the Lord and others.

---

[14] Isa. 6:1.
[15] Isa. 8:19.

Uzziah was a leader of far-reaching vision whose accomplishments included both domestic and foreign projects. He built Eloth and restored it to Judah. Eloth (modern Eilat) was the port city at the southern tip of Israel on what is today called the Gulf of Aqaba. Furthermore, he subdued a number of Philistine cities to the west of Jerusalem and built Israeli cities in their region.[16] He conquered the Arabians and Meunites to the south, and the Ammonites to the east paid him tribute.[17] Uzziah also fortified Jerusalem, thus restoring the defense against the Northern Kingdom which his father had lost.[18] Furthermore, he built towers for the defense of his vast agricultural and livestock holdings in the outlying countryside; Uzziah "loved the soil"[19] and the land prospered under him.

Uzziah also developed a strong army which "could wage war with great power."[20] In addition to the traditional weapons,[21] Uzziah installed the latest military hardware in Jerusalem—great catapults and arrow-shooting devices.[22] As a result, we read twice[23] of his widespread fame.

Whenever God grants that kind of success and fame to a person, it should be used for the Lord and His purpose. Fame is simply an opportunity to tell more people of the greatness of God, so that His name is exalted. It also provides the opening to do more for the Lord's work and for His people to see them established in His ways. George Washington Carver said that the only advantage of fame is that it gives us a platform for service. So, we ought to view any measure of success God gives us as a trust to be managed for His glory and kingdom.

The hinge of Uzziah's story is at the end of 2 Chron. 26:15: "... for he was marvelously helped until he was strong." Uzziah's problem was precisely that—he became strong. Uzziah's success and strength led to his downfall.

---

[16] 2 Chron. 26:6.
[17] Ibid., vv. 7–8.
[18] Ibid., v. 9.
[19] Ibid., v. 10.
[20] Ibid., v. 13.
[21] Ibid., v. 14.
[22] Ibid., v. 15.
[23] Ibid., vv.8,15.

James D. Martin

Success is a great Danger if we do not Guard against Pride

Someone has said that a human being is the only animal that can be patted on the back and his head swells up. Uzziah, like so many pastor CEOs today, started believing his own press clippings, and his pride led to his fall. In one hour, he ruined a prosperous lifetime as a successful king. When Uzziah became strong, his heart was lifted up and that led him to enter the holy place in the temple to offer incense to the Lord. However, the Law of Moses restricted that duty to priests, and Uzziah was not a priest.[24] Only the Messiah Jesus would combine the offices of Priest and King.

We cannot know for sure what Uzziah was thinking when he decided to enter the temple and offer incense. No doubt there would be many reasons and excuses, but the problem was that God had forbidden it. Like another man in the Bible with a similar name, Uzzah,[25] who was struck dead for touching the Ark of the Covenant, Uzziah presumed on the holiness of God. As a result of taking upon himself a task that required holiness, Uzziah was rendered ceremonially unclean for the rest of his life by being struck with leprosy. Here, we should learn that pride is at the heart of all sin.

In Isaiah 14:13–14, the prophet is speaking of the king of Babylon, but most Bible scholars agree that he goes beyond the human king and speaks of Satan's fall: "But you said in your heart, 'I will ascend to heaven; I will raise my throne above the stars of God, and I will sit on the mount of assembly, in the recesses of the north. I will ascend above the heights of the clouds; I will make myself like the Most High.'"

Satan's original sin was pride that led him to exalt himself against God. He dangled the same temptation in front of Eve: "For God knows that when you eat from it your eyes will be opened, and you will be like God, knowing good and evil."[26] That was the beginning of the self-esteem movement, which invariably pulls God down and lifts man up. Satan was implying that God was keeping Eve from realizing her full potential. However, if she would only eat the fruit, she would be fulfilled. Ever since the human race fell into sin, all sin at its core consists of the arrogance of

---

[24] Num. 18:1–7.

[25] 2 Sam. 6:6–7.

[26] Gen. 3:5. New International Version.

saying, "I know better than God and His ways. I don't need to submit to God's authority. I am an authority unto myself. I can be like God."

Nevertheless, scripture is clear: "Pride goes before destruction,/ And a haughty spirit before stumbling;"[27] "God is opposed to the proud, but gives grace to the humble."[28] If we want to avoid being opposed by God and if we want His grace in our lives, we must judge every proud thought and grow in humility.

The closer we draw to God through His Word, the more it confronts our proud, self-reliant nature and drives us to find out all in Christ. Even the Apostle Paul had to be given a thorn in the flesh to keep him from exalting himself.[29] He wrote: "And what do you have that you did not receive? But if you did receive it, why do you boast as if you had not received it?"[30] as well as "Therefore let him who thinks he stands take heed that he does not fall"[31] and "For if anyone thinks he is something when he is nothing, he deceives himself."[32]

How is it that the contemporary church has widely embraced a teaching for which there is absolutely no support in the Bible; that the church should model and market itself in the same manner as secular institutions? Pride is the root and at the heart of all sins.

When Uzziah arrogantly went in to offer incense, Azariah and eighty other priests courageously confronted him.[33] Here, we should learn that pride is revealed by an angry response to godly correction.

There are other marks of pride, but when a person is filled with pride, they react with indignation when a godly person tries to warn or correct them. When an individual becomes as powerful and successful as Uzziah, they start thinking that they are accountable to no one. They feel that their hard work and intelligence is the reason for their success. They stop listening to those who challenge them and gather "yes men" around themselves. Earlier in his career, Uzziah accepted the counsel of the godly

---

[27] Prov. 16:18. New American Standard Bible.

[28] 1 Pet. 5:5.

[29] 2 Cor. 12:7.

[30] 1 Cor. 4:7. World English Bible

[31] 1 Cor. 10:12. New American Standard Bible.

[32] Gal. 6:3. English Standard Version.

[33] 2 Chron. 26:17–18.

Zechariah, but now he angrily rejects the counsel of eighty-one godly priests: "I'm the king! These priests can't tell me what to do!"[34] Ironically, Uzziah sought honor for himself, but these priests tell him plainly, "You have been unfaithful, and you will have no honor from the Lord God."[35] So, Uzziah was angered. Here, we can see that Uzziah failed the test of humility and learned that unjudged pride results in God's discipline.

If Uzziah would have repented on the spot, God probably would have been gracious in restoring him. However, Uzziah did not repent until he realized that he had been struck with leprosy. Then, he realized that God had struck him, so he hastened to get out of the temple, probably so he would not get struck dead.[36] The Lord never healed Uzziah—he remained a leper until he died. He spent his final years living inseparate quarters. He never again worshipped in the house of the Lord.[37] His son had to carry on the daily affairs of the household and kingdom. When Uzziah died, they did not put him in the same tomb with the other kings but buried him in the field nearby, so that they would not defile the tomb. The final comment on his life was: "He is a leper."[38]

God will not share His glory with proud men or women. If believing men or women honor the Lord, the Lord will honor them.[39]However, if they think they are free to disregard God's Word and begin exalting themselves, they will come under God's discipline. The more successful we become, the more it ought to drive us to our knees with the awareness of our own weakness and sin, so that we cling to God alone as our strength and salvation.

---

[34] Ibid., v. 18.

[35] Ibid., v. 18.

[36] Ibid., v.20.

[37] Ibid., v.21.

[38] Ibid., v. 21.

[39] 1 Sam. 2:30.

Background Information

Pastor as CEO

One of the most business-like aspects of the contemporary church is the CEO. The pastor is the CEO, and in today's ministries, that position can be held by a male or a female. These individuals achieve power through charismatic means and are usually very personable and charming. They are extremely influential in making primary decisions that direct the church in every facet of the ministry. Consequently, their personalities can be seen reflected in everything, from the vision statement down to how office activities are carried out at the church on daily basis. These individuals are highly skilled at establishing programs within the church to provide the needs, both social and economic, to its members. They are adept at fundraising, connected politically, and skillful orators, who can present a biblical nexus with their visionary programs and objectives. Pastor CEOs, who are successful at wielding these attributes, have no problem convincing their followers to agree to their demand for six-and seven-figure salaries, perks, and unchecked autonomy. The organizational demands of the programs require worldly bureaucratic operations coupled with a leader, who possesses strong organizational, charismatic, and administrative skill sets. This results in a pastor CEO with an executive board.

The executive board is a governing body of the church, similar to a board in a business. An even distribution of ministerial power appears to be the key goal when these boards are formed. The board is supposed to function and act as a type of check and balance. However, even the best attempts at equal distribution of power end up flawed. The pastor CEO often plays a key role either in choosing those that reside on the board, or in influencing who is chosen for positions on the board. The result is what is termed a "yes board," which is a collection of individuals whose function is to implement the ideas of the pastor, inspire plans, and act as liaisons to the general population of a church. In most cases, it has been observed that the pastor CEO ends up with all of the control. Just like the owner of a business has the final say in all decisions, so does the pastor CEO.

Scott Thumma clearly observed such a phenomenon in his examination[40] of Chapel Hill Harvester, a church that he studied in depth. Drawing from Lyle Schaller,[41] Thumma found that the organizational structures of a successful charismatic leader, centralized power, few checks from external authorities, and inadequate management of leadership training all allow for the possibility of complete pastoral control of a large church body.

Similar to how some large corporations flounder and stocks plunge when a successful CEO resigns, churches also experience great difficulty functioning when the pastor leaves for greener pastures or other reasons. Transition from the presiding pastor to a new pastor is also difficult. Often, the former pastor refuses to relinquish control, leaves, and forms a new church. Some members leave or follow the pastor to his new church or cease to attend a church altogether. Outcomes tend to vary greatly among congregations. Some churches continue to grow as pastoral control goes through transition after transition. Others fall by the wayside, ineffective without the show's leading actor. This transition appears to be more difficult for mega churches because of the large amount of control that these pastors have in their roles as CEOs.

The Emergence of the Pastor as CEO

The emergence of mega churches marked the dawn of an age where the ability to lead appeared higher on the list of job qualifications for pastors than their ability to preach and teach. James Mellado suggests that in recent years, the leadership demands required to manage a complex organization outgrew the capacity of most of the preachers.[42] Most ministers entered the ministry to preach and teach but not to lead. George Barna further indicates that the future of the church largely depends upon the emergence of leaders—not seminary graduates, pastors, or professional clergy, but individuals called by God to lead—who will commit their lives to the

---

[40] Scott Thumma, "The Kingdom, the Power, and the Glory: The Mega Church in Modern American Society" (diss., Emory University, 1996).

[41] Lyle E. Schaller, "Discontinuity and Hope" (Nashville, TN: Abingdon, 1999).

[42] James Mellado, *Willow Creek Community Church* (N.p.: Harvard Business School, 1991), 15.

church and cast God's vision for ministry without "flinching."[43] This new leadership imperative calls pastors into an unfamiliar domain and marks another way that the church is aligning its message with the world.

These mega churches are a direct response to individuals' consumerism mentality, thus each church competes to service the most needs: "the biggest churches offer not only spiritual attractions but such features as movie theaters, weight rooms, saunas, roller rinks, and racquetball courts."[44] In other words, the church adjusts their typical format by including amenities to appeal to the masses, thus adding credence to Peter Berger's[45] idea that for the church to survive it must be marketed. Studies indicate that when the church organization has attained a state where it holds a critical mass of 1,000, the sky is the limit for its financial and organizational potential for further growth through a myriad of dazzling modern insights and technologies.[46] Twenty years ago, such terms as "financial and organizational potential" would have been thought to be heretical when describing the church, but the rhetoric has changed. The difference between secular and sacred has become less definitive than clearer. Management guru Peter Drucker suggests:

> "All institutions, including governments, churches, universities, and so on, will become more interdependent, more market-and customer-driven. Today is a world of infinite choices. With churches, it used to be that you were born into a denomination and stayed there. In the fast-growing pastoral churches, which are the most significant social development in this country, 90 percent of the members were not born into the denomination. So competition in all realms is acute."[47]

---

[43] George Barna, *The Second Coming of the Church* (Nashville: Word Publishing, 1998), 34.

[44] Os Guinness, *Dining with the Devil: The Mega church Movement Flirts with Modernity* (Grand Rapids: Baker Books, 1993), 12.

[45] Peter Berger, *"The Sacred Canopy: Elements for a Sociological Theory of Religion"* (Garden City, NY: Doubleday, 1967).

[46] Os Guinness, *Dining with the Devil*, 12.

[47] Peter Drucker, "The Shape of Things to Come," *Leader to Leader*, no. 1 (Summer 1996): 12–18.

This similar expectation is placed on today's churches in the same way that it is placed on businesses in the marketplace. This result in a situation where churches have to meet the expectations of their "customers," and in so doing, the church leaders have to function just like business leaders in the marketplace.

Bill Hybels embraces this ideology as he believes that as churches continue to grow in size, the pastors will "provide much of what a Chief Executive Officer provides for a for-profit company. These leaders would cast the church's vision, attract people of high state caliber, give them unique gifts, and they will all go in the same direction."[48] The CEO parallel continues into dictating Hybels' salary. In a *Time* magazine article, Hybels explains that he calculated the average salary for non-profit CEOs, but in a move unparalleled in the business community, he placed a self-imposed freeze of $80,000 on his salary.

This business imperative within the church is not limited to Willow Creek. Churches across the nation are hiring clergy and non-clergy alike to serve as their CEOs. For instance, the First Presbyterian Church, located in Winston-Salem, North Carolina, hired Steve Lineberger,[49] a former Sara Lee executive, to serve as their first CEO. Lineberger served as Chief Operating Officer from June 1999 to May 2006. Over the last five years, First Presbyterian Church has added two new services and a plethora of new ministries. As a result, they found it necessary to hire a CEO to lessen the burden on the senior pastor, Russ Mitchell. Much like the marketplace, bigger churches provide an overwhelming amount of competition for smaller churches by offering a more desirable product. In short, due to the pervasive consumerism mentality of Americans, mega churches are flourishing because of their abilities to align their numerous services to meet most of the needs of those attending. As a result of these expanded services, pastors' roles within these churches have shifted from preaching and teaching to leading. Hybels heads the pack of pastors, who see themselves as leaders. A careful study of Hybels' rhetoric reveals that vision casting, empowering, and managing are the three main tenets to

---

[48] Mellado, *Willow Creek Community Church*, 15.

[49] "Steven A. Lineberger," *Bloomberg Businessweek*, n.d., accessed June 23, 2013, http://investing.businessweek.com/research/stocks/people/person.asp?personId=24001424&ticker=KKD.

this post-contemporary leadership imperative that propels Hybels into the role of CEO. Hybels is one of several post contemporary pastors, who through their language and worldly ideology have shifted the traditional head pastoral emphasis from teacher and preacher to CEO. Unfortunately, this approach and their success have become the gold standard for pastors of other churches seeking worldly recognition and status.

Theoretical Basis for the Project

Schaller provides important insight on the context of mega churches. He provides the distinctive issues of mega churches as highlighted below:

1. The common misconception held concerning large congregations are that they enjoy the status of leadership.
2. The larger the congregation, the increased chances of conflict.
3. The larger number of individuals in the group, the more demand they have toward leaders to be the initiators.
4. The larger the congregation, the more importance is given to the need for and in carefully designing internal communication.
5. The larger the congregation, the more temptations lure leaders to focus on other investments rather than on the role, mission, and purpose.
6. The larger the congregation, the more senior ministers have to accept and recognize that they cannot be effective pastors or shepherds to each church member.
7. The larger the congregation, the more institutional pressure is put on senior ministers to place priority on administration and not to spend too much time on pastoral roles with members of the church.
8. A larger church also means that program planning plays a crucial role in the use of both the large group model and the small group model in program development.
9. A bigger congregation also means a greater need for decision-making and organizational structure that emphasizes performance.

10. A bigger congregation also means a great need to prepare and plan every program or event carefully.[50]

The items on the list, among others that have been suggested by Schaller, show the potential pressure that is placed on the pastor CEO. In a church where the corporate model prevails, various things stand out as being relevant. There is the need for the pastor CEO to provide systematic management, administration, and care on these issues for the overall success of the organization. He also has to provide proper care when dealing with other pastoral staff in the church. The critical issue is on the establishment of performance quality and measurement. This administrative burden makes it necessary to have an administrative or executive pastor. There are three main points mentioned by Schaller that have to be taken into consideration. One is on the issue of the "Volunteer Intensive" organization that is mentioned by Hybels. This is an organization where the ministry leaders and servants are involved in the managerial and administrative activities through careful planning.[51] In such an organization, there is the need for intentional placement and development in an administrative-led system. The second is the senior pastor tenure. In such an organization, the credibility and integrity as well as the longevity of the pastor play a critical role in the welfare and health of the assembly. Schaller urges that though there is a lack of evidence to prove that the expansion of program staff and long pastorates will increase the congregation size of the church, there is persuasive data which suggests that it is almost impossible to see a growing congregation that has achieved its growth which was not due to the benefits of a program staff and long pastorate.[52] This is a point that is affirmed by Rick Warren in his book *The Purpose Driven Church*. He says that pastors who have been in the church for a long time have led successful large churches. However, the long pastorate does not guarantee the growth of the church, but constant pastor changes means that the church will never

---

[50] Lyle E. Schaller, *The Multiple Staff and the Larger Church* (Nashville: Abingdon Press, 1980), 17–27.

[51] Bill Hybels, *Creating a Volunteer Intensive Organization*.1997.Willow Creek Association DF9704), Audiocassette.

[52] Schaller, *The Multiple Staff*, 57.

grow.[53] The third issue is that with the growth of churches, pastors are very limited in the provision of direct care to the members of their church. They have to use other people to help them be in touch with their members. This enables pastors to be more like "ranchers", rather than shepherds. Carl George defines this design as a strategy.[54] Moses demonstrates this strategy of cell leadership in the book of Exodus. In chapter 18, Moses practices care in dealing with the people of God as he accepts and implements the advice of his father-in-law Jethro to share his leadership responsibilities with others. The principle of multiplication is also repeated in 2 Tim. 2:2. Lawrence Richards is against this form of leadership; according to him, it is simply a hierarchical model of the Old Testament. This study supports the biblical shepherding model that is enhanced through team-building and humble servant leadership[55] in the organic church.

This means that the support staff, church pastors, and other spiritual leaders have to develop an appropriate pastoral care system. Gary McIntosh presents various best practices concerning congregational size. In a group of 200 members, the pastor can make use of the shepherding model by getting in touch with every individual personally. In a congregation of 400 members, the pastor delegates his role to a volunteer to shepherd all members. In a congregation of 600 members, the pastor's role of a shepherd is transferred to other leaders to be in touch with the members. A congregation of more than 800 members means that the pastor transfers his roles and responsibilities to a pastoral staff to provide for the members.[56]

McIntosh further explores the change in pastoral roles in becoming a corporate model. This is where one moves from a volunteer worker, to a skilled worker, to a lead man, to a supervisor, to middle and top management, then to being the leader of a congregation of more than 800 people. This is when the church pastor has attained the position

---

[53] Rick Warren, *The Purpose Driven Church: Growth Without Compromising Your Message & Mission* (Grand Rapids: Zondervan, 1995), 31.

[54] Carl F. George, *Prepare Your Church for the Future* (Tarrytown: Revell, 1991), 121ff, 40.

[55] Lawrence O. Richards and Clyde Hoeldtke, *A Theology of Church Leadership* (Grand Rapids: Zondervan, 1980), 23, 138–41.

[56] Gary L. McIntosh, *Staff Your Church for Growth: Building Team Ministry in the 21st Century* (Grand Rapids: Baker Books, 2000), 78.

similar to that of a corporate president with 2,000 members.[57] Though this relation may be arbitrary, there is a direct connection in style and size of leadership. According to George, large churches have over 1,000 members, while churches with over 3,000 members are referred to as mega churches. Churches with more than 10,000 members are defined as a meta church.[58]

The Ministry and Team Theory

John Vaughan gave a comment that joining a large church means to be lost in the large crowd. Pastoral care provision has become a strategic issue with the increasing number of congregation members. This is mainly the result of the numerous tasks that need to be shared. The pastor CEO needs to involve other shepherds to ensure that people do not get lost in the crowd. As a church grows in both depth and volume, it will require teamwork and reproduction of leaders. Christian and secular authors agree that leadership development is a primary necessity for successful organizations at all levels. Therefore, the development of effective leaders is one of the core competencies that separate successful organizations from losing organizations.

Growth can take various forms. When an assembly attains its growth as a result of spiritual renewal, it will end up being in need of structure reformation. According to author and pastor Bill Hull, the real work begins after revival. Revival comes with transformations and brings power that brings lasting change.[59] Growth can also occur through spiritual health that is operating in the church through diligent leadership guidance. In addition, with the growth of the church comes the need for leadership development and the need for structure. The failure in senior ministers comes from the lack of establishing team members.[60] This is because the church calls for the need to have cooperative leadership that is committed in developing leaders and adequate infrastructure.

---

[57] Ibid, 79.

[58] George, *Prepare Your Church*, 54.

[59] Bill Hull, *Revival That Reforms: Making It Last* (Grand Rapids: Fleming H. Revell Company, 1998), 11.

[60] W. Steven Brown, *13 Fatal Errors Managers Make and How You Can Aviod Them*, 21st ed. (New York: Berkley Books, 1985), 19–32.

Marketing also plays a critical role in ensuring the sustainability and success of a product. This means that without marketing, a product is likely to fail. For instance, before the 1980s, most Americans did not consider the necessity of having a personal computer. However, given the vision of computer companies, such as IBM, innovators have come up with new technologies that have prospered because of lack of competition. Entrepreneurs like Bill Gates and the late Steve Jobs were successful in acquiring an unadulterated niche for themselves. In their success, Gates has emphasized the importance of developing a need, and then providing the mechanism for fulfilling that need. With time, the needs fluctuate according to the population's desires.

Just like other institutions that need to survive, the church feels pressured to align itself with the plausibility structures that are ever fluctuating. The aim of this alignment is to present itself in a way that fits the desires of the population. These are the needs that are connected together, and the society validates them. Berger suggests that society has to be linked to these needs to establish plausible structures.[61] This means that these structures guide people in determining the issues that are incredible and credible. Plausibility structures in the past have had the least effect in modern churches. These structures are the broad social norms and consensus.

Berger, however, believes that this has changed. In his book *The Sacred Canopy*, he suggests that the church is among the institutions that are currently competing for its allegiance to fit the constituency of human beings. This is because its traditional form lacked effectiveness. Just like all the other institutions, the church has to align itself in order to survive with the plausibility structures that are fluctuating. Through this alignment, an organization positions itself through stimulating the 'consumers' desires on 'purchasing.' This is evidenced in the way the mainline denominations are trying to increase membership via means of providing contemporary services. John Railey says that this happens even when worshipers pass by to attend to services provided by charismatic mega churches.[62]

---

[61] Peter L. Berger and Thomas Luckmann, *The Social Construction of Reality: A Treatise in the Sociology of Knowledge* (New York: Anchor, 1967), 154–55.

[62] John Railey, "Images of Religion Tradition: Face of Mainline Churches No Longer Reflects the Faith of the Fathers" *Winston-Salem Journal*, August 23, 11.

Barna, a marketing and demographic research expert, postulates his premise by saying that as the world prepares itself to join a new century in the ministry, it has to address the inescapable conclusion. This conclusion is that, despite the activity portrayed in thousands of congregations, the American churches are losing their adherents and influences much faster than other large institutions in the country. This can be solved only when there is a radical solution for the Christian churches' revival in the United States that has to be adopted and implemented in the soonest possible time. Without this immediate response, many Americans will fail to meet their spiritual hunger needs and will not be satisfied with what is provided by other faith organizations.[63]

In his book, *Basic Christianity*, prominent theologian John Scott calls upon the modern day pastors to first begin by providing the fundamental Christian message and this message should be presented in competition with other philosophies and religions. This is a point that also confirms that the church is an organization that has to compete for its survival.

As a youth minister, Hybels was among the first ministers to sense this trend and put his thoughts into action. He conducted a thorough research with the hope of finding out the main reasons for the declining number of worshipers attending church services. Hybels' research involved door-to-door interviews throughout Palatine, a suburb of Chicago. An analysis of the interview data revealed that the majority of the respondents felt that church services were lifeless and irrelevant. Others said that the services were predictable and boring, and they felt beaten up after the services and more tired than when they arrived. Others were not happy with supporting these churches in terms of financial support.[64]

With these findings, Hybels and other youth came up with the decision to be the church themselves. They were zealous with the desire to pass the Gospel with sincerity in a way that would appeal to many people. Hybels and his group decided to focus on an audience who had not been attending the church and listened to their needs. They were able to identify the gap that had to be filled in worship services in order to meet the worshippers' needs. This resulted in the development of a new product that has been

---

[63] Barna. *The Second Coming of the Church*, 1.

[64] Lynne Hybels and Bill Hybels, *Rediscovering Church* (Grand Rapids: Zondervan, 1997), 58.

adapting to the needs of the multiple constituents over the years. The church leaders also implemented various Leadership Summits[65] and conferences[66] to help other churches and to provide resources to other churches.[67] As a result of the support, cutting-edge mentality, and initiatives, the Willow Creek Church is perceived as the modern and futuristic church.

Berger and Luckmann suggest that plausibility alignment for modern institutions is a linguistic exercise in that institutions have to legitimize themselves internally and externally according to their constituencies via language.[68] In keeping with this notion, it enables the churches to align with the needs of the population. The churches that have applied the plausibility alignment formulas have grown in size and structure. The number of worshipers in mega churches requires a leadership model that articulates the requirements of its membership. The testimony of most churches is a clear purpose of glorifying God, obeying His commands, and following His mission. God's mission to Christian leaders is to make disciples, mature them, and help them in conducting the same process of discipleship, evangelism, and reproduction. Whether or not the churches utilize this mission statement, they have the mandate to this mission both in theory and practice. Worshipers expect their leaders to direct and support them in this mission. This means that the main influencers and responsibility takers are the senior pastors.

In various multiple staff churches, senior pastors are commonly seen as acceptable icons. There is also the position of the executive pastor, but this position lacks a commonly agreed upon job description. In addition, there is no proof to show that the role of executive pastor is biblically acceptable. The position of a senior pastor has changed mainly because of the large culture. This is in relation to the earlier statement that in a large church of over 800 worshipers, pastors cannot be the shepherds to

---

[65] Leadership Summits are designed to increase the leadership effectiveness of church leaders.

[66] Church Leadership Conferences help church leaders find new ways to fulfill and expand their ministries.

[67] The Willow Creek Association (WCA) was created to assist churches in recruiting key staff or ministry positions but primarily to augment ministry resources in areas of leadership, evangelism, spiritual gifts, small groups, and contemporary music.

[68] Berger and Luckmann, *The Social Construction of Reality*, 201.

every member of the congregation. The senior pastors have to change their emphasis from conducting the work of the ministry such as administering, pastoring, and teaching to delegating the work, so that they can rely on general preaching and vision casting. In so doing, it is essential to recognize that most ministers and churches do not allow the shift of duties for senior pastors because they believe this to be scripturally wrong. According to them, senior pastors should not take the position of CEOs and should not stop the traditional role of being ministers. They also believe that senior pastors should not provide oversight and pastoral care to the whole church at large. This is a responsibility that has to be assigned to others. In real life, it can be difficult, if not impossible, for the pastors to be in touch with every member of the congregation. As a result, the senior pastors must have help from other church leaders to meet the needs of the church. It naturally follows then that there is a need for staff members, the congregation, and the ministry leaders to acknowledge and allow this shift or transition to occur.

Schaller shows that it is possible for mega churches to be accessible and reach youths, the un-churched, singles, and other seekers in a more effective way than smaller churches. The question as to why mega churches allow senior pastors to be less accessible and why they do not allow staff members to have more power compared to the board now arises. In many ways, the duties of these mega church pastors are to unify people, set the vision, and design and implement change, which are responsibilities that are more like a CEO than a shepherd. Many challenges arise from this form of pastor-CEO leadership because it can easily result in pastors, who are not in touch with the spiritual needs of the worshipers. It is necessary to have a macro level form of leadership, but not when the micro level form of pastoral care is neglected. The main challenge for pastors is to find ways to balance between these two levels and to work in equipping their team and staff to minister various needs to the congregation that they cannot manage or address because of other responsibilities. In so doing, pastors will require a strong theological center, humility, and accountability among other things. The literature review section that follows will look into various literature materials that have presented the problem of the pastor as CEO in contemporary churches and in their balancing of a large church leadership.

Literature Review

The main focus and concern in Christian ministry in providing guidance to pastoral ministry has been the struggle for leadership more than the struggle in discerning theology. Barna, in his effort to establish organizational behavior and its impact to the ministry, is convinced that there are a few key strategies to establishing a successful ministry. He goes on to state that leadership is the indispensable characteristic concerning a life-transforming ministry. However, only a few churches have managed to establish the desired form of leadership, and those churches that do not establish the desired form of leadership have little to no impact in the lives of people.[69]

Earlier scholars have largely agreed with Barna's argument for the need of leadership in churches. Robert Dale has explored the issue of leadership as a form of keeping up with the changing focus and growing demands of the population.[70] In support of this perspective, he draws views from the biblical, managerial, and social understanding on leadership. In his arguments, he understands that the changing culture in the society has an impact on leadership.

In his book *Working the Angles*, Eugene Peterson describes current pastoral leaders as being metamorphosed to a shopkeeper's company, in case shops are referred to churches. The leaders of churches in the United States today are concerned with making their customers happy and are focused on how to market themselves and compete with other denominations to increase membership. These church leaders are also concerned with the packaging of goods to make them attractive, and customers are willing to lay out more money for this kind of production. Peterson goes on to describe some church pastors as very good shopkeepers, who can attract a large number of customers, attain financial wealth, as well as attain global recognition. These are the church leaders who are adept in marketing strategies and are preoccupied with franchise success.

---

[69] George Barna, *Today's Pastors: A Revealing Look at What Pastors Are Saying About Themselves, Their Peers, and the Pressures They Face* (Ventura: Regal Books, 1993), 117.

[70] Robert D. Dale, *Pastoral Leadership: A Handbook of Resources for Effective Congregational Leadership* (Nashville: Abingdon Press, 2001), 13.

They are also cognizant about worldly recognition and use media coverage throughout the world.[71]

Roger Heuser and Norman Shawchuck further show that church members enhance this problem with their growing distrust towards church leaders. Leadership in religious organizations has become the center of great skepticism and distrust because many members have been disappointed by their leader's moral failings.[72] Henri Nouwen also explored the issue of moral failings among church leaders, and he says that the moral failures are mainly related to physical and spiritual temptations that they are confronted with as they exercise their leadership roles in the ministry. Nouwen says that these pastors are unaware of how to develop intimate and healthy relationships and have instead chosen control and power.[73]

Alan Nelson, however, states that though it may seem that the topic of leadership calls for Christians to keep pace with secular and business fields, there is little hope in dealing with the leadership crisis that faces the church. The leadership problems that arise are a result of moral failings, lack of skills, and giftedness in leadership skills. The focus in church leadership is that which focuses on pastorate.[74]

A research project on *Leadership Development in the New Millennium*, directed by Gregg Morrison, highlighted that the pastoral leadership nature is a major concern to divinity schools and seminaries whose existence is based on the need to equip ministers for the church that Christ built.[75] On the same note, John McDonald also points out the need to develop strong

[71] Eugene H. Peterson, *Working the Angles: The Shape of Pastoral Integrity* (Grand Rapids: William B. Eerdmans Publishing Company, 1989), 2.

[72] Roger Heuser and Norman Shawchuck, *Leading the Congregation: Caring for Yourself While Serving the People,* Revisedhowarde ed. (Nashville: Abingdon Press, 2010), 8-9.

[73] Henri J.M. Nouwen, *In the Name of Jesus: Reflections On Christian Leadership with Study Guide for Groups and Individuals* (New York: The Crossroad Publishing Company, 2002), 60.

[74] Alan E. Nelson, *Leading Your Ministry: A Moment of Insight is Worth a Lifetime of Experience*, Leadership Insight Series, ed. Herb Miller (Nashville: Abingdon Press, 1996), 46.

[75] Gregg Morrison, "Being a Pastor Today," *Christianity Today*, 5 February 2001, 78–112, accessed September 15, 2013, http://seminarygradschool.com/article/The-Changing-Landscape-of-Pastoral-Leadership.

biblical leaders in the church.[76] Despite this goal, there are numerous doubts related to whether this focus will change in the years to come. Barna also expressed his opinion concerning North American churches. He wondered if these churches would ever adopt the kind of leadership that is necessary to influence the American culture. He blames the lack of pastoral leadership for the failure of church revitalization. According to Barna, the churches' strategy to revitalize the church failed because it already had an assumption that people in the leadership position had the skills and ability to be leaders. He says that in spite of leaders being great people, they lacked the skills expected of them to be leaders.[77]

Given the examination of literature materials on the issue of leadership in churches, one will wonder how various opinions on leadership have shaped the way we understand the pastoral role. Some of the questions include: Is leadership the main role of a pastor only as shown by Barna and other scholars? Is the term "pastor" synonymous with leader? Does the role of a pastor CEO aligned with the biblical standard? Does being an effective pastor also mean that one has to deal with the issue of leadership? If leadership is the main issue in providing effective pastoring, are the models of leadership described in various publications appropriate for effective pastoring? The word "pastor" has been mainly presented to function as an adjective that describes leadership and not a word that describes the essence of church life. The main point remains that leadership in the church has to be different from other forms of leadership outside the church. Therefore, it is essential for the church to engage in finding out the means of enabling leaders to serve in a pastoral role. The role of the pastor CEO then has to be questioned on the basis of whether or not it is pastoral, or has fallen out of Christ's intention when Peter was commanded[78] and reinstated to take care of His sheep.

---

[76] John McDonald, "Teaching Pastors to Lead," *Christianity Today*, 5 February 2001, 80–84, accessed September 15, 2013, http://seminarygradschool.com/article/Teaching-Pastors-to-Lead.

[77] Tim Stafford, "The Third Coming of George Barna," *Christianity Today*, 5 August 2002, 34. accessed September 15, 2013

[78] John 21:16.

James D. Martin

How the Position of Pastor CEO Came Into Being

Nouwen provides insights on the hectic role of pastors in the 1970s. These insights provide a rationale for the reaction for embracing a new style of leadership. Pastors during this time brought a new model of leadership that had successfully been implemented in the business world. Nouwen writes that the form of the earlier church leadership mainly consisted of the "oughts" and "musts" that have been handed down from the leaders. These are the values and customs that the churches had to live by and were perceived as authentic translations from the Lord. Nouwen goes on to state that in reality there is the need to motivate people to attend church, for the youth to be entertained, and for the contributions of money to support various programs. He also sees the need of church leaders to move up in their ranks, earn a good salary, and lead a comfortable life. Therefore, just like any other businessperson, pastors also are busy people and need to be rewarded for their effort.[79]

The clear issue about pastoral leadership is that as pastors embrace the subject matter contained in secular leadership courses, there are certain things that have to be taken into consideration. This means that it may go beyond the set "oughts" and "musts" in order to be successful and effective leaders. This calls for the need to define the pastoral role. Literature materials have postulated that pastoring, besides being related to the understanding of leadership, is also regarded as a role that maintains the status quo.

Carlyle Fielding Stewart III relates that pastors are sometimes viewed as caretakers and managers in some parishes. Pastors work according to a set time and hardly challenge the spirituality of the people of God or move the church towards new spiritual frontiers.[80] Nelson indicates that pastors define themselves as shepherds, and with this image of being caretakers, they have to focus on other activities that affect the ministry. However, Nelson warns that the manager approach, comprising of programs and

---

[79] Henri J. M. Nouwen, *The Way of the Heart*, Reprint ed. (New York: Ballantine Books, 2003), 22.

[80] Carlyle Fielding Stewart III, *The Empowerment Church: Speaking a New Language for Church Growth* (Nashville: Abingdon Press, 2001), 71.

activities, will not succeed in times of crisis when there is the need for acute changes and when there is the need to have a visionary leader.[81]

As a response to the crisis, the question whether leadership should be emphasized as a pastorate calling needs to be answered. What are pastors required to do? If pastoring should be about leadership, what should the leadership look like? In most literature material, leadership is viewed as a solution to the pastoring crisis. In responding to this crisis, the leaders turn to secular understanding and not the theological and biblical informed understanding about leadership.

Secular Understanding of Leadership in Churches

In assessing what is actually meant by being an effective pastor in the church, the majority of the literature examined defined the term "pastor" by using secular sources rather than theological and biblical sources. The secular sources define the role of pastors by comparison with various leadership models rooted in politics, business, psychology, sociology, and military studies. Olan Hendrix credits John Maxwell as being the first person to teach him about leadership principles and Christian Management. He assumes pastoring and leadership as being similar and views that leadership is primarily a success-oriented and pragmatic term, mainly in relation to the task that the leadership principle accomplishes. He views pastoral leadership skills in the same context as those of a vice president, executive director, president, or CEO.[82]

Nelson also makes the same comment in saying that to gain a better understanding in church leadership, it is essential to look beyond the biblical sources. He adds that Christians have not maintained the pace by thinking that the Bible is the only manual on leadership. He warns that the Bible's main goal was not meant to be a leadership text, even when it provides illustrations through stories on the concept of leadership. To Nelson, the Bible talks about leaders and passes the message about their

---

[81] Nelson, *Leading Your Ministry*, cover flap.

[82] John C. Maxwell, *Developing the Leader Within You* (Grand Rapids: Thomas Nelson, 2005), 98.

characteristics to all who desire to lead and excel in their duties. However, it does not give Christians the fine points on the leadership process.[83]

On the same note, Duane Litfin, in his search for a metaphor on the role of a pastor, says that the pastoral role is highly comprehensive compared to the shepherding metaphor, which seems inadequate. This is because it does not touch on all aspects that are expected in a minister's role in the context of a pastoral role into sociological sources so as to find a more comprehensive metaphor.[84]

Based on a sociological framework, leadership is defined as any behavior that assists a group to fulfill its purpose and meet its goal, and a leader is anyone assigned to carry out this behavior. Therefore, the role of the leader is to fulfill an issue that is lacking within the group. According to Litfin, its implication to the pastoral ministry is that it is focused on the maintenance and task that is needed by the church and it has to be managed well. Litfin concludes that the role of a pastor is that of running an organization, which is the church.[85]

In order to provide pastors with a theological paradigm that will help them gain insight on and appreciate the mission of the church, much has to be done in the search for literature beyond ecclesial insights on the issue of christianization when referring to leadership. This has to be a theologically informed activity that focuses on the metaphors and understandings related to the Christian community and scriptures. With this kind of literature, it will be possible to attain foundational premises rather than relying on leadership literature based on social sciences. There is a need for Christian pastors to reflect theologically and biblically, so as to establish how pastoring should be conducted. This is through establishing a different purpose and telos beyond the leadership models seen in the corporate business world.

The pastor metaphor has been defined through the espousal that those individuals who are serious about management and growth will opt to become ranchers and not shepherds.[86] This is through seeking to

---

[83] Nelson, *Leading Your Ministry*, 48.

[84] Duane Litfin, "The Nature of the Pastoral Role: The Leader as Completer", *Bibliotheca Sacra* 139 (January–March 1982): 57. accessed June 26, 2013.

[85] Ibid, 65.

[86] Ibid., 66.

become the pastor CEO or chairman with the responsibility of directing the church organization,[87] and in their efforts to grow the churches they end up adopting the program-oriented mega church.[88] In his study of the Christian leadership crisis, Ernest White relates the CEO model as one that is becoming highly prevalent in most churches. This is whereby the churches have undertaken the corporation ethos, and the mega churches have become the ideal churches.[89]

On the contrary, others have shown that the CEO model is one that dilutes the pastoral role. E. Glenn Wagner says that this model of leadership is more focused on the issue of leading. Rather than dealing with the leadership crisis, it is a model that indicates the crisis of the church as a result of the growing number of Christian dropouts from other churches who have been abused, hurt, and viewed as objects. Wagner continues to say that many pastors are totally dismissed because they do abide by the corporate model.[90] He further says that most churches in North America have forgotten about the essence of doing ministry and being the church.[91] Peterson says that the calling of being a pastor is that of guiding followers on the scripture of God, providing spiritual direction, and through prayer.[92] The pastor is also a shepherd with the responsibility of guiding the flock entrusted upon him. Scripture informs the church leaders to follow the warning of the Lord by surrendering and diminishing their roles as a pastoral calling and shepherds. Ezek. 34:1–10 and Jer. 23:1–4 give prophetic warnings concerning the abuse of the shepherd's role given to church leaders.

Pastoral Leadership of American Pastors between 1900 and 1980

During modern decades, a significant amount of attention has been placed on church leadership by number of authors, carrying out

---

[87] Peterson, *Working the Angles*, 12.

[88] Ibid., 56.

[89] Ernest White, "The Crisis of Christian Leadership", *Review and Expositor* 83, (1989): 549.

[90] E. Glenn Wagner, *Escape from Church, Inc.* (Grand Rapids: Zondervan, 2001), 10.

[91] Ibid.

[92] Peterson, *Working the Angles*, 4.

an important dialogue with the corporate world.[93] Recent literature has brought more focus on organization and internationality of the Church ministry. In this regard, great strides have been made and attempts are continuously being made for making church accessible to followers.[94]

According to David S. Schuller, Merton P. Strommen, and Milo L. Brekke the winds of change started striding during 1960s and 1970s as American pastors were overwhelmed with futility and frustration and the growth movement of church was in complete swing.[95] Several large, mega churches started to emerge and large conference were held in order to share the growth of churches. Irrespective of the method and means, megachurches started to emerge all across the nation, growing out of several spiritual persuasions and denominations.

The extraordinary church growth in the modern period of 60s, 70s and 80s brought a deepening sense that the way church have been practicing in the past would not sustain in future with the growth that is being experienced at present. With the increasing size of the church, there was a major change occurring in the American Protestant churches. While predicting the perceived future of church, Russell Chandler cited:

> "Jim Dethmer, one of the teacher-pastors at Willow Creek Church even predicts that by 2001 many major U.S. cities will support evangelical meta-churches with 100,000 to 300,000 members! But, he says 'They will be incredibly personal (with) deep personal connectedness at the small group level.'
>
> Leadership Network's Robert Buford believes the super church is the coming successor to both the neighborhood church and the para-church organization. The large church, he told Fortune Magazine's reporter, Thomas Stewart, is 'like a shopping mall. It contains all

---

[93] Such as, Anderson, L., *A Church for the 21ˢᵗ Century*; George Barna, *The Habits of Highly Effective Churches*; Berger, Peter L. *A Rumor of Angels*, etc.

[94] Ibid.

[95] David S. Schuller, Merton P. Strommen, and Milo L. Brekke, *Ministry in America*, (San Francisco: Harper & Row Publishers, 1980), 3.

the specialized ministries of para-church groups under one roof."[96]

However, in the middle of all this, some underlying assumptions have penetrated from corporate world into the church environment, which tend to blur the priorities of pastoral leadership and increase the vulnerability of the church.

History of Church Leadership

The history of leadership mainly starts with civilization. Since the existence of man, issues such as influence, work, and dominance have been seen as ways of effectively providing for the society, family, and self.

Leadership has been developed over two centuries now and has been scrutinized in relation to aspects of the work environment, motivation, work, leadership styles, and the follower's response. With time, different theories have been offered that help us to understand the leadership phenomenon. Among these theories, we find the history of leadership. The pursuit of leadership is tied to the concept of influence, leverage and movement.

In the past decade, various theories have come up to explain the topic of leadership. The book *Work in the 21st Century: an Introduction to Industrial and Organizational Psychology* by Frank J. Landy and Jeffrey M. Conte provides a list of some of the traditional theories on leadership developed in the past decade.[97] Some of the theories mentioned are Great Woman/man, trait theory, power approach, behavioral, situation, constituency, scientific management, path-goal charismatic, and servant leader theories. These leadership theories have been developed to explain the phenomena of leadership since time immemorial. These theories have not only explained leadership styles in businesses and organizations but have also impacted church leadership.

---

[96] Russell Chandler, *Racing Toward 2001* (Grand Rapids: Zondervan Publishing House, 1992), 162.

[97] Frank Landy and Jeffrey Conte, *Work in the 21st Century—An Introduction to Industrial and Organizational Psychology, 2004 Publication* (Boston: McGraw-Hill, 2004), 369.

In his book *What Leaders Really Do*, John Kotter defines leadership as a means of developing strategies and vision and the enlightening of individuals behind the proposed strategies. It is also a means of empowering individuals to realize their shared vision despite the obstacles they may face.[98] This definition in relation to church leadership can mean that the dynamic of church leaders is essential because they are the ones to undertake the purpose of the gospel. This purpose is that of guiding the church attendees in true discipleship and saving the lost[99].

Management vs. Leadership

There is a difference between leadership and management, yet students and scholars often confuse the distinction. In his book[100] *Common Sense Leadership,* Roger Fulton distinguishes the two by saying that leadership deals with process and people orientation while management is about result and task orientation.

Kotter, however, defines leadership as the development of strategies, vision, and the alignment of individuals to follow these strategies. People are empowered to achieve the vision despite facing challenges. According to Kotter, management has a clear purpose, which is distinct and important for the attainment of said goals. Management involves ensuring that the organization is operating through staffing, organizing, budgeting, and problem solving.[101] The definitions clearly show that there is a difference between leadership and management, yet both play an important role.

Kotter also emphasizes that leadership behaviors are desired more so than management behaviors. This is because the main force in the attainment of successful change is more a matter of leadership and not management. This statement is especially applicable and true for for-profit organizations in the business world, but it may not be applicable in a non-profit context as is the case of an ecclesiology such as the church. This is

---

[98] John Kotter, "What Leaders Really Do," *Harvard Business* Review 68, no. 3 (1990), 83.

[99] Matt 28:19–20; Luke 19:10.

[100] Roger Fulton, *Common Sense Leadership: a Handbook for Success as a Leader* (Berkeley: Ten Speed Press, 1995), 130.

[101] Kotter, "What Leaders Really Do," 2.

an argument that has been addressed by scholars, including Bob Whitesel and Kent Hunter[102] who have seen the importance of management among church leaders.

Transformational leadership in the Church

Transformational leadership has its roots in charismatic leadership theory, but there is a distinction between a transformational leader and a charismatic church. Charismatic leaderships are the style and personality of a leader. A charismatic church is one that is based on how they express their church gatherings and services. The study of transformational leadership is a concept that affects the academic and business world in their overall application of leadership concepts.

This section examines church leadership style development from the 1900s to the 1980s. During this time, people were frustrated with the church movements and the lack of leaders opting for change. The frustration stemmed from the early church leadership style that maintained the old traditions that had been established. The early church leaders perceived that maintaining the old traditions was an effective way for the church to conduct its *Missio Dei*. *Missio Dei* is a Latin term that means "mission of God." This is a concept that developed over the centuries to become a church movement in fulfilling the mission of God.

Dutch theologian Karl Hartenstein first coined this phrase in 1934. Missio Dei has since then continued to become a conversation that refers to the overall mission of God. John G. Flett states, "He uses God's mission also known as the *missio Dei* because it is a concept that recognizes the connection of the church in the world as being that which can only be answered by God alone. This is a justified mission for it accomplishes the mission of God on earth."[103]

Though the term was coined by Hartenstein and has been adopted in current mission circles, it is a concept that focuses on the history of

---

[102] Bob Whitesel and Kent R. Hunter, *A House Divided: Bridging the Generation Gaps in Your Church* (Nashville: Abingdon Press, 2001), 26-27.

[103] John G. Flett, *The Witness of God: The Trinity, Missio Dei, Karl Barth, and the Nature of Christian Community* (Grand Rapids: William B. Eerdmans Publishing Company, 2010), 4.

theology, especially Karl Barth theology that puts much emphasis on *actio Dei*. The *actio Dei* is a concept that indicates that all human action has to be that which serves the mission of God; it is the participation in God's redemptive world.

The phrase Missio Dei has since then developed and adopted in major mission circles as seen in the 1952 conference. This conference is known as The World Missionary Conference of Willingen, which further made God's own mission, Missio Dei, to be known internationally. This popularity occurred in the discussions on the missions and overall direction of man in carrying out the gospel mandate. Missio Dei has become a term that is commonly accepted for it effectively urges out the reality of the defect and habitual overestimation of the mission actions and achievement of human beings. Missio Dei is based within the heart of an organized church of God. It means the personal actions of God are calling the world to Him. The concept was later encased in the whole horizon of human and divine history.

In church history, there have been many struggles with the overall mission of the church and fulfilling the goal of attaining humanity. This is because many have the notion that Missio Dei was developed as a relief after the realization that the mission of God is not that of human beings. In its proper understanding, Missio Dei as a whole emphasizes that the responsibility of redemption is God's alone and not that of a man. This is a concept that has always guided the leadership of churches. It is the concept that did not define ways that the church could research the Gospel or reaching God's people with the Word. Instead, it is a notion that originates from God Himself, and the efforts of the church and its leaders are to participate within the set plan of God. This means that the presentation of the Gospel, or evangelism, does have an impact on individuals and groups of people to a point of redemption and transformation.[104]

Since the early 1900s, there were various historical movements such as the Church Growth Movement (1960–present), crusade evangelisms (1920s–1960s) and the Sunday school movement (in early 1900s). There were also the church measurement tools such as Patterns of Mission

---

[104] Donald McGavran, *Bridges of God: A Study in the Strategy of Missions* (Eugene: Wipf and Stock Publishers, 2005), 329.

Faithfulness and the Natural Church Development (1990–to date). There is also the Mission movement that is still ongoing, which began in 1985.

In order to understand the issue of church growth and the concept of Missio Dei in guiding church leadership, it is vital to highlight some of the developments and history of the church growth in past centuries. This will enable us to expose the current discussions on ecclesiology on church leadership, church effectiveness, and church growth. The issue on church growth is plagued with confusion because church growth is realized solely in regard to the number of people attending the church. This notion is in sharp contrast with the concept of church growth that mainly focuses on Missio Dei, which is not just about church attendance. This difference helps us to find out how effective the church is to continue with God's mission to the world. Church growth is an aspect that mainly focuses on the effectiveness in the church and mass movement to the world according to God's wish.

Many epistles in the New Testament mainly based their teachings on the effectiveness of the church. For example, Paul helped the church to attain and remain effective through dealing with the challenges faced within the life of the faith group. Paul's examples can be used as a tool to evaluate the effectiveness of the church in identifying the areas that are ineffective or unhealthy and develop ways of improving the church. This goal is found in a commission of 1933 by J. Waskom Picket[105] to undertake a study on mass movements of God in the early 1900s. This similar goal is also seen to be at the center of postmodern or modern analysts of today who aim at finding the effectiveness, validity of mass movements, and growth of churches in the current century.

The earliest studies on church growth and those dealing with the analysis of God's movements are mainly linked to the world of Picket. His main study was an examination of mass movements in people of groups starting in the early 1900s to the 1940s. The thoughts and concepts presented in the books[106] of Pickett are instrumental to Donald McGavran, who is now referred to as the father of church growth movements. The

---

[105] Wikipedia contributors, "J. Waskom Pickett," *Wikipedia, The Free Encyclopedia,* accessed June 30, 2013. http://en.wikipedia.org/wiki/J._Waskom_Pickett.

[106] J. Waskom Pickett, *Christian Mass Movements in India* (New York: The Abingdon Press, 1933), 324.

research and impact of Pickett's work was one that would spur what is now referred to as the Church Growth movement. The work of Pickett starting from 1933 to 1963 shows a shift from the previous two centuries, which had a focus on mission station and colony approach. This work documents the shift towards the movements of people and the undertaking of the growth of churches in a totally new lens. Pickett notes that the concept of church growth has been interchangeably referred to as mass movements and group and revivals movements. In the current church economy, the mega churches can be included in examining the growth of churches and their effectiveness.

Harold D. Hunter showed that there is a need for church leadership to lose their focus on a mission and purpose. He goes on to describe the condition of an unhealthy church by saying:

> The church is a living organism which becomes an institution and an organization. Christians in these institutions end up becoming spectators and preaching becomes an irrelevant part of the church. The Lord's Supper is perceived as being a ritual. The pastor's job is evangelism and spiritual growth and is only viewed to be for Sunday school children. Generally, in this church the spirit of God is frustrated because the growth of this church is not only a matter of seeking the Holy Spirit for help. Instead, it seeks advice from people to find solutions to barriers they face in attaining effective growth.[107]

In the search for renewal, and effectiveness in churches today, Towns and McIntosh present the following challenge:

> "The growth of churches has occurred throughout the era of Christianity. The current day growth of churches is a pressure to the thoughts presented by Gisbertus Voetius (1589–1676), a Dutch missiologist. Voetius belief was that the central goal of his mission was the heathen conversion.

---

[107] Harold D. Hunter, *Spirit Baptism: A Pentecostal Alternative* (Lanham: Wipf and Stock Publishers, 2009), 163.

Biblical Pastors were not and are not CEOs.

His second mission was that of establishing churches and at the highest level glorifying God."[108]

The 20th Century Church

In the years between 1890 and 1940, the church attendance level in the United States was low. Most of the church members were not regular attendees of vicarious sealing, endowment or baptism ceremonies. However, many changes in church practices and doctrines took place that led to an increase in church attendance. Attending church became a vital aspect for faithful membership in churches. There was also the importance of every family attending the church.

The dropping of the law of adoption occurred in 1894, in which members of the church were linked to prominent church leaders. However, with the dropping of this law, members were to find their identity with their ancestors in establishing an unbroken line to their forefathers based on their research finding. In addition, the Churches in the United States in 1894 supported the Genealogical Society of Utah.

These changes in the church practices and doctrines are still supported by faithful church members today. The church leadership encouraged members to carry out their personal research on their ancestral lines. The church leaders also encouraged the members to conduct vicarious ordinances for the people and groups.

By the 19th century, most members of American society were attending church services on a regular basis, but most of them failed to attend church. Additionally, the developing and founding settlements of the 19th century impacted church leadership because the settlements required priesthood holders. This was noted especially with the call of church members all around the world to serve in proselytizing the Mission Dei. The conditions changed, and leadership did not call upon members to observe the right interpretation of the Word of Wisdom[109] on the need to abstain from additive beverages, such as alcohol, tobacco, tea, and coffee.

---

[108] Gary L. McIntosh, *Evaluating the Church Growth Movement: 5 Views,* Counterpoints: Church Life, (Grand Rapids: Zondervan, 2010), 9.

[109] Wikipedia contributors, "Word of Wisdom," *Wikipedia, The Free Encyclopedia,* accessed June, 30, 2013. http://en.wikipedia.org/wiki/Word_of_Wisdom.

However, after 1900, these practices went into major changes, especially due to the measures perceived to constitute full activity in churches. Leaders began to emphasize more on the Word of Wisdom, and by 1921, adherence to the Word of Wisdom was a prerequisite for church attendance. Though the church continued to place emphasis on married men to conduct missions after 1900, it mainly called on the young single priesthood, more than those committed with families.

Furthermore, the church leaders started to pay close attention to the number in attendance at church meetings and to encourage members to attend church meetings as a sign of worthiness. Moreover, leaders regularized meetings of the church that can be held in various times in various wards of the church. After experimenting with different meeting configurations and also on conducting priesthood meetings on weekdays, the church leadership gave instructions to wards to conduct Sacrament meetings. The Sacrament meetings were to be done on Sunday. Church leadership also began writing lessons for priesthood auxiliaries and quorums. The Young Men's Mutual Improvement Association (YMMIA)[110] and Quorums of the Seventy[111] were among the earliest organizations to be assigned lessons. These changes had an impact on the rising percentage of membership attendances to Sacrament meetings ranging from 5% to 15% at the turn of the 20th century. By the 1930s, the percentage had risen to 35%. There was also an increase in auxiliary and priesthood attendance.

In the early 20th century, the leadership of churches began to place more control on the auxiliaries. This shows a slight change from the leadership style of the 19th century that did not accept the challenge of adopting a new design to fit the post-industrial revolutionized society. The 20th century church leaders did not accept the challenge of an institution-based society.

---

[110] Wikipedia contributors, "Young Men (organization)," *Wikipedia, The Free Encyclopedia*, accessed June 30, 2013. http://en.wikipedia.org/wiki/Young_Men_(organization)).

[111] Wikipedia contributors, "Seventy (LDS Church)," *Wikipedia, The Free Encyclopedia*, June 30, 2013. http://en.wikipedia.org/wiki/Quorums_of_the_Seventy.

Biblical Pastors were not and are not CEOs.

A Secularization of Modern Day Churches

Secularization is a concept that is often misunderstood to mean a decline of religion, yet its actual meaning is on the declining religious scope. The emphasis on religious authority is related to the contemporary developments in social theory more than on the religious issues. The concept of secularization develops and draws more on the sociological analysis of religion. Various theoretical and descriptive concepts on secularization have presented new hypotheses to explain the relationship between social and religious movements. These efforts depict the enhanced capacity on the need to investigate and conceptually apprehend the issue of secularization among organizations, societies, and individuals. These efforts have shown that there is a clear connection between sociological and secularization literature.

Secularization is a process through which the traditional practices and beliefs of the church are made to be more non-religious and secular in their nature. Secularization involves the presence of those activities and governments that are not religious and does not represent or codify a specific religion. This change has become the norm in modern day democratic countries. This means that the individuals in such a government can follow any religion they feel like. The government does not specify or impose any specific religious practice on the people. Therefore, secularization means human decisions and activities based on evidence and facts that are unbiased by religious influences. This is associated with the freedom of individuals to be independent in the selection of the norms and values for their lives, leading to the weakening of their religious values. For example, interfaith marriage is viewed as a violation of the Christian code of conduct just like the rest of the world's religion. Owing to the open government system and secular systems, individuals will focus more on establishing the true match with their terms of material expressions such as social economical and educational background similarity and not religious congruity.

Secularization encompasses a wide range of conceptions. It defines the decline of religiosity in society. Secularization is also the decentralization of society and the Word. It is the differentiation of activities, practices, and institutions from religion. Secularization also means the transportation of religious norms to suit those of the world. Finally, it also means the conformity of religion to fit the world. The main causes of secularization are urbanization, industrialization, and some practices and beliefs of Christianity have led to some secularization forms. The central and core thesis of secularization theory is a conceptualization of the societal modernization process as being the emancipation of the secular issues and functional differentiation from the religious concerns. It also means the specialization and diffraction of religion within its religious sphere.

Differentiation Theory and the Secularization

Viewing the modern historical change from the secularization perspective implies viewing reality on the religious perspective. The Differentiation theory[112] is a theory that is related to secularization. Secularization theories have a different view on the perspective of each sphere. These different ions are seen in various spheres such as the formation of modern day states, protestant reformation, modern capitalism growth, and scientific revolution. These developmental spheres acts as carriers of secularization, however, economic development is the only one that impacts on secularization rate. The development of modern science is among the main developments that influence the secularization process. Scientific developments have impacted scientific worldview, in which its assertions have replaced religious worldview. Therefore, the scientific paradigm has replaced the traditional way of thinking. Secularization can best be undertaken as a decline of religious authority scope more than the decline of religion. This understanding is vital to avoid the theoretical cul-de-sacs that are modern day sociology of religious issues.

Religions in modern day societies are social and based on different institutional spheres that are differentiated from religions. Religion based on its concept is understood as being ambiguous. In one view, it is seen as referring to both the differentiated spheres of religious institutions and role to a set of beliefs and values, which are considered by some to provide the social glue vital to counteract the forces of differentiation. The ambiguity

---

[112] Wikipedia contributors, "Differentiation (sociology)," *Wikipedia, The Free Encyclopedia,* accessed July 2, 2013. http://en.wikipedia.org/wiki/Differentiation_(sociology).

is not as a result of social approach to religion, and neither is considered a virtue. The Parsonian social theory[113] has, however, enabled us to think based on this heritage. The differentiation theory is mainly useful for analyzing secularization.

The differential theory mainly gives an attempt to rethink and reevaluate the institutional differentiation process that is vital in the vision of the social system as presented by Parson's. The main theoretical task deals with the separation of the problematic and unsustainable influential diffraction formulation as presented by Parson in his paradigm of evolutionary change. The differentiation theory understands no particular sector as being the primary in having an essential goal in itself for the whole society.

This is a major shift in perspective that properly highlights the conflicting political and contingent nature of relations in various societal institutions and especially among religions to other spheres. Therefore, the society is understood in terms of being an inter institutions system more than the moral community. Within this type of system, religion is best understood as being just like any other institutions or organizational sector. Thus, the church in this society cannot claim to have a necessary functional primacy. The religious sphere may have its domain of occurrences in the place or time as the state, science, or market dictates. At other places and times, religion can circumscribe the possibilities of other spheres. This means that there is no assumed trend, and no contentious notion that religion provides the moral integration that is highly necessary and not proclaim on certain institutions as being dominant and primary more than others. Religion has no privilege in holding this position, and it does not languish in an unprivileged position. Religion holds gelatinized spheres among many other spheres, with an elite goal of increasing or even maintaining control on organizational resources, human actions and other spheres in society.

Religion represents an institutional sphere like many others with its own interests and concerns. The church is perhaps gaining its influence and power, and may at the same time be losing it. Unlike the classical versions of secularization hypothesis, which includes theorization of other

---

[113] Nelson N. Foote, "Parsonian Theory of Family Process: Family, Socialization and Interaction Process," *Sociometry* 19, no. 1 (1956): 40–46, accessed on July 26, 2013 http://www.jstor.org/stable/2786102.

societal spheres (such as science and the state) for increasingly dominating the social life keeping religion at stake, the differentiation theory places a question openly for the investigation. The differentiation theory also opens up a new approach of secularization—one that places religious change and religion in a concrete institutional and historical context. Secularization does occur or not occur as a result of political and social conflicts between various social actors that can reduce religious issues. Karel Dobbelaere pointed out that secularization is acted upon by social actors and at the same time is resisted by others.[114] Religious sphere has its social significance at a specified place and time, and it is the outcome of other conflicts. Explaining and understanding secularization call for the need to address rising conflicting issues. Differentiation theory provides the right context for explaining how religion is to be conceptualized within contemporized society. The modern day differentiated society provides an adequate sociological approach for secularization. This calls for the need to place attention away from resurgence or decline of religion and towards the decreasing or despising religious authority scope.

The impact of secular governments has caused secularism to become more prominent in the west as a result of the advancement of technology and sciences, as well as the prevalence of a multicultural environment. Because of the increase of immigration, there is a high frequency of people coming together with different cultures and religions. This is a change of pattern that is mainly seen in the United States. Matthijs Kalmijn pointed out the increase of inter religious marriage incidence since the early 1920s, and this is attributed to the increasing decline of religious boundaries.[115] The classical sociological theories such as Max Weber, Emile Durkheim, and Karl Marx gave their thoughts that religion in the modern time would reduce in its significance. They believed that religion is an illusion in a fundamental sense. The advocates of various faiths may be persuaded by their beliefs, values, and the rituals they participate in, yet the very religious

---

[114] Karel Dobbelaere, "Secularization: A Multi-Dimensional Concept", *Current Sociology* 29, no. 2 (1981): 30.

[115] Matthijs Kalmijn, "Shifting Boundaries: Trends in Religious and Educational Homogamy," *American Sociological Review* 56, no. 6 (Dec, 1991), 786, accessed September 29, 2013, http://www.jstor.org/stable/2096256.

diversity and the connections they share in society make these claims implausible according to these early thinkers.

In a study by Anthony Giddens, he states that the secularization theory posits that with the advances of society, there is a retreat of religion.[116] This infers that the scientific and intellectual developments have undermined the supernatural, spiritual, paranormal, and superstitious ideas that are part of the legitimacy of religion. Religion, therefore, becomes hollow, surviving on emptiness and becomes obscure. The secularization theory means that as society moves towards its modernity, it becomes more secular and begins to lose its religious importance.

The sociologist's predictions have proven to be true to some extent. Western societies are shifting away from institutionalized religion. There has been a decrease in the number of people attending churches and a lowered rate of funerals, baptisms, and marriages conducted in a religious manner. In religions like Hinduism and Islam, people are following the religious dogmas more than before. This is through the ability to expand their education social sciences to help their understanding of the world and humanity in issues that have been for a long time viewed as being mystical. This leads to a decrease of the supernatural and lowers the rate of being scared of the supernaturals. Kalmijn shows that religious monogamy is decreasing, while educational monogamy is increasing.[117] With increased urbanization, industrialization and secularization in eastern and western societies, religion has been viewed as more of a social identity rather than a representation of the core identity source. This lowering of religious values has made people more concerned with their current life and not the afterlife. Thus, whenever dealing with a marriage decision, religious views do not play a vital role. Marital matching is determined by various factors, such as cultural upbringing, education, financial status, and physiological issues.

---

[116] Anthony Giddens, *Sociology*, 3rd ed. (Cambridge: Polity, 1997), 441.

[117] Kalmijn, "Shifting Boundaries."

James D. Martin

Review on Pastoral Leadership as Understood and Defined Within the Mega Church and Church Growth Literature

This section presents the literature review on how pastoral leadership is understood and defined within the mega churches and church growth literature. Many literatures on mega churches and the church growth movement devote major sections to defining the pastoral role according to leadership responsibilities. An author like Maxwell, who used church contexts to begin his ministries, no longer, speaks about the pastoral ministry. He now makes a living through hosting conferences that are based on leadership principles with the assumption that the principles have relevance to any context, including the way pastors have to implement ministry within church life.[118]

The Pastor from a Shepherd to a Leader

According to most literature, pastors seem to only have a focus on pastoring and not on shepherding. They have accepted a definition of the pastoral role in terms of other dimensions of leadership and have not examined the shepherding aspects and its implications.

Peter Wagner on the Role of Growth in Churches

Wagner is mainly known as the spearhead in speaking about the need for pastoral shifts. He is a professor on church growth and focus on factors that have enabled churches to grow. His conclusion is that the pastor is the main catalytic factor that contributes to the growth of any church. The pastors of these local churches have dynamic leadership traits that they can use to catalyze the church into attaining its growth. He defines the pastoral as being focused on two main aspects. In his definition, he puts emphasis on equipping the laity as a response to charisma that was an active component in the church system. He is, however, against the pastoral model that was part of the equipping movement that emphasize on the servant role played by pastors. This is because the pastor was viewed

---

[118] Maxwell, John C. *Developing the Leader Within You.* (Grand Rapids: Thomas Nelson, 2005), 44, 98.

as an enabler and a synonym of being an initiator rather than a calling. The pastor is also expected to be aggressive and not take leadership as a form of responsibility,[119] thus he redefined the pastoral role as being both an equipper and a leader.

Through this redefinition, Wagner defines an effective pastor as one who instills church growth, who is a leader, and who sets goals to be followed by the congregation. These goals are aligned to God's will but are owned by the people. All members of the congregation are equipped and motivated to carry out their roles in accomplishing set goals.[120] This is a definition that defines a job description that many boards of the church seek in a pastor. In a research project conducted by Robert L. Wilson and Jackson W. Carroll, Wagner says that the pastor is highly demanded for he is the source of strong leadership and is one who makes things to happen, just like an entrepreneur.[121] This clearly shows that Wagner refers to the traditional role of a pastor as one that is passive, and that there is a need to redefine the current pastoral role in order to include engagement as an active form of leadership. Wagner views the shepherding metaphor as being an obstacle to church growth through the way it focuses on church life. He defines a pastor as a shepherd who provides one-to-one relationship and contact with every parishioner. This is, however, a traditional model of defining a pastor. According to Wagner, a pastor is an individual who knows the names of every family member and even the homes of the parishioners. He can also visit the sick, perform baptism, counsel, and attend to funerals and weddings. The pastor can generally enjoy that close family relationship with his followers. However, in defining the new form of a pastoral role, especially leaders of mega churches, Wagner indicates that these pastors are ranchers. He says that a church led by a rancher still needs shepherding of the sheep, but this is not done by the rancher; the rancher assigns this duty to others.[122]

---

[119] Ibid., 75, citing Lyle E. Schaller, *Effective Church Planning* (Nashville: Abingdon Press, 1979), 162.

[120] Ibid., 79.

[121] Ibid., 80, citing Jackson W. Carroll and Robert L. Wilson, *Too Many Pastors? The Clergy Job Market* (New York: Pilgrim Press, 1980), 118.

[122] Peter Wagner, *Your Church Can Grow: Seven Vital Signs of a Health Church* (Glendale: Regal Books, 1976), 55, 57.

Through the definitions given by Wagner, we can access that the pastoral role has shifted from being people-oriented to a more task-oriented role. This presents the question whether this shift engages the mission given by God that calls for the need to adopt a people-oriented form of leadership into embracing a task-oriented one so as to work according to God's telos to humanity. Wagner thinks that this has to happen because he advocates that with the growth of the church, leadership has to change as pastors will be expected to create ecclesiologies that are solidities and not modalities. He says that through ecclesiology, a form of mission-focused solidarity, it will be possible to provide a new paradigm shift that understands the church. Through this solidarity, a task-oriented structure will be formed. Based on this concern on the growth of the church, Wagner presents the decisive question on the people of the church and pastors to take on the characteristic of solidarity. From this argument, we can question the theological views in defining the pastoral role, and whether the fulfillment of God's mission calls for a form of leadership whose main goal is to focus on a ministry that is deeply oriented on the people. Through Wagner's definition, we clearly get the pastoral role redefinition as that which calls for the need to understand the current nature of the church.

Leadership Development in Christian Literature Genre

The growth of church movement in Wagner's redefinition of pastoral role regarding the shift of focus in leadership can be seen in the genre of Christian literature. Christian literature focuses on the role of pastors in helping their congregation to understand the leadership process. In its response to the new awareness on pastoral role, an article in an issue of Christianity Today's *Leadership Journal* gave its practical guidance for church leaders.[123] The organization has also managed to produce a series on leadership such as the Leadership Library and Leaders: Learning Leadership from Some of Christianity's Best. The editor of these volumes, Harold Myra, says that leadership is a paradoxical and puzzling art that demands both attention and vision. It is a process that calls for hardheaded

---

[123] *Leadership Journal* began publication with its first issue in Fall 1980.

and an uncanny intuition analysis. He also says that leadership is for one to standalone and proves an ability to rally other people.[124]

Myra's statement presents the new trend of comments provided by many authors in addressing the pastoral role regarding setting direction and leadership dimensions. Kennon Callahan indicates that pastors have to show strong leadership skills in major planning areas such as programs, personnel, and policy—decisions that determine the future and financial objectives that concern the congregation's outreach and mission.[125]Marvin Thompson, however, argues that the Lutheran Church has not well emphasized the issue of leadership in context of church growth, and he calls for new leadership styles to be implemented within churches. Though he attributes this form of pastoral leadership towards spiritual aspects, he says that leadership growth is a crying need within the Christian community, and that this is a time for leadership.[126]

Changing Image in the Ministry

Heuser and Shawchuck indicate that the shift in pastoral leadership is mainly in consideration of the ministry imagery. For example, Kent Hughes indicates that the pastoral ministry can no longer be viewed through a singular passion; he calls for the need to be concerned with complexity in the pastoral leadership role of coordinating various aspects so as to foster an effective ministry.[127] Paul Cedar similarly relates an effective pastoral leadership as one that involves discerning when to respond and when to lead. This means that leadership is all about taking the initiative and also ensuring that our ears and eyes open to God's will and His people. In addition, pastoral leadership calls for one to be accountable and to continuously test ideas on life experiences and other crucial debates. The

---

[124] Harold Myra, ed., *Leaders: Learning Leadership from Some of Christianity's Best.* TheLeadership Library, (Waco: Word Books, 1987): 7.

[125] Kennon L. Callahan, *Twelve Keys to an Effective Church: Strong, Healthy Congregations Living in the Grace of God*, 2nd ed. (San Francisco: Jossey-Bass, 2010): 45.

[126] Mervin E. Thompson, "Leadership for Growth," Word & World13 (Winter 1993): 25.

[127] Paul Cedar, Kent Hughes, and Ben Patterson, Mastering the Pastoral Role (Portland: Multnomah Press, 1991), 43.

leader has to constantly observe, correct, and be eager to absorb new ideas and information.[128]

Based on the changes and shifts on pastoral role, Heuser and Shawchuck indicate the metaphors of leadership in the Christian sense are often related to the traits of Jesus of being a shepherd and a servant. However, they note that these definitions no longer fit well in modern day practices and understanding of church leadership.[129] Donald E. Messer also supports this reconsideration and reconstruction by stating that the ministry imagery call for the need to revise theological and biblical understandings in the current metaphors that are appropriate to this age. He says that for many past centuries, the symbols of servant, pastor, prophet, priest, and shepherd have been used in the ministry without differentiating them according to their impact and influence on Christian communities in many different cultures. He acknowledges that in the past decade, other secular models have been developed in the ministry, such as administrator, pastoral director, counselor, player coach, enabler, midwife, and professional. Within these new dimensions in the church, he calls upon the need to revise and review these portraits in the ministry and to find new contemporary images that show meaning and motivation.[130]

In addition, Nelson calls for a shift in the pastoral role imagery by stating that the Bible does not provide a clear pastoral model. He says that the current church paradigm is a result of the many years of evolution and tradition. Basic human needs have remained the same, but there is a need to structure the way these needs are met and acknowledge the changes that have taken place since the last 1,900 years.[131] Nelson, therefore, defines a pastor as an individual within great responsibility in the church product and assuring that the effectiveness of the church is within the individual talent of the pastor.

Heuser and Shawchuck view a leader as one who ensures that the right things are done at all times. Warren Bennis and Bert Nanus, in their attempt to explain the shift in the pastoral role from that of management

---

[128] Ibid., 63.

[129] Heuser and Shawchuck, Leading the Congregation, 19.

[130] Donald E. Messer, Contemporary Images of Christian Ministry (Nashville: Abingdon Press, 1989), 14.

[131] Nelson, Leading Your Ministry, 28.

to leadership, portray sharp differences of these to extend. In the focus on attention, a leader operates on spiritual and emotional resources of the church and on its aspirations, commitments, and values. On the contrary, the manager operates based on the physical resources provided by the organization such as human skills, capital, technology, and raw material. In demonstrating the new metaphor for the pastoral ministry that focus on leadership, Heuser and Shawchuck outline six main aspects to define a healthy pastor as needed by growing churches for pastors to carry out their leadership tasks. The characteristics were compiled from interviews they conducted on more than 1,000 large congregations. The main responses from these churches are that they mainly needed directive leadership.[132]

Fostering Institutional Change

Nelson places emphasis on leadership as a main element in the pastoral role. He says that leadership is a relational process where individuals provide special influences over one or more people, who in turn enable the group to pursue the changes that they intend to do. He believes that leaders are supposed to make dynamic changes for them to be considered as effective leaders.[133]

Many other leaders have also expressed the pastoral role in terms of the changes they contribute to the church. George presents the meta church model and shows how these large-sized churches related to church staff and pastoral leadership. He says that these meta church calls for the need to manage leadership development in its structures through organizing leadership and caring formation.[134] Within this organizational context of the meta church, the main role of the pastor is to serve as the CEO. According to George, in large churches in the United States today, the senior pastor's position is that of being the chief executive officer, just like those in the business world. The CEO's role in decision-making is minimal, but the role has a major influence in vision casting.[135]

---

[132] Warren Bennis and Burt Nanus, Leaders: The Strategies for Taking Charge (New York: Harper and Row, 1985), p. 21, cited in Heuser and Shawchuck, 114.

[133] Nelson, Leading Your Ministry, 49.

[134] George, *Prepare Your Church*, 59–60.

[135] Ibid., 185.

On the contrary, Leith Anderson argues for a shift in viewing pastoral leadership from a passive transactional perspective to one that can be characterized by transformational leadership. He describes transactional leaders as consensus implementers who determine the mind of the followers and help them do what they want done. Anderson's main concern with effective leaders is related to negotiating change. The four main characteristics of a transformational leader, as suggested by Anderson, include: one who stays close to action, excelling in the midst of diversity, gets authority from followers, and undertakes initiatives on change.[136]

Statement of Limitations

This survey explores various church and denominational issues that result from the pastor CEO model of leadership. It reflects on contemporary pastoral practices, church leadership, and provides an overview on Old Testament and New Testament concepts of spiritual leaders. It provides a plausible rational basis for why contemporary pastors model CEOs of secular organizations and presents a challenge to pastors to assess their leadership styles and return to biblical standards of leadership. It provides biblical standards for pastors who have abandoned the biblical model of leadership in favor of secular business practices.

---

[136] Leith Anderson, *Dying for Change:An Arresting Look at the New Realities Confronting Churches and Para-Church Ministries* (Minneapolis: Bethany House, 1990), 188–195.

✠

Chapter 2

Survey On Leadership

The Old Testament

The Old Testament focuses greatly on principles of leadership that leaders in the church and other secular settings can learn from. This can be seen in the teachings in Neh. 1:4 where we learn the principle of seeking God's guidance and listening to Him: "When I heard these words, I sat down and wept and mourned for days; and I was fasting and praying before the God of heaven.[137]" This is a principle that calls upon leaders to sit down and ask themselves whether they care to conduct their duties according to God's will. In this process, leaders have to be patient and will eventually listen to God's answer informing them of their duties as leaders. This means that it is vital for leaders to know whether or not they have received a call from God and know what they have been called to do.[138]

Another vital principle we learn in the in the Old Testament is to have God's vision. Just like in Exod. 21–24, the way Moses received confirmation from God through his vision or calling is similar to how the leaders can be assured of the direction that they are to be heading. God also uses other people to give directions of their leadership. It can also be confirmed through the Word of God, direct communication with the Lord, and in life circumstance. In Neh. 2:4–5, Nehemiah also says that

---

[137] Nehemiah 1, New American Standard Bible

[138] Reggie McNeal, *A Work of Heart: Understanding How God Shapes Spiritual Leaders*, Updated ed. (San Francisco: Jossey-Bass, 2011), 98.

he prayed to the heavens to give him an answer to the question asked by the King. His answer was, "Then the king said to me, 'What would you request?' So I prayed to the God of heaven. I said to the king, 'If it pleases the king, and if your servant has found favor before you, send me to Judah, to the city of my fathers' tombs, that I may rebuild it.'" This is the city where the fathers of Nehemiah lived and were buried. This means that for individuals, in order to have peace within themselves, they should first have a sense of direction that is sustained and pardoned by the supreme power. As a result they will feel that they are in the right direction and they will know that God destined them to be in accordance with God's will. This type of faith will give them a sense of calm and strength. This call may be private but would have a public validation.

Leadership is also about sharing the vision. This is when one has heard God's vision and has confirmed it; the leader can share this vision with others. God gives the ability to share this vision with others. This marks the beginning of the true leadership journey. In Neh. 2:17–18, Nehemiah acknowledges the trouble that they faced in Jerusalem, in which the city lies in ruins and its walls and gates have been destroyed by fire. He calls upon his fellow city men to rebuild Jerusalem's walls so that they may no longer be disgraced. He manages to call his people together through God's gracious hand on him and through the commandment from the King. This message clearly defines that leadership is all about having a vision that provides people with guidance. Having a sense of direction gives the church goals to reach in the same way as organizations establish regulations, policies and rules, and charts to gives its members a sense of direction. This means that the true direction of an organization is to build on its vision, and it starts when the leaders believe and accept this direction. Through the leader's vision, they act as role models for others to follow and to respond to this vision.[139]

In an effort to fulfill the mission and vision, leaders should anticipate challenges and oppositions along the way. Through these challenges, they should never lose their focus towards the mission. By anticipating these challenges, it is possible for them to decide before hand how to deal with these challenges rather than wait for them to become an emergency. Neh. 4:15–18 clearly elaborates on how men rebuilt Jerusalem while at the same

---

[139] Maxwell, *Developing the Leaders Around You*, 8.

time protecting themselves from their enemies. While a group was working in rebuilding the walls of Jerusalem, another group was equipped with armor, bows, shields, and spears. There was also a man with a trumpet who stayed with Nehemiah to alert the others at any signs of attack. This teaches that a leader has to have the ability to recognize challenges before they become an emergency. Church leaders who are the spiritual leaders have to welcome conflict as a shaping tool to keep God's will.[140]

Leaders also learn from the Old Testament that it is important to practice humility. This means that, in the leaders' efforts to fulfill their vision and a mission, they must know someone is greater than they are. This one, who is more important than their mission, is God. In Neh. 4:21–23, Nehemiah narrates that everyone had a sense of duty. This teaches that it is vital to forego our selfish interests that make us lose our sense of commitment, humility, and balance.[141]

Good leaders have to reflect on accountability and ensure that their team members are also responsible. Accountability is a vital aspect to leaders because they are held accountable to the lives and all the spiritual and social needs of their followers. This means that leaders should not be the only one to inspire others to be faithful and accountable, but they also need to be faithful and accountable. This will make their followers be able to follow their track records and also ensure people keep up to their promises because failure will cause people to lose their trust in their leaders. Therefore, accountability enables leaders to be role models for others. Nehemiah says that he summoned the priests and made the officials and nobles take the oath of doing as they had stated in their promise. He also kneeled and asked God to take out the possessions and house of anyone who failed to abide by their promise[142].

The Old Testament also provides us with the specific character traits of a leader. One of the traits is the ability to seek good judgments and to be ethically sensitive. This can be seen in 1 Kings 3:9, where it depicts the story of Solomon after he became the king. He first had to seek a discerning heart that would help him govern and to separate the right from wrong.

---

[140] McNeal, *A Work of Heart*, 156.

[141] William Borden, *Living Like Benjamin: Making Dreams Come True* (Bloomington: Author House, 2007), 137.

[142] Nehemiah 5:13, Cambridge Bible for Schools and Colleges

This is considered to be symbolic and shows that becoming ethically sensitive and seeking good judgment skills from God are prerequisites of an effective leader. On the contrary, a leader who does not consider these issues as part of his leadership traits will be involved in scandals and disaster, as we have seen in modern churches.

A leader is also one who gains gradual assumptions and training of his authority as seen in the way Joshua transcended into power in a remarkably smooth way. He succeeded Moses by taking orders from Moses as seen in Exod. 7, and he served as Moses' aid to his work as depicted in Exod. 24. In addition, Num. 14 shows how Joshua managed to face challenges that came his way, and Deut. 34 shows how he later received blessings and a commission as he took up full leadership duties as seen in Josh. 1.

Another quality of a leader is the ability to show restraint when cursed or confronted. This can be seen in the case of David when he was cursed and confronted by Shimei in 2 Sam. 16. David's aide Abishai, upon seeing this, wanted to kill Shimei, but in 2 Sam. 16:11, David told him not to do so but to let him continue cursing him. This shows that leaders can make wise decisions to ignore the wrong done to them.

Good leaders can also tests the integrity of their close associates. This can be seen in the case of Joseph, who tested the integrity of his brothers in Gen. 44, and at the end, Joseph managed to forgive them for mistreating him, as described in Gen. 50. Another vital trait of a leader is courage. This can be seen in Esther 7 when Queen Esther acted in a decisive manner when faced with danger and at the time when the cause was just. She seriously took into consideration the admonition from Mordecai by informing him in Esther 4:14 that his coming to the royal position was at the right time. Good leaders also have compassion toward the poor and the alienated members. This is exemplified in Ruth 2:4 in the way Boaz interacted with his workers and greeted them at any time he had the chance. He was compassionate toward them, and he was not an aloof leader. Good leaders also seek wisdom and ethical sensitivity. They carefully plan for their succession and know when to ignore the wrongs done against them. This clearly shows that the actions of a leader are a valuable tool that enables the casting of a vision and staying on the right track.[143] Leaders are responsible for directing people to the right as they are the one who understand and know which way to go.[144]

New Testament

Paul's greatest letter to the Church, the Book of Ephesians clearly shows the purpose of God on leadership. His message in Eph. 4:1–20 is that the gifts of leadership are created in mature communities that proclaim and perform the news of redeeming the lost world. God's mission is reaching the world and making disciples. He says that disciples should be like their masters. The metaphor on the new and old wines skin clearly elaborates on leadership structure that has to be adaptable.[145]

The New Testament also shows that leadership is not all about the measurement of success through wealth, position, or church growth in terms of numbers. Instead, discipleship has to focus on specific outcomes and practices. Discipleship is also based on Christological principles that are character-based and kingdom-centered. The orientation of leadership is based around the Cross and Incarnation, sacrifice and love, and the community.

The word leaders in the New Testament are mentioned four times in relation to Christians. In Matt. 23:10, leaders are mentioned in how Jesus spoke to his disciples and the multitude. Jesus informs them that the Pharisees and Scribes have sat at the chair of Moses, and they are responsible for telling them what they should observe and do. However, these leaders do not follow their creed because they do not obey what they tell people to obey. They also place a huge burden on the shoulders of them, which they themselves are not willing to move. The actions of the Pharisees and the Scribes are only aimed at being seen by men through lengthening the tassels of their clothing and broadening their phylacteries. These leaders also adore and desire for places of honor at the synagogues seats and in banquets. They also love respectful greetings and being called

---

[143] McNeal, *A Work of Heart*, 169.

[144] Carl Tuchy Palmieri, *Satisfying Success: And the Ways to Achieve It* (BookSurge Publishing, 2009), 21.

[145] Howard A. Snyder, *The Problem of Wine Skins: Church Structure in a Technological Age* (Downers Grove: Intervarsity Press, 1975), 165.

Rabbi by men. Jesus warns the multitudes against worshiping these early leaders because they are all equal and no one on earth is the Father. This is because there is only one Father seated at the throne in heaven, who is God the Almighty. There is also one leader who is Jesus Christ. In Matt. 23: 1–12, Jesus continues to say that those who are the greatest in the eyes of men are the servants, for whoever exalts himself will be humbled, and one who is humble will be exalted.

In addition, Matt. 23:10 make use of the Greek word *kathegetes* to mean leaders or guide. This is the word that is only used in Matt. 23:10 and not anywhere else in the books of the New Testament because Jesus is referring to his disciples who obeyed what He told them. Jesus' message to these disciples is that they should not allow anyone to refer to them as leaders or Rabbi and warns against the use of these titles associated with teaching. Jesus informs us that God is the only one who deserves to be referred to when using these terms. He informs His disciples that they are all brothers and sisters; therefore, equal in the eyes of God because they all belong to one family. Jesus was quick to point out that Peter is not their leader but a servant, and the servant is the one who is great amongst them. Therefore, the greatest one among people is not a leader but the servants.

The commandment of Jesus is that His disciples should refrain from receiving titles that show clear-cut distinctions amongst themselves because these titles imply that they have control and authority in the conduct and opinions of others. The titles also signify that they should be acknowledged as superiors. This is a very powerful message that most Church leaders of today should acknowledge. The Scriptures and the Word of God clearly state that church leaders have to be servants and not be referred to as leaders, pastors, CEOs, Rabbis, or Fathers because this shows the congregation that they are more superior that anyone of them. The New Testament clearly shows that no one should be referred to through special names, such as Reverend Peter, Minister John, Pastor Paul, or Priest James.

The New Testament writers did not refer to themselves using titles that are used today. In Rom 1:1, Paul refers to himself as an apostle or the bond slave of Jesus Christ. In James 1:1, James is also referred to as a bond slave of the Lord Jesus and God. In 2 Pet. 1:1, Simon Peter is an apostle and bond slave of Jesus Christ. Jude is also a bond slave to Christ the Lord as seen in Jude 1:1. In the Revelation of Jesus Christ, God assigned Him with the duty of showing His bond slaves on the things that will happen, and He communicated and sent this message through His angel to John, one of His bond slaves as depicted in Rev. 1:1. These examples clearly show that the writers of the New Testament acknowledged that they were the authors of their life and referred to themselves as bondservants and bond slaves of God. It is also vital to note that the people of God are referred to as the bond slaves, as is stated in Rev. 1:1, to show they had given up themselves to become slaves of God to work as per God's will and not according to their individual interest. Bond slave, therefore, refers to absolute submission to God as their Master, who is fully committed and loves Him with all their heart.

In Luke 22:13–30, we see that Jesus is informing His disciples about how one of them will betray Him. On hearing this, the disciples began to discuss among themselves who among them would do such a thing. They also disputed on who among them would be the greatest. Jesus replied that the kings of the Gentiles exercised lordship over them, and those with authority more than them are offered to as the benefactors. However, this is not the case with His disciples because the one considered as the greatest among them is the youngest and a servant instead of a leader. In Luke 22:13–30, Jesus continues to tell that this definition of the greatest one is the one who serves.

In Luke 22:26, the Greek word *hegeomai* as a verb, is used to mean guide or lead. *Servant* is also a Greek word that means one who serves. The New Testament clearly shows that the actions of leadership are a biblical concept, and the freedom of Christ shows that any person of God has the ability to lead. Leading is a role of serving others through showing care and love to others. This means that a person is not specially described as a leader or a unique person of God. This is because there is only one leader who is Jesus Christ. Christianity today is highly obsessed with being leaders or with the leaders of groups, congregations, and movements more than being the servants of others or the followers of Jesus.

A leader is defined in the English dictionary as a person who leads or occupies a forefront or first position.[146] We relate this term to a person in authority and in charge. God's intention for man was not to appoint one to

---

[146] Leader. *Oxford Dictionaries-language matters, OUP*, accessed September 29, 2013, http://www.oxforddictionaries.com/definition/american_english/leader

be in charge because he was already the ruler of the world. This means that we lose our freedom and equality in our daily lives when we exalt ourselves as leaders or other people claiming to be leaders, yet we should only exalt Christ alone. We have failed to humble ourselves by referring to ourselves as "servant leader," and this makes us ignore the commandment given by God against putting ourselves in higher positions than others.

Jesus referred to himself as a true leader, but He saw His function on earth as being that of serving the people of God. Therefore, the message here is that we need servants and not servant leaders. Many leaders are not against being servant, but they hate to be treated like servants. This can be seen in the bible where Jesus cleaned His disciple's feet. He humbled himself and was ready to be crucified on the cross to save man from sin. This is an example that the church servants of today have not practiced. The example that Jesus showed us has very deep meaning. Jesus did not go around the early cities calling Himself Christ Jesus or Messiah Jesus. There are many instances where we see Jesus being discrete about his identity. In John 4:25–26, a woman spoke to Jesus telling Him that when the Messiah comes, He will unveil all things to them. Jesus replied, "I who speak to you am He." In another instance in Luke 22:70, Jesus is asked if He is actually the Son of God. Jesus replies to them, "Yes I am."[147] In Mark 15:2, Pilate also asked Jesus if He was the King of the Jews, and he replied by saying, "It is as you say."

Being referred to as a leader or other religious titles is problematic because it allows one to be viewed as being greater than others, yet all children of God are equal and all fall under the same family of God that is united by and in Jesus Christ. There is nothing like being a servant leader because it may mean first among equals, yet this beats logic. The definitions such as prophets, leaders, pastor CEOs, priests, and bishops show that the church elders are above the rest of the congregation members. The Bible clearly shows that every follower of Christ lives within the same spirit given by Jesus Christ. The exaltation of men through the use of titles is disarming and discouraging. God's intention for leaders is for them to be servants because He is the only one who is the Leader, and all of humanity is supposed to act as brothers and sisters.

---

[147] Luke 22:70, New American Standard.

The Biblical Standard

Various studies have used the biblical perspective in defining leadership. This is with the aim of redefining the present understanding of pastoring and on pastoral leadership without diminishing the pastoral role as a main concern in the maintenance of the status quo.

The Body of Christ

Paul used the body of Christ metaphor in several ways:

1. In 1 Cor. 12:27, the metaphor refers to a local congregation.
2. In Rom. 12:4–5 and 16:3–15, the metaphor refers to Christians who are not necessarily members of the same congregation.
3. In 1 Cor. 12:12–13, the metaphor refers to a wider group possibly inclusive of all believers in Christ.

Regardless of the application, in 1 Cor. 12:21, it is clear that Paul sets the idea that every person within the soma is important and necessary: "And the eye cannot say to the hand, 'I have no need of you,' nor again the head to the feet, 'I have no need of you; or again the head to the feet, I have no need of you.'" Every person within the body of Christ possesses a unique gift that is vital for the body's wellbeing and health, yet not one gift is more important than any other.

Pastors of a church are no more important than the maintenance personnel. They simply have different gifts and serve different functions. This would become readily apparent if the maintenance personnel failed to perform their functions because over a period of time, the church and the facilities would fall into disrepair. Similarly, if pastors failed to perform their functions, the spiritual life of the church would fall into disrepair. The point is this: There is no hierarchy within the kingdom of God, and there should be no hierarchy within the church. Each person is important though each serves a different function.

However, there is often a disconnection between theology and praxis when it comes to giftedness within the church. Pastors may have a special parking space near the door, while others are forced to park in less privileged spaces. Pulpits in some sanctuaries are lofty and can send the message that the proclamation of the Word is more important than other elements of the service that are delivered from less lofty spaces. In short, scripture may speak of equality of persons and interdependence of gifts, yet churches may send other messages that often are quite subtle.

Charismata

In his first letter to the church at Corinth in 1 Cor. 12, Paul says, "Now there are different gifts (charismata), but the same Spirit[148]. There are also different ministries but all serve the same God.[149] To each person the manifestation of the Spirit is given for the benefit of all.[150]" Paul says there are different charismata, different *diakonia* (services or ministries), and different *energema* (activities), but one God. The charismata, *diakonia*, and *energema* are given for the glory of God and for the service of God's kingdom, not for the glorification of one or more gifted persons.

Charisma, which is derived from charismata, is currently used quite differently compared to the first century. Corporations, both for-profit and not-for-profit, seek charismatic persons who can generate business, inspire employees, and be the public face of the corporation. One only need read a few ads for churches seeking pastors to find that many churches are searching for the rare charismatic type who can do much the same for the church that the charismatic leader can do for a business. Yet, the biblical understanding of charisma is that everyone possesses it. It is not in short supply. It is plentiful in the community of faith.

Corporate Personality

Hebrew theology had a concept of "corporate personality" where one person would incorporate into himself those persons represented. For example, according to Rom. 5, sin came into the world through one man and that the gift of the grace of God through one man. In a similar way, Queen Esther metaphysically and spiritually incorporates into herself the

---

[148] 1 Cor. 12:4, NET Bible.
[149] 1 Cor. 12:5, New American Standard Bible.
[150] 1 Cor. 12:7, NET Bible.

Hebrews who would have experienced genocide were it not for her courage. As such, the notion may not have been a foreign concept for Paul's intended audience.

Perhaps the first experience of the corporate personality occurred when the Hebrews crossed the Red Sea and then entered the wilderness. Through the waters of the sea, they were "baptized" new people—an elected, covenant people, who became more than a loose federation of tribes. This experience did not broach the notion of one's individual experience before the Lord, rather to one's life as it was interconnected and intertwined with other elect persons. Manna in the morning and quail in the evening did not depend on one's individual piety or one's personal relationship with YHWH, but rather on YHWH's promise of provision to the elect and the fulfillment of that promise.

Each person, regardless of gender, age, or education, possesses gifts to serve Christ's Church. The service is not for the glorification of self-satisfaction of the individual, but for the good of the faith community. In most churches today, pastors are the fundamental figures within the church who are met with praise, accolades, and reliance upon to dispel the Word of God to the masses. Pastors are most often at the top of the hierarchical ladder or are positioned as the main focal figure to render out theological interpretations within the church institution. They are often trained and graduated as professionals from seminaries and have met the criteria or qualifications to maintain their position. As a result, the pastoral office is a coveted position desired by most Christians who feel they have been called by God to feed His sheep.

What may come as a surprise is that the pastoral office in the Early Church looks quite different than the pastoral office in the churches of today. Jesus and His teachings were the main focus of the Early Church. However, the main focus of the contemporary church today is based on individuals and their own agendas. The facts of history and Scriptural context serve as evidence that this is the truth.

There are some important things to consider from the only singular verse that appears in the New Testament in Eph. 4:11: "And He gave some as apostles, and some as prophets; and some as evangelists, and some as pastors and teachers." The word "pastor" is used in plural form, which means that there is no Scriptural evidence that there was a singular pastoral practice in the Early Church. "Pastor" is the Latin word for shepherd, and the Greek word for "pastors" is rendered as *poimenas,* which also means shepherds. This would mean that a pastor is not a professional title but a metaphor for one of the many functions of the church. A shepherd is a person who cares for and nurtures the people of God but not within the context of a professional hierarchical title. Upon closer inspection of Eph. 4:11, it appears that man has added to and distorted the true definition, description, and function of a pastor, which has created the office of the head or senior pastor in the institutionalized churches of today.

The man-made idea of a prominent head pastor comes from a desire of people to have someone revered to bring them to God, someone who is specially trained and is to stand out from amongst the crowd. The following verses from Num. 11:26–29 give an example of Moses opposing hierarchical or "special" positions that would suppress all of God's people from using their gifts in His service:

> But two men had remained in the camp; the name of the one was Eldad, and the name of the other Medad. And the spirit rested upon them (now they were among those who had been registered, but had not gone out of the tent), and they prophesied in the camp. So a young man ran and told Moses and said "Eldad and Medad are prophesying in the camp." Then Joshua the son of Nun, the attendant of Moses from his youth, said, "Moses, my lord, restrain them." But Moses said to him, "Are you jealous for my sake? Would that all the LORD'S people were prophets, that the LORD would put HIS SPIRIT upon them!"

A very good example of domineering leadership presented in the New Testament is of Diotrephes. In 3 John 9–10, John states:

> "I wrote something to the church; but Diotrephes, who loves to be the first among them, does not accept what we say. For this reason, if I come, I will call attention to his deeds which he does, unjustly accusing us with wicked words; and not satisfied with this, he himself does

not receive the brethren, either, and he forbids those who desire to do so and puts them out of the church."

In the book of Rev. 2:6, John-the apostle wrote under a prophetic spirit to the Churches of Ephesus and Pergamum. While opposing the idea of making distinct hierarchical classes of people within the church, who are considered themselves as powerful by lording themselves over others, Jesus Christ who was against Nicolaitans, which in Greek means, "conquering the people" stated that "Yet this you do have, that you hate the deeds of the Nicolaitans, which I also hate."[151]

The application and structure (see Figure 2) of the pastoral office in our western society is not based on Biblical concepts and standards (see Figure 1), rather based on man-made system that is a distortion of the gift given by the God. This means that today's pastoral offices have taken the form of corporate organization, where pastors instead of acting as shepherds, they act as CEOs of the organization. The early church was solely led by the headship of Jesus Christ, where all men were considered to be equal and recognized His body. People used to be recognized by the level of their spiritual involvement and maturity, rather than by their position or hierarchical exclusivity. The apostles never used to reside in one place, but were temporal as *church planters*, who moved to places where they were called by God to oversee for a short time period.

---

[151] Rev. 2:6, New American Standard Bible.

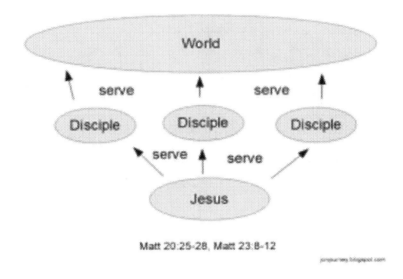

Matt 20:25-28, Matt 23:8-12

Figure 1: Early Church Scriptural Structure.
Source: planksandnails.hubpages.com [152]

This type of deviation from the biblical standard based pastoral office can be traced back to Ignatius of Antioch (A.D. 35–107) and the role performed by bishop. The bishop was in total power and authority and required complete obedience in the church. During the third century, Cyprian of Carthage started making more distinct classification among Christians giving them the terms of laity and clergy. He was a pagan speaker, who turned as Christian, and did not abandon the traditions of pagans, instead incorporated them into the overall system. Eventually, the role of bishop evolved into the head of the church, and the delegated responsibilities were forwarded to the presbyter. Later, the presbyter transformed into the Catholic priest with the broadening of the hierarchical structure of the church and pastoral office.

By the fourth century, another position was taken by deacons under the presbyters and under them were the laymen. By the time the Protestant Reformation occurred in the sixteenth century, lots of questions were

---

[152] The Pastoral Office of the Modern Church is not Biblical. (Hub pages, 2014), accessed on October 2, 2013, http://planksandnails.hubpages.com/hub/The-Pastoral-Office-is-not-Biblical

raised related to the Catholic Church practices. As a result the priesthood and the bishop's office were reduced to the presbyter. Instead of raising questions about the status classification or division between laity and clergy, the Protestants incorporated these divisions into their own classification system. They divided the people into the one who must be "ordained" and who are "special" and "called" into the ministry. Moreover, there is no difference found between the duties performed by the Catholic priest and a Protestant pastor except of the slight reformation in the office and hierarchical structure.

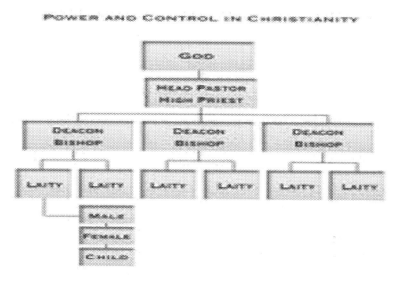

Figure 2: Contemporary Secular Church Structure

Source: planksandnails.hubpages.com[153]

The biblical standard of having a church office among the participatory body has significantly transformed into a ruling of single pastor (*sola pastora*). Similarly, the bishop was given the status where all the authority and power for him was absolute. This means that the bishop was in complete power of making decisions alone. It was stated by Ignatius:

---

[153] Ibid.

"He that honors the bishop is honored of God."[154] Fallen men are always seeking to have someone who would mediate a connection between them and God, for which they look up to bishops. An example of this can be observed in Exodus when the Israelites were seeing Moses' help to mediate everything for them. In modern scenario, it is observed that pastors have taken similar role and conducts everything from marriages, baptism, and sermons, controlling influence over various other activities within the institutional church.

This hierarchical system penetrated the church due to the influential cultural impact of Greco-Roman. The church, these days, have turned into an institution where official people do their ministry. Figure 1 demonstrated the true picture of Scriptural church, which was led by the Holy spirit, and shared and functioned by all believers, but has soon become the past. As observed in Figure 2, the pagan organizational pattern/ structure have penetrated and become the backbone of what is known as modern church hierarchy.

A true believer of Jesus Christ must have faith and understand that God has sanctified how a person should do in everyday life; therefore, there is no for any higher person to call into the ministry against the worldly work and actions. The dichotomy of deciding what is "worldly" and what is "scared", is a concept borrowed from pagan. Furthermore, there are no grounds for ordaining spiritual elitism since all believers and followers have the discernment from God to identify the ones specially gifted by God. In the early church, the term "ordain" was not used in context of putting an official title, rather it was used as an affirmation of the gift given by God and the character of a person that is recognized. It was considered to be a blessing related to the function, not a custom. Ordination into church office has stemmed from pagans traditions, which involves empowering individual through divine flow for becoming honorable, separated, and vulnerable. It is considered to be an incorporation of Old testament priesthood with Greek hierarchy. One the contrary, the people part of early church did not consider themselves above each other, serving each other in humility and humanity.

---

[154] Viola, F. and Barna. G. Pagan Christianity?: Exploring the Roots of Our Church Practices. (Tyndale House Publishers, Inc.2010). 111 accessed on October 2, 2013

Biblical Pastors were not and are not CEOs.

As is written in 1 Pet. 5:2–3: "Shepherd the flock of God among you, exercising oversight not under compulsion, but voluntarily, according to the will of God; and not for sordid gain, but with eagerness; nor yet as lording it over those allotted to your charge, but proving to be examples to the flock." Thus, it is not mentioned anywhere in the New Testament, where marriage, baptizing, preaching, and so on were found to be specifically limited to the people with "special" authority and power. Every Christian has immediate access to God and a true church is a set of believers, who tend to share the Word of God with each other, rather than communicated by single paid mediator to a passive audience without any two-way interaction.

According to John Calvin, "The pastoral office is necessary to preserve the church on earth in a greater way than the sun, food, and drink are necessary to nourish and sustain the present life.[155]" It is clear that the majority of the churches have adopte Calvin's model of the church, but it needs to be understood that the model is in no way shape, or form similar to the model that was developed and implemented by the apostles in the early church. Both the Protestant and Catholic practice performed by church are built on the same man-made traditions and humanistic ideologies. The structure of modern pastoral office has become an obstacle for the true function of the church. True functional believers of Jesus Christ are not suppose to just listen passively to the very "Words of God" that are spewed by pastorals from the platform every Sunday morning.

The Greek word for minister is *diakonos*, which means servant. It has incorrectly become synonyms with pastor, who is a professional salaried person. What has the office of modern church's head pastor has done to the followers of Jesus Christ that is observed in contemporary churches of today? What actually stands out is the classification of Christians into different divisions and sects where the more privileged and special people are only allowed to serve Jesus Christ in certain ways. The human-tailored system chokes the rest of the church body to become content with on-man ministry and rule that only reaches to a mute audience. Basically, they want the people to just follow powerful people without raising voices for their rights. On the contrary, the early church system used to encourage every individual following Jesus Christ to practice their rights and have privilege

---

[155] Institutes, IV: 3:2, 1055

to be a part of church assembly. Unfortunately, the head pastor's office on the modern church has found a way towards acquiring the headship of Jesus Christ by taking over the centrality and taking away the functional headship from other followers and believers. When Jesus Christ is the actual headship, it is obvious that everyone is openly and freely able to contribute, and that all parts of the body of Jesus Christ, are functioning they way they should.

Today's modern and professional pastor has become a slave to the office and position, oppressively manifesting in different ways, such as morality failures, stress, marital issues, emotional breakdown, burnout, depression, and *plastic fantastic* are some of the few. This is not an outcome of becoming a pastor, rather a result of the modern office and church structure.

Scriptures have not been observed supporting one person wearing so many hats one time, i.e. one person must not take away all the privilege of serving Jesus Christ alone. There is a very high obligation and expectation for entertaining, "tickle ears" and keep other people happy and content. This type of system is a form of artificial Christianity, which is deceptive and dishonest. The head pastor of modern church is just like a Hollywood star, who wins an Oscar award for the main role by playing the part of a person who is always cheerful, disciplined, perfectly dressed, and spiritual in different walks and disciplines of life. The unquestioning and unapproachable behaviors clearly demonstrate the political and corrupt nature of office of the contemporary churches, which many times results in isolating from *among* the people (laity) to the ones who are *over and above* the people (clergy) in the church. They often have no value or importance outside of their own groups. The evidence has revealed the head pastor's office by the way they function in modern church does not exist and has not been supported in Scriptures.

The Roles of Church Leadership

Elders

An elder is defined based by his ability to teach. Titus 1:9 and 1 Tim. 3:2 use the term *didaktikos* to describe an elder who has to hold firm and ensure that the world of the Lord is taught. The term is related to the word *Zaqen* in the Old Testament to mean mature men who can provide leadership in God's teaching. The elders of Israel in the Old Testament are seen in the story of Moses and bondage in Egypt. In Exod. 3:16, the Lord instructs Moses to gather the Israel elders. In Num. 11:25, during the wandering in the wilderness, the Lord placed the Spirit on other elders that was initially on Moses. An anointing on the elders occurred in Num. 11:17, so that they too can bear the burden that Moses had. Though the Old Testament does not spell out the details on the origin of the Israelites eldership system, it is clear that at the time of enduring to the Promised Land, most of these elders had an experience and were capable to do their duties and be respected among the peoples. These are the seventy leaders who were later referred to as the Sanhedrin. Their role was to provide the Israelites community with leadership and each city and tribe was under each of the elderly leaders, as seen in Deut. 5:23 and 19:12.

These elders of Israel are mentioned more than fifty times in the Old Testament, but their specific role is not mentioned. Looking at how the elders are referred to in the Old Testament, we gain insight on their overall responsibilities. One of the tasks that they had to accomplish was serving as representatives for the people, as seen in Exod. 19:7–8. In Lev. 4:13–15, they were responsible for leading people into repentance, and in Deut. 19:11–12, for administering justice based on scripture. According to Deut. 27:1, they taught the people following the Word of God and advised them to obey the Holy Scriptures. In Deut. 21:18–21, the elders were also responsible for providing ministerial services in family situations. The leaders in the Old Testament also had the responsibility for providing people with advice for declining godly counsel and discerning leadership, as depicted in Ezek.7:26 and Job 12:20. The elder gave sound instruction and had the responsibility of confuting those who contradicted what was taught to them by the Lord. Confusion, however, arises when looking at the definition of the role of elders in the church. Being an elder does not only mean the ability of a person to teach. The New Testament clearly shows that believers should also have the ability to teach. Heb. 5:12 define the spiritual meat eater as one who is capable of teaching others. Titus 2:1 and Col. 3:16 indicate that the ability to teach does not just mean a person who has biblical language skills or one who has attended the seminary to be trained on Bible studies. This can be seen in Titus 1:5–9, where the

Gentile Christians became the first elders in churches even when they were not Hebrews.

1 Tim. 5:17 recognizes the possibility of some elders being gifted with teaching skills and would exercise their gift. This implies that not all Christian elders have the ability to teach equally. The main qualification for one to become a teacher is to teach based on the doctrines that will correctly guide the church in its intended direction. One way to ensure that the elders meet their role of teaching is to oversee various home bible studies. This is a role that elders mainly play in mini-churches, and it is very biblical. This can be likened to the activities of the early churches when they met in a member's home on a weekly basis. Each home had an elder who prepared the teaching, and if needed, also led the teaching.

Boards

In the modern churches of today, church leaders are generally "laymen" groups who help the pastor in different practical matters or work as the church board. The elders' roles in these modern churches rarely involve pastoral oversight, laboring in the world, or praying for the sick. The role of the board members is to affirm the senior pastor's vision through discerning of God's voice and through prayers. They have to affirm and direct the big picture and values of the ministry with the senior pastor. The board is also responsible for determining the values and pace on finance and facilities. They act as the discerning partners of the pastor in social, political theological, and community issues as well as other key issues in the public position. They are responsible to put across reproductive questions and to contribute in the provision of solutions. Their responsibility is that of making decisions on major issues that impact the church's business, such as the decision to purchase land. The board members of the church also function as the prayer warriors for all the church ministries, and they also are the spear headers of positive influence to the congregation.

According to the Bible, the role of the church board members is described in Eph. 4:11. This is where God appoints a government through choosing, calling, and equipping persons to be the leaders of the church. They are responsible for delegating and investing on their authority as per the will of God. These are individuals known as the elders. They guide in various degree on aspects of spirituality and other measures according to the ability and grace given unto them by God. According to Eph. 4:11, the mantle of leadership is placed on one person, who is the senior pastor, with the responsibility to teach, be an evangelist, prophet, apostle, and a pastor.

The elders of the church and the senior pastor make up the board of directors. They give the church a direction, but the senior pastor is the one who makes the final decision. The group of elders agrees and confers on the decisions. These elders have to possess spiritual maturity and believe in Jesus Christ. They are individuals who have agreed to the Constitution, by-laws, and statement of Faith of the church. Elders are also expected to lead by example.[156] This means that the people selected to be board members of the church are those with firm understanding and conviction of leadership to serve the needs of other individuals.[157] A member of the board is also an individual with outstanding temperance, morals, is gentle, honest, prudent and devout, have a sense of humor, self-control, and not covetous. The board member has to be in a heterosexual and monogamous relationship. The board has to demonstrate a form of giftedness to ensure that their board role is conducted well. This is especially with the board chairperson, who is expected to provide a certain form of spiritual influence to the whole church.

According to the Bible, leadership is not a form of hierarchy; true eldership is one with the only place of prominence and authority who is Jesus Christ. This does not mean that it is a theological concept; rather it is an operational reality. The elder-overseers in eldership do not have the final authority. Instead, these elders function as a collegial group and can confirm to one another through God's will. Their work is to protect the assembly from engaging in human error.

Congregational

The congregation comprises those who are being led. They do not have an inactive role to play because if the shepherd's role is to care and protect the sheep, the sheep cannot be stagnant but active and moving. This is the same role that God's people are expected to play. The leader, who is the

---

[156] Titus 1:5–9; 1 Tim. 3:1–7; 1 Pet. 5:3

[157] Rom. 14:13–23; 1 Cor. 10:22–33

pastor and other elders, should not be the only active individuals in the church. The leaders are giving God's leadership and leadership calls for people to live by the Truth that they believe in and know. Leadership is a responsibility, according to Eph. 4:12. This is a responsibility that deals with the preparation of individuals to live in one body of Christ and to serve other people. Act 6:1–7 shows that Stephen was among the chosen one to provide pastoral leadership and to maintain by the Word of God.

Peter was also called by God to provide emphasis and practice leadership on the Word of God. Congregations today also have the same role of fulfilling responsibilities and needs. They should help their leaders in their own capabilities. This is because leadership is all about the preparation of people to take up responsibilities of providing services. This is the same as Paul's comment: "so in Christ we, though many, form one body, and each member belongs to all the others."[158] Based upon the grace that the Holy Spirit has bestowed upon us, we have different gifts that we can use to encourage prophecy and contribute to other people's needs. In doing these services, the scriptures such as in Rom. 12:5–8 call upon us to do it diligently, to be cheerful, and to show mercy to others.

The Role of the Pastor

Biblical Role

Though the role of the pastor in Christian churches can be confusing, the correct approach in defining the pastoral role is through the biblical approach. This is based on the belief that the Bible is the guide on issues concerning our faith and practice. This assertion calls for the need to evaluate the pastor's role by looking at the pastoral role from the original concept in the New Testament church. The New Testament presents many words that have to be evaluated in order to understand the pastoral role from the biblical perspective. The terms *poimen* (pastor), *episkopos* (bishop) and *presbyteros* (elder) are used in the New Testament. These terms will help us to examine how the Bible defines the role of the pastor.

---

[158] Romans 12:5, New International Version

Presbyteros

Presbyteros is generally a Greek term that means the elder. According to the Jews, a presbyter is an official who leads a synagogue congregation in Jerusalem. This is a term that was used before 70 A.D. to denote officers. The term *presbyteroi* is used in both the Old Testament to refer to a group of local council members representing various cities, as described in Ruth 4:2 and Josh 20:4.[159]

In the New Testament, the term "presbyteros" is also used to refer to group members in the Sanhedrin.[160]The word "presbyteroi" is used among Christians to designate both the religious and civic officials. The English word "priest" is from the Latin word *presbyteries*. The word "presbyter" was used by early Christians to refer to church leaders. Another word is *presbuteros*, which means the noun "older," and *presbus*, which means "the comparative of elderly". This is a term that denotes seniority among the Sanhedrims who were Israelites. This term is sometimes figuratively used to mean a member of the celestial council or presbyter to mean a Christian leader.[161]

Liddell and Scott indicate that the term "presbuteros" means an elder or a person who is superior by birth, therefore, regarded as being higher, greater, and more important.[162] Mounce defines the term as used in the New Testament to mean an older, senior or elder who is advanced in years.[163] 1Tim. 5:1, 2 uses this term to mean fathers, ancestors and ancients. Luke 7:3 uses the term "presbuteros" to mean an elder among the Jewish Sanhedrin. Matt. 16:21 refers to the presbyter or elder to the Christian

---

[159] William Amdt and Frederick Danker, *A Greek English Lexicon of Early ChristianLiterature and New Testament* (Chicago: University of Chicago Press, 2000), 862.

[160] Matt. 27:41; Mark 8:31, 11:27, 14:43, 53, 15:1; Luke 9:22, 20:1.

[161] Edward W. Goodrick and John R. Kohlenberger III, *Zondervan NIV Exhaustive Concordance,* Premier Reference Series,2nded.(Grand Rapids: Zondervan, 1999), 1,584.

[162] *Liddell and Scott's Greek-English Lexicon*(Oxford: Oxford University Press, 1997), s.v. "presbuteros.".

[163] William D. Mounce, *The Analytical Lexicon to the Greek New Testament,* (Grand Rapids: Zondervan Publishing House, 1993), 389; Acts 2: 17; John 8:9; Luke 15:25

Church. For the Jewish, the presbuteros are the Pharisees and scribes of the synagogue.

H.M. Shepherd indicates that the presbyteries are those with a general oversight of Jewish communities performing administrative roles as assigned to them by Roman authorities. Their main duties include the interpretation of law, judicial duties, and punishing of offenders.[164] In Acts 15:4, 6, 22–23; 16:4 *presbytero* and *apostoloi* are terms clearly used for normative teaching and Supreme Court office for the entire Church. James 5:14 also uses the term "apostolic" to mean the elders of the church who are summoned whenever a person is sick. These church leaders prayed over the sick and anointed them with oil in the name of the Lord; however, this is in sharp contrast with contemporary church leadership. Contemporary leaders are the holders of the office and not the older men who have been charismatically endowed.[165]

Benjamin Merkle indicates that presbyteros can mean an old woman or a man, or one can use it in comparative context of one who is elder than the other person.[166] However, commonly, presbyteros is used to denote Judaism officials from the synagogue, Sanhedrin, and the church. Presbyteros has been used in a few places to mean forefathers.[167] Just like the way this term has been used in the Old Testament, there are various designations related to the elderly people as seen in Luke 22:66 and Matt. 21:23; the Jewish elders in Acts 15:15 and Luke 7:3; church elders in 1Tim. 5:17, 19; Israel elders in Acts 4:8; and Christian and Jewish assemblies in James 5:14.[168]

The term "presbyteros" in the Bible denotes that it bears a doctrinal tradition with reference to the dignity of a community, as seen in1 Clem. 1:3 and 1 Pet. 5:5. Presbyterian refers more on a local authority such as

---

[164] M.H. Shepherd, Jr., *The Interpreter's Dictionary of the Bible* (New York: Abington Press, 1962), 73, s.v. "elders in the New Testament."

[165] Ibid., 664.

[166] Tim. 5:1–2; Luke 15:25.

[167] Heb. 11:2; Mark 7:2, 3; Matt. 15:2.

[168] Benjamin L. Merkle, *The Elder and Overseer*, Studies in Biblical Literature, ed. Hemchand Gossai vol. 57. (New York: Peter Lang International Academic Publishers, 2003), 43.

the Sanhedrin and other governing bodies of the churches or synagogues. These individuals are appointed and have a specific function to carry out.[169]

Keith Schooley comments:

> The word *presbyteros* appears sixty-seven times in the New Testament of which there are nineteen that refer to "elders" as an office in the early church. Most of these reference simply assume the existence of elders and describe dealings with them as representatives of the church (Lam. 5:14; Pet. 5:1, 5, Acts 11:30, 15:2, 14:23. 21:18, 20:17, 4, 6, 15:2, 1Tim. 5:1). The ordination of church elders is only found in Titus 1:5 and Acts 14:23. In 2 In. 1 and 3 In. 1, John identifies himself as "the elder". Similarly, Peter also identifies himself as an elder in his writing to other elders of the church (1 Pet. 5:1). In the early and late section of the book of Acts, the term presbyteros is commonly used in reference to the Jewish leaders mainly in reference to the elders and chiefs priests. Other adjectives in reference to the elderly are also used, for example, the older brother of the prodigal son and other elders in general. The book of Hebrews uses the term presbyteros to mean the "ancients." The book of Revelation makes use of this term to refer to the "twenty-four elders" seated beside god's throne according to the vision of John. This term has been used in this book twelve times.[170]

In the book of Acts, the Jerusalem church elders are first mentioned to refer to a Christian Group (Acts 11:30). This is where the term is used to refer to an Antioch collection that Barnabas and Paul brought to

---

[169] Gerhard Kittel and Gerhard Friedrich, eds.,*Theological Dictionary of the New Testament*, vol. vi, trans. Geoffrey.W. Bromiley (Grand Rapids: William B. Eerdmans Publishing Company, 1968), 654.

[170] Keith Schooley, "What is a Pastor?" *Quodlibet Journal*2, no.2 (Spring 2000), accessed on October 10, 2013, 16th para, http://www.quodlibet.net/articles/schooley-pastor.shtml.

Jerusalem. The term "presbyteroi" is used to refer to the foundation of both the apostolic council and apostolic decree (Acts 15:2, 4, 6, 22).[171] According to Thomas Oden, there is considerable evidence in the Bible to show a general pastoral guidance to followers through breaking bread, preaching, resurrection witness, and teaching. These teachings also appear in the incidence where Paul comes to Jerusalem as shown in James 21:18. In addition, in Acts 14:23, there is the work of the church in ordaining elders. In Titus 1: 5–6, Christians understand that the church elders were placed in every town.[172]

The use of the term "presbyteros" in the book of Acts, according to Gunther Bornkamn, shows the main role and duties of the presbyters[173]. These church leaders played a significant role during the post-apostolic churches. After Barnabas and Paul left the congregation, they chose elders for the churches everywhere and commanded them to fast and pray according to the Lord's will, as described in Acts 14:23. The major address that Paul provides to the Ephesians Elders indicates the significance of the duty that they had been assigned. These are the elders who had been appointed by the Holy Spirit to act as the shepherds and overseers of the congregation. The apostle also appointed these elders to be a whole council to pass God's will. According to Acts 20:18–35, their duty was to administer the apostle's legacy, protect the churches from danger of sin, and to act as God's examples. For the first time, we see the elders being appointed guardians to the apostle's traditions, who entrusted and appointed them to guide their congregation.[174]

Additionally, in relation to the pastoral charge assigned to the church elders in the Book of Acts, Paul writes a letter informing them to guard themselves, as well as their flocks through the announcing of the Holy Spirit that has made to be the overseers (*episkopos*) and to be the shepherds (*poimen*) of the church of God, as seen in Acts 20:28.

Oden responds that the collection of Paul acts as a demonstration of the intricate role of integrating various ministry images. Elders in the book

---

[171] Kittel and Friedrich, eds., *Theological Dictionary*, 663.

[172] Thomas C. Oden, *Pastoral Theology: Essentials of Ministry* (San Francisco: HarperOne, 1983), 68.

[173] Kittel and Friedrich, eds., *Theological Dictionary*, 665

[174] Ibid, 665.

of 1Peter are viewed as an institution trusted with the role of guiding the church. Just like Acts 20:28, the book of 1Pet. 5:2 also sums up the office as playing the role of a shepherd. These two passages suggest that there is a close relationship between pastoral care and eldership.

Gunther indicates that a pastoral is related to presbyteros in four passages, but its usage is not consistent. In the book of 1 Tim. 5:1, the term presbyteros is used as an indication of age reference. However, it should not be assumed that its meaning should be used in all other aspects. The term "presbyteros" was used in the early churches to refer to the office of leadership. In 1 Tim. 4:14, elders are referred to as a college that is referenced during the ordination of Timothy as he laid hands to the chosen apostles. Another instance on the use of the term "presbyteros" is when Titus appointed the local congregation to instill order in the churches.[175] It is quiet surprising for the pastorals that the bishop plays a significant role here as well as the presbyters and that his functions are similar. Therefore, it is generally assumed that the church offices play the same role as the current pastorals.

The term "presbyteros" in 1Tim. 5:17 is not used in its literal sense to mean older men but in a much more technical sense to mean elder. This latter meaning indicates the dimension on experience and maturity in guiding the church and has the connotation that the best teaching can be provided by the ruling elder and the teaching elder. The term "presbyteros," in *Pastoral Theology: Essentials of Ministry* does not necessary mean an old man in terms of age. Instead, it means the qualification or position in understanding or maturity in the Word of God.[176] Therefore, it is clear that the role of the elder has to be that of enhancing spiritual maturity of Christians through their wisdom and experience. According to John Piper, the elders of the New Testament mainly had the responsibility of providing oversight for the church and were the primary leaders of the church.[177]

Dale indicates that leaders have to be the shepherds and guardians of their flock. They also have other responsibilities of leading and ruling as

---

[175] Titus 1:5.

[176] Oden, *Pastoral Theology*, 49.

[177] John Piper, "Christian Elders in the New Testament," Desiring God, last modified November 1, 1976, accessed October 12, 2013, http://www.desiringgod.org/articles/christian-elders-in-the-new-testament.

well as instilling hope to the sick.[178] According to Acts 15:1–6, the pastors based on their leading and ruling ability, have a role to guide others in different matters related to faith and practice. Dale points out that elders with effective leading skills will be recognized by the congregation, as is mentioned in 1 Tim 5:17. The role of the elders is to provide guidelines to the church in times of controversies and in other ordinary normal growth issues. This is possible when they use sound interpretation of the Bible in providing judgments and in solving issues based on biblical issues.

The congregation will have the obligation of obeying their elders because, as is written in Heb. 13:17, these elders provide an account for their souls. Therefore, this means that the elders have the duty in providing judgments on matters that impact their flock's lives. Their decisions on issues relating to personal conflicts, doctrine, ethical and moral dilemmas as well as the general programs and plans of the church have to be for the good of the congregation.

Paul informed the elders of the Ephesians on the need to provide care and guide their own personal lives and to protect their moral conduct and testimonies. They have the responsibility of caring for their flock through the Holy Spirit guidelines.[179] Those who are physically and spiritually sick have to ask for assistance from the elders of the church.[180] Paul's main purpose for summoning the elders was to call upon them to be spiritual leaders in the provision of physical needs of their followers. They have to pray at times of sickness and deal with any form of sin that arises from their flock. Peter also called upon the leaders to be their flock's shepherds through leading, protecting, and feeding them, as seen in 1 Pet. 5:1–3. This means that the leaders have to show personal concern and involvement to the lives of their followers.

Another role of the church ministry leaders is to teach and preach to the congregation.[181] All church leaders should be able to educate and teach the flock through instructing them on the doctrine of the church and God. Tim. 5:17 may imply that public exhortation is not an aspect that

[178] Dale, The Leading Edge: Leadership Strategies from the New Testament, (Nashville: Abington Press, 1996), 59.
[179] Acts 20:28.
[180] James 5:14.
[181] 1 Tim. 5:17.

all elders are expected to do. A statement that strongly relates to this point is in the book of Titus 1:9–11. This is where Paul calls upon the elders to hold on to the truth of the world, to defend the truth, not compromising the Scriptures. This means that they are responsible to exhort believers through the provision of doctrinal counseling and teaching as well as in the refuting of errors[182].

Other literature texts have also shown the duties of the church, but they have no reference as to whether this is an oversight or bishopric duty. The Epistles indicate that due to necessities, their duties had to be differentiated to become a distinct organizational ministry. In addition, through following the synagogue custom, some leaders have been committed to the historic role of providing an oversight and bishopric role. In fact, the position of an overseer or bishop in the early churches was not the highest position. Paul does not show the order in the ministry through these positions, which he assigned, to the Ephesians. These positions are pastors, evangelist, teachers, prophets, and apostles. Timothy, in his role of providing oversight on the presbyters or elders, is seen through him being joined by Paul to rebuke the sinners, as is written in1 Tim 5:19–20. This indicates the foundational trial of a person in authority of individuals who are inferior to him in positions.

Contemporary Role

Various current views on the pastoral role, as appropriated through theological perspectives, have been tackled in various practical theologies in the works of Oden, Wayne E. Oates, Jacob Firet, Ray Anderson, William Willimon, and Thomas H. Groome.

Jacob Firet's book *Dynamics in Pastoring* forms the foundation of contemporary analysis on the pastoral role. He makes use of the term "pastoral role fulfillment"[183] as the main concept in understanding the task of a pastor. This is the official activity of an individual who is referred to as the pastor. Firet uses three modes to define the pastoral role: the *paraklesis, didache,* and the *kerygma. Kerygma* is the proclamation of a new and current state of affairs, which is a mode that accentuates and places

---

[182] Ibid, 52.

[183] Jacob, Firet, *"Dynamics in Pastoring"*, (Wm. B. Eerdmans Pub. Co, 1986), 14.

importance on the present pastoral role. For the *didache* mode, the pastor is involved in teaching people on discipleship and wisdom as part of the challenges and complexities of everyday life through God's power. The last mode is known as the *paraklesis*, which describes the coming of God's Word via the intermediary of pastoral fulfillment.[184] These modes show the pastors roles in working with the community so as to fulfill God's will through spiritual, scripture, and prayer direction. This means that the pastoral role is to change the lives of people. This is with the belief that people's lives will change when they come into contact with God.[185] This is a form of leadership that is focused on organizational change. This is a kind of leader that is also supported by Nelson and others.

Another unique way of understanding the pastoral role can be seen in the work of Oates. He views the pastoral task as mainly being in relation to a person's life and crisis issues of an individual. However, the pastoral duty is more than just providing care giving because other tasks can be delegated to others. Oates views the pastoral role in terms of symbolic power in ministering to the community of believers[186]. Oden provides a foundation in thinking about the pastoral ministry by saying that the pastoral image forms a central paradigm that combines courage and vigilance, with trust and tenderness.[187]

In regards to the nature of current pastoral ministry, Oates believes that it involves a unique relationship with the community of Christ. Some missiologists refer to the pastoring role as being one that is task-oriented and forms an entrepreneurial spirit. On the contrary, Oates believes that pastoring is a role that does not necessarily focus on the tasks that person carryout, but the significance of undertaking this role is based on both being-centered and identity-centered integrity. This is a role that pastors carry out as a vocational calling and will guide them on how to serve people and to follow God.[188] This same perspective on the modern role of churches is also addressed by Oden, who says that the Christian ministry

---

[184] Firet, *Dynamics in Pastoring*, 14.

[185] Ibid., 99f.

[186] Wayne E. Oates, *The Christian Pastor. 3rd ed.* (Philadelphia: Westminster John Knox Press, 1982), 66.

[187] Ibid, 66.

[188] Ibid., 128.

is energized through its conviction to Christ who established and ordained the pastoral office for the guidance and edification of the church. He goes on to state that the main intention of Christ for modern day ministries is to embody His initial ministry in the world. He also informs us about the promise Jesus made that He be in our midst and will nourish and sustain the church.[189]

On reference to the shepherding role as pastoring, Oden states that the congregation is served by a central image of the ministry, which is life enabling, nurturing, and non-combative. To him, the pastoring image forms central paradigms. Through this argument, he means that authority and leadership is part of pastoral.[190] Oden says that pastoring authority is not a coercive one, but it is an authority that is based on covenant caring, mutuality, caring, and expectation on empathic understanding.[191] This means that the concept of pastoring leadership can be understood as coercive and one coming from above to provide guidelines. Oden's main element in the understanding of pastoral role is not just the sociological function on the needs of leadership but is a continuation of Christ's personal ministry. Christ is the head of the church, and the church celebrates His ability to discern what is needed to continue His ministry.[192]

William Willimon presents various images on the pastoral role as being a resident activist, manager, therapist, political negotiator, media mogul, preacher, and servant.[193] Based on this image, Willimon indicates that the image of a servant is one who is critical for the church and the Gospel.[194]

This is a new picture that tries to reflect the reality in current day pastoral images that have changed within the cultural context and time. Willimon proposes three caveats for guiding the current ministerial world. First, he says that the Christian ministry is mainly countercultural within

---

[189] Oden, *Pastoral Theology*, 28, 50.

[190] Ibid., 52–53.

[191] Ibid., 53.

[192] Ibid., 67.

[193] William H. Willimon, *Pastor: The Theology and Practice of Ordained Ministry* (Nashville: Abingdon Press, 2002), 56–69.

[194] Ibid., 69.

a predominant culture. He also warns that it is necessary to be wary of the Christian leadership style that is mainly one of accommodations.[195]

He shows that in the attempt of the church to be "relevant" to the Word, we may fail to offer a purely spiritual form of leadership. He also advocates that we need to draw from the classical styles of Christian ministry as our foundation for the pastoral role. This means that he aims to recovery the classical form of the ministry in the provision of preaching, evangelical, and teaching through the ministries order, sacrament, and worship. He says that pastors have to be prepared for moral formation, regenerate the people of God, and lead in catechesis.[196]

Willimon also expresses the need for pastors to continue with a critical assessment of congregational needs and denominational families because each of these families has differentiated values and qualities in their pastoral leaders. This means that pastors should be willing to adopt new models of leadership for the good of the Church and for Christ. According to his caveats, Willimon relates the pastoral role as one that involves metaphors of an interpreter of the Scriptures, as a priest to lead in worships, as a counselor, teacher, preacher, prophet and evangelist. In addressing the issues of leadership, Willimon remarks on the peculiar aspects of Christian leadership. Though he supports the need for congregational leadership as the main responsibility of the pastor, the ordained leaders of the church can rarely and extremely carefully examine the cues in secular models of leadership. This is because the Christian form of leadership should be that which is congruent to the leadership of Jesus Christ. Willimon, like many other theologians, have recognized the shift in leadership, but in this case it is different from the change spoken about by Firet on agony. He speaks about the leadership rules like the transformational leadership in churches.

Groome, a religious educator, presents a new perspective that focuses on the ministry of Jesus Christ. In regard to the commitments of Jesus, Groome presents three main missions of Christ: (1) He undertook the personal initiate of personally being in the presence of God without exception; (2) He called upon individuals into the community and

[195] Ibid., 70.
[196] Ibid., 71.

partnership; (3) He acted as a motivator and empowered individuals so as to have their freedom and knowledge of truth as agent subjects.[197]

Based on the dynamics in Jesus' ministry, Groome states that Jesus informed people to recognize their historical praxis and reality in the world. He also states that Jesus led the people into a state of vital consciousness concerning the reign of God and enabled them to be reoriented. Third, Jesus' authority acted as a life giving means that He used to empower against ignorance, suffering of the evil, and to empower them to live by the reign of God. This means that Jesus' authority is not that which comes from social or ranking positions but from his life-giving nature and his personal integrity of his ministry. He further elaborates that in Jesus' call for discipleship, He had respect for the decision making and discernment, and there is no place in the Bible that hints that He tried to control people to simply repeat what He said. Based on these aspects, Groome provides the foundation that is possible to reflect on the essential issues that relate to pastoral ministry.[198]

Messer indicates that the pastoral ministry is one with a servant nature. He states that servant leaders understand the ministry and not status in their service to humanity.[199]According to Ray Anderson, leadership is the inner logic within the ministry. Leadership according to him is locus and rooted in the ministry of Jesus Christ, which is known as the Christopraxis servant leadership. He relates this definition of leadership by saying that pastors as effective leaders require three main things. First is to have a creative vision that inspirers others. Second is to have the spiritual gift in the ministry, and third is to have power in the delegation that enables.[200] However, Anderson focuses on the primary role of a leader as that which deals with the elevation of responsibilities expected in servant hood. He says that pastors should act as servant leaders to God's congregation. This means that the pastor does not hold a position between God and man but

---

[197] Thomas H. Groome, *Sharing Faith: A Comprehensive Approach to Religious Education and Pastoral Ministry: The Way of Shared Praxis* (San Francisco: Harper San Francisco, 1991), 303.

[198] Ibid., 308.

[199] Messer, *Contemporary Images of Christian Ministry*, 106.

[200] Ray S. Anderson, *The Soul of Ministry: Forming Leaders for God's People* (Louisville: Westminster John Knox Press, 1997), 204.

stands with the rest of the congregation as a faithful steward, to provide correction and discipline and to prepare the path for the coming of Jesus Christ. Therefore, in order to understand the actual role a pastor in modern day churches, it is essential to examine five main aspects: theology of transformation, charisma, discernment, reconciliation theology, reading the signs of the current times and the prophetic vocation.[201] This helps us to know that leadership in churches is situated in a relation of matrix. This means that leadership theology is one that focuses on individuals within a transformative context and not the sociological function of leading.

We would all be well advised to heed the example of the Apostle Paul concerning the characteristics of godly leadership as described in Acts.

Godly Leadership

Acts 20: 17–21 has recorded the last encounter of Peter with the Ephesians' elders. The elders included pastors from different house churches, who use to meet all over Ephesus city. Ephesus is a Greek ancient city, situated on the coast of Iona. This city is famous as most of the events from Acts 18–20 have been set in the areas around Ephesus. According to Acts 19: 1–10, a number of these "elders" were the original twelve men, Peter has met in the school of Tyrannus. The term "elder" is referred to the maturity required for handling office matters. In Acts 20:28, these same men are referred by Paul as "overseers" (bishops), which is focused on the main tasks performed by these men, to supervise matters in the church office.

Apparently, some of the critics of Paul have been at work in Ephesus, who continuously tried to undermine him as a leader and a more specifically as a man of God.[202] This can be observed when he repeatedly states: "You yourselves know"[203] and reminds them of his characters and the way he behaved when he had been with them. He has been clearly

---

[201] Diane Kennedy, "A Contextual Theology of Leadership", *Theological Education* 37, no. 1 (2000), 67

[202] Lannon, Keith. *A Backward Look at the Big Picture as Paul Left Ephesus Behind. (1 Corinthians 3:10).* WordPress.com October 15, 2013, 13th para. accessed on October 12, 2013 http://keithlannon.wordpress.com/2013/08/04/a-backward-look-at-the-big-picture-as-paul-left-ephesus-behind-1-corinthians-310/

[203] Acts 20:18, 34

defending himself and has been simultaneously demonstrating qualities and characteristics of godly church leadership. In scenarios when a number of church leaders have fallen for serious sin and have moved away from their actual responsibilities, the validity of the churches depends upon the way they recover their godly leadership characteristics and qualities. Observing the example of Paul, every Christian leader should develop the following qualities:

A Godly Leader must portray a Servant Leadership Behavior

Majority of the Christian institutions are being run in the same way as any business organization, with a line of positions. In such structures, President is at the top and Vice President (VP) reports to him. Likewise, managers report to VP and so forth. The church follows the same hierarchical structure. However, the church is supposed to follow a different structure, i.e. the biblical structure.

Godly leadership generally comes from servanthood, not by position within the church organizations. This message has been clearly demonstrated by Paul's attitude; however, he has specifically mentioned that he was "serving the Lord".[204] The term "serving" is a verb that is referred to the noun slave or bond-servant. This practice of relating servant and leader has originated from the Bible. Throughout the biblical narrative, kings, leaders, and rulers have referred themselves as servants, albeit, with highly different and distinct meanings and intentions.[205]

Observing to Paul's example, he often referred himself as the bond-servant of God.[206] It was the way Paul use to view himself and it is the way every Christian must view him/herself. Jesus informs His followers, in Mark 9:35, "If anyone wants to be first, he must be the very last, and the servant of all. We are slaves of Jesus Christ, and do not belong to ourselves. Whatever we do, must always be in order to please Him. We must also

---

[204] Ibid., v.19.

[205] Anthony P. Celelli, The Just Pastor: An Ethical Hermeneutic Of Biblical Justice, Positional Power Theory, And The Theology And Practice Of Pastoral Leadership, (ProQuest, 2012), 64.

[206] Rom. 1:1; Gal. 1:10; Col. 1:7, 4:7; Titus 1:1.

recognize that if we have the quality of service, we have received all from Him.[207]

This means that the primary responsibility of the church leaders is to serve the Lord, and secondary comes serving the church. They will have to answer God one day for the way they have fulfilled the stewardship entrusted upon them. Nevertheless, there is a logical sense in which godly church leader consider he has to answer God someday, which also keeps them away from becoming man-pleasers. In Gal. 1:10, it was stated by Paul: "For am I now seeking the favor of men, or of God? Or am I striving to please men? If I were still trying to please men, I would not be a bond-servant of Christ."[208] The sense of serving and pleasing God instead of men enables godly leaders to face and confront sins and to preach and convey difficult truth when necessary. As reported in John 13: 1–17, when Christians will be able to see themselves as true servants of Jesus Christ, they will take up the basin and towel like Jesus and will serve other humans out of care and love. Ruling and commanding over others is the world's way for leadership. On the contrary, Jesus states in Mathews 23:11 and Mark 10: 42–45, "The greatest among you will be your servant."

The message is clear related to the responsibility of servant leaders to be person of string character. According to Philippians 2: 3–4, "Do nothing out of selfish ambition or vain conceit, but in humility consider others better than yourselves."

A Godly Leaders must possess Transparent Integrity

Another significant quality learned from emphasizing upon Paul's character development is the one that leads from within oneself. What is valued by a leader will be the foundation for all of his behavior. The godly leader can only lead with complete integrity if they incorporate their competencies with their character, i.e. integrating what they do with what they are.

In Acts 20:18, Paul states: "You yourselves know, from the first day that I set foot in Asia, how I was with you the whole time." In Acts 20:31, referring to the time he spent with, he further mentions: "night and day for

---

[207] Acts 20:24.
[208] See also 1 Thess. 2:4.

a period of three years I did not cease to admonish each one with tears". In this statement, where he was talking about so much time he has spent with these men, he was also referring to the way he openly spend his life before them. They have observed how he used to live. He never pretended to be something in front of them, and lived differently when he was away from them. He never had to hide anything about the way he lived from these men. In this reference, integrity is referred to what one is in private or at home is the same among people. Webster's explain integrity as an "unimpaired condition."[209] It is described as being sound. A person with integrity is also explained as one who still survives to do things with excellence, even when there is no one to watch or notice. Our life is a single foundation. This integrity significantly emerges from the first godly leadership discussed in this section, that is we need to understand that we are here to serve the Lord, who knows every motive and thought of our hearts. In reference to this, Paul stated: "This is our boast. Our conscience testifies that we have conducted ourselves in the world, especially in our relations with you, in the holiness and sincerity that are from God."[210]

A Godly Leaders should portray Godly Characteristics

Gal. 52:22–23 provides a list of qualities that are demonstrated by godly character, such as the fruit of the Spirit. However, three qualities are of particular note for those serving as pastors.

A.   Humility-as part of Godly Character

Humility is considered to be the foundation, upon which the Virtues are built, that a person may become a force of God that brings Him brilliance and live a life of Godly Masculinity. Such humility is necessarily direct by the fear of the Lord, which keeps an individual from turning towards to humility for pleasing men, instead constantly keeps him aware of a humility directed towards pleasing God.

What does being humble means? In a spiritual sense, biblical humility is a conscious awareness of our utter dependence on Jesus Christ. This can

---

[209]   Merriam-Webster's Collegiate Dictionary, 10th ed. See "integrity.
[210]   2 Cor. 1:12, New International Version

be observed in Paul's character, when in 2 Cor. 3:5, he states: "Not that we are adequate in ourselves to consider anything as coming from ourselves, but our adequacy is from God." It can also be observed when he states in 2 Cor. 4:4, "But we have this treasure in earthen vessels, so that the surpassing greatness of the power will be of God and not from ourselves." He then faces the pride of the Corinthians, when in Cor. 4:7, he asks them: "What do you have that you did not receive? And if you did receive it, why do you boast as if you had not received it?"

Humble people remain continuously aware that whatever they are is by the Grace of God. They understand that whatever skills or privilege they have is given by God. Their confidence does not lie within themselves, rather lies within their God, so that they quickly give the glory to the Lord no matter what the situation is. A godly leader is a true humble person. This is not a fake humility that is for pleasing people or to manipulate them.[211] The true humility understands that we are nothing without our God, and have nothing that God has not given us. A true humble leader understands that followers try to seek the same things that leaders seek, such as acceptance, contentment, understanding, love and most importantly peace. Paul has experienced the highs and lows of poverty and privilege, of debasement and authority, and of insult and respect.[212] Going through all of this, he never stopped leading humbly.

B.   Love, concern, and compassion-part of Godly Character

In Acts 20:19, Paul talked about his ministry: "Serving the Lord with all humility of mind, and with many tears, and temptations, which befell me by the lying in wait of the Jews." The qualities of compassion, love and concern are behind the terms tears. He further mentions his tears in Acts 20:31, in terms of warning these elders, specifically in context of false teaching. There are more tears shed by the elders as well as Paul, when the elders accompany Paul to the ship for saying their final goodbyes, as mentioned in Acts 20:37. His tears showed how much love and care he

---

[211] Brentm Riggs, Godly Leadership – Character Traits 1 – Part 2, BrentRiggs (blog), accessed on October 16, 2013 http://www.brentriggsblog.com/2009/08/godly-leadership-character-traits-1-part-2/

[212] Ibid.

had for these elders, and the tears on both end showed that the feeling is mutual. According to a famous quote stated by Maxwell in this reference: "People don't care how much you know unless they know how much you care."

When Paul heard about Christians who were not following the Word of God and not walking to God obediently, he was moved to tears. In 2 Cor. 2:4, he wrote to the Corinthians: "For out of much affliction and anguish of heart I wrote to you with many tears; not so that you would be made sorrowful, but that you might know the love which I have especially for you." We should understand that if a person wants to correct someone, who has committed serious error or fallen into sin, it is important they we do so with genuine concern, love and affection. Analyzing Paul's example, it is observed that he is full of compassion and his writings were filled with strong feelings of love and concern for his followers.

Furthermore, throughout the Bible, it has been observed that compassion lies within the core of the Godly character. God is consistently referred to being merciful, compassionate, and loving. In addition, throughout New and Old Testaments, we are asked to imitate or adopt God's compassion for others. In Zechariah 7:9, we are reminded that God wants us to show compassion and mercy to one another.

C.   Steadfastness in trials-part of Godly Character

As stated in Acts 20:19, the Ephesian elders had witnessed Paul going through the trails that came upon him throughout the plotting of the Jews. The Book of Acts does not have any record related to such plotting in Ephesus, even though it has reported several similar plans and schemes of the Jews in other cities.[213] Therefore, it is not difficult or impossible to assume that similar might have also happened in Ephesus. The Ephesian elders have also witnessed behavior of Paul when the Gentiles rioted and went against hm. In all these situations and circumstances, they have seen Paul trust even more in the Lord, even though he was in extreme despair of life itself.[214] Facing all such situation did not turn him into bitter person or did not create any kind of rage against God in his heart regarding His

---

[213] Acts 9:23, 20:3, 23:12.
[214] 2 Cor. 1:8–10.

fairness. His bad days did not make him lash out at the Jews in anger and vengeance. He was composed and had faith on God, submitting to God's might hand, and casted his care upon Him.[215] Paul's example shows that we should remain patient and have strong faith in God in times of trial. We need to have endurance in such situations.

Thus, a godly leader is identified through his servant attitude, transparent integrity, and includes love, steadfastness in times of trail, and humility.

A Godly Leader is identified by his Faithful Biblical Teaching

Acts 20:20–21 highlight the following five main aspects of biblical teaching:

A.   Faithful teaching involves not hiding or manipulating difficult/ harsh truth

"I did not shrink from declaring to you anything that was profitable."[216] This verse implies that some certain things that are beneficial are hard to acquire, therefore also it is also difficult to teach them. If Paul would have aimed his life in pleasing men, he would have denied these truths. If would have wanted to become famous and popular speaker, he would not have chosen these subjects rather would have opted to talk about things that please other people. But, since Paul always seek to please the Lord, and he knew and understood that these truths were profitable for spiritual health and growth; he always taught what God wanted to him to teach to other people.

By reading Ephesians, the writings of Paul to the church, we can learn and understand some of these truths. In Eph. 1:4–5, Paul began by talking about the doctrines of sovereign election and predestination of God. He further talked about human wickedness in Eph. 2:1, telling that we were all buried under our sins and trespasses. Due to this, we can only acquire salvation by the grace of God, neither from our works nor

---

[215] 1 Pet. 5:6–7.

[216] Act 20:20.

our merit, as explained in Eph. 2:5–9. Paul demonstrates how the wall of separation between Gentiles and Jesus is brought down in Christ.[217] All these principles, lowers the human pride and praises the cross of Jesus. As these truths involve people to ignore their pride, people generally hesitate in adapting them. However, like healthy food, these truths are beneficial for spiritual health; therefore we should choose to teach and practices them as Paul did.

B.   Faithful teaching involves practically applying and helping people to grow in their faith.

Paul has taught us what is profitable and beneficial for our spiritual growth and health. He warned Timothy in 1Tim. 1:4–7, about the teachings that lead to fruitless discussions and sheer speculations, instead of teaching and extending upon God's provision, by having strong faith. As a faithful Bible teacher reads Bible, he/ she always have this question, "So, what? What difference should this Scripture make first in my life, and then in the lives of those people who I will teach this?" Strongly applying the teachings always stems out of strong interpretation and understanding of biblical text in its actual context. We should be able to look at the bible and say, "yes, I know what God wants me to do."

C.   Faithful biblical teachings must be provided both in informal as well as formal settings.

Analyzing Paul's example, it was observed that Paul use to teach these men from house to house and also collectively in public. He went to school of Tyrannus to teach them. Furthermore, he taught people in the church house meetings, when they heard him preaching in the Jewish synagogues, and also taught some in their homes in some social gathering or when they sat together to have meals. Sometimes, it used to be the entire group together. Other times, he used to meet them individually in order to help them in understanding some principles or solve their problem under the light of biblical studies. During informal settings or gatherings, Paul

---

[217] Eph. 2:11–22.

always liked talking about the things and Words of Gods with these men. He used to always interact with these men about Scripture as it was the central purpose of life.

   D.   Faithful biblical teaching requires reflecting seriousness about the everlasting truths.

Faithful teaching involves a person to seriously reflect upon the biblical texts, so other people can understand and practice it seriously. Paul has seriously testified both to the Greeks and the Jews about the faith and repentance. The term "testifying" pictures a person in courtroom, who is under oath, solemnly swears to tell the truth, the complete truth, and nothing but the truth. Considering that the entire destiny of souls was at risk, Paul never took his preaching assignment lightly and always taught the truth with complete dedication and sincerity.

Although there is some space for humor at the platform where teaching is taking place, but many times humor is abused as it is conveyed that we are not dead serious about eternal matters. Many times, if the humor element is included frequently in the sermon, a lot of people come out feeling they have seen a stand-up comedy show. The content of the preacher is fine if he conveys the message with utter seriousness, rather than incorporating humor frequently, conveying the message not to take things seriously. Therefore, it is highly important for a biblical preacher to convey the seriousness and solemnity of the gospel. This will make people to take things seriously and understand the repercussion of not obeying to God.

   E.   Faithful biblical teaching must assert that faith and repentance are the core requirements for the people who want to be right with God.

According to some people, faith in God applies to the Jews, and repentance towards the Lord is applicable to Gentiles. However, there is no reason to believe in this, and the fact is that both the Jew as well as the Gentiles needs to have both the qualities. Faith and repentance are considered to be the flip sides of the same coin. Although they both are different ways of seeing the requirement for salvation, however, they cannot be separated from one another. Repentance has been significantly emphasized in the teaching of the New Testament. Repentance means turning away from our sins and moving towards God. It also states that one can never turn towards the God, while continuously holding on their sins. Repentance is the heart-felt plea to God for forgiveness and salvation, "O God, I have sinned against You, but I don't want to live that way any longer. Have mercy on me, the sinner!" While preaching to Gentiles, Paul asserted that "God is now declaring to men that all everywhere should repent."[218]

Faith is considered to be the hand that lays hold of provision of God in Christ. Faith is looking to Jesus as the righteousness and believing that we need to stand before a Holy God. Faith involves looking up to Jesus as the forgiveness for all our sins and wrong doings through His bloodshed. Having faith in the Lord Christ means that instead of trusting our own righteousness, we consider Jesus to be our sole advocate and mediator. Both repentance and faith are the gift of God, not the outcome of our merit.[219]

As stated in Col. 2:6, just like we start our Christian life through faith and repentance, thus, we should continue living our lives through faith and repentance.[220] As the word of God shines in the dark areas of our lives, we move away from our sins and start trusting in all that Jesus is for us.

---

[218] Acts17:30.
[219] Acts 11:18; Eph. 2:8–9.
[220] Col. 2:6.

✠

Chapter 3

Cultural Influences On Church Leadership

The Contemporary State of the Church

Many churches today are influenced by external factors, yet many of them deny and have no insights in acknowledging that they are misaligned to modern practices and thoughts. Factors of consumerism mentality, mass media, and changes in demographics have led to various changes in the churches of today. These churches are also failing to address their needs in a credible version as seen in the arguments provided by Thumma, Barna, and Berger. Larger churches may appear to be more credible compared to smaller churches. This is seen in the larger proportions of individuals attending mega churches that comprise 14% of the total church population.[221] In the past, church attendance did not comprise a total number of followers exceeding 1,000 people. On the contrary, some churches today comprise thousands of members, extensive support staff and multiple pastors among other leaders. The duration of the service last only for an hour and the sermon takes only 27 minutes. The churches also use multiple approaches to reach member through counseling, affinity evangelism, discovery classes

---

[221] L. Anderson, *Dying for Change*, 50.

on spiritual matters and other forms to get in touch with the smaller sub groups of the church.[222]

There is no longer a church that can be seen as the "typical" one, but churches today can be classified into three main categories. One of the categories is a small church with less than one hundred people living within the community. The second is the middle growth church with at least 400 people and are seeking to attract more members. The mega churches are those on the extreme end with more than 1,000 members that offer a wide range of programs to meet various needs.[223] In the recent past, the media highlighted the emergence of mega churches, such as in the case of Zion Dominion Global Ministries led by Roderick Hennings, Brooklyn Tabernacle with 10,000 attendees; Christian Cultural Center with 13,000; Mount Pleasant Church and Ministries, and Empowerment Temple and Real Life Ministries among others.

In much the same way, the church leadership has also gone through major changes. The previous role of the pastor was to teach the Word of God as the main pillar of their leadership role. In the past, leaders did not have the critical role in ensuring the growth of churches as they do today.[224] Pastors believed that as long as they preached God's Word and were committed to the living faith of the Lord, they did not have to worry for God was always there to provide for all their needs.[225]

However, in past decades, the churches have placed emphasis on the spiritual gifts of the Bible that proclaims that God gives every believer a spiritual gift to use in the service of Jesus Christ. This means that every gift plays a critical role in enhancing the health of the church. This is a concept that plays a critical part in helping us to understand the reasons of power decentralization in churches. Though pastors are revered, they are now called by God to possess virtuous character and lead, mobilize resources, motivate, and to direct people to embrace a vision from God and His fulfillment.[226] The laity especially carries out the vision of the church, and the senior pastors' role is that which has shifted in that the act of inspiring

---

[222] Ibid., 14.

[223] Barna, *The Second Coming*, 15–17.

[224] Ibid., 102.

[225] Ibid.,102

[226] Ibid.,, 107.

others, vision casting and management of the people is the first priority for them on a daily basis unlike in past generations.

Nowadays, pastors are not simply expected to preach but to create a community, envision, equip others, plan, organize, celebrate, and to relate to every member of the church.[227] These widespread demands on the pastor are insurmountable and even oppressive.

America today has become the nation of the niche market and the place of specialists. Churches are placing demands on ministry specialists who are the pastors. On a weekly basis, pastors in the protestant churches work up to sixty-five hours in dealing with sixteen significant dimensions in a single activity. This tedious job has made most of them experience common burnout.[228] The pastors also perceive their work as a calling by God and by other elders of the church, including other constituents, to participate in every piece of activity within their congregation.

With the effort of decreasing the burden on the pastors, many churches have embraced the multiple pastor staff. This is an effective way for the pastors to be in touch with every member of the congregation. Anderson says that the best practice for Christian churches is for one pastor to serve a group of 150 members of the church.[229] As churches continue to grow, the senior pastors' responsibilities also expand. This in turn leads to heightened expectations of the senior pastors toward both volunteer and paid staff. Women in the past have mainly participated in volunteer jobs in the churches, as well as the community in the same way as they do in modern day churches. In past decades, women's number in the work force has significantly increased, and this means that their dedication to volunteer services in the church has declined.[230] Therefore, this calls upon the modern day and future pastors to focus on how to motivate and influence individuals to take up the necessary actions in order to fill the gap that resulted from the decreased volunteer population.

The church, therefore, has undergone significant changes in terms of leadership styles size and volunteer base. There is also a change in the

[227] John Jackson, "How to Be a Pastor and Manager," *The Christian Ministry* 20, 1989, 8–10.
[228] Barna, *The Second Coming*, 5.
[229] L. Anderson, *Dying for Change*, 55.
[230] Ibid., 30.

Biblical Pastors were not and are not CEOs.

nature of constituents in churches. Most churches have failed to adjust to the cultural changes taking place in modern day American society. Berger shows the need for American churches to change along with societal changes, so that they can survive in the coming years. He also shows that there is a need for churches to align themselves as a result of plausible ever-changing structures that signify society. Furthermore, he states that for the churches to be successful in the coming century, they have to keep up with the pace that society perceives as being credible as well as formulate messages they pass to their congregation accordingly. The church leaders need to identify the desires, needs, and longing of the different constituents of the churches that keep on changing. Therefore, this is not an option but a major necessity of current churches.

The Influence of Culture on Church Leadership

The constantly changing American culture has also impacted the face-lifts of churches today. In the last few decades, there have been staggering cultural changes, and this has made the members of the church and other prospective church members to think, act, and perceive differently on various issues that impact their lives unlike in past decades. In order to understand the changing faces of the church, it is essential to examine the major factors that have affected the church, and the way they have influenced our culture, particularly issues regarding changing demographics, consumerism, and mass media. These are the factors that affect the church leadership through three major ways: business principles, congregational, and materialism.

Business Principles

With the advent of new technologies, consumer expectations for various organizations as well the churches have increased. Americans are encouraged by technology to strive to attain the greatest and latest. These new technologies have also led to a lack of commitment and loyalty to institutions, ideas, and individuals.[231] This means that individuals are driven with the need to climb and reach limits beyond their reach, outweigh

---

[231] Barna, *The Second Coming*, 63.

their commitment to invest and plant stakes for long-term purposes. This way of thinking is also employed by church members. Robert Bellah indicates that religion has been attacked by the market mentality and has become consumer driven in many ways. The consumer Christians, as he refers to them, are constantly shopping for a church that is convenient to fulfill their needs and can switch churches casually in the same way as they switch goods or brands. This means that whenever Christian consumers feel that a church is not meeting their views or demands, they shift to another church where they think they will find a more desirable package.[232]

This is a demand that has significantly impacted churches as they have to develop a "better package" to become full service churches that offer a wide variety of quality music, diverse educational opportunities, extensive programs for youth, children and adults, support groups, counseling, athletic activities, singles' ministry, modern nursery, multiple Sunday services, and many other programs and services that can only be found in mega churches.[233]

The movements from one church to another, as seen in many church members today, were not observed in the past. The churches are viewed by too many people as destination in a way that when their consumer appetites are satisfied, they would attend churches. Alternatively, when they find the church they wanted to join and that suits their appetite, they will stay in it in both good and difficult times.[234] However, this should not be in the case true followers of Christ. In spite of the theological debates around church attendance, cultural influence has resulted in bringing significant changes in the church. For instance, with the hope to meet the changing needs of Americans, the churches have shifted towards special taskforce assignments, one-day seminars, and stand-alone sermons.[235]

Church loyalty is no longer the norm in modern day churches, and this means that pastors and other church leaders are now at a point where they have to persuade individuals to be committed to the church and to attend church frequently. Every American today is a consumer, which means

---

[232] Robert Bellah, *The Good Society* (New York: Random House, 1991), 183.
[233] L. Anderson, *Dying for Change*, 51.
[234] Ibid., 27.
[235] Ibid., 36.

that religion is viewed on the basis of preference and not as a necessity.[236] This indicates that there is the need to question how the consumer can choose one church at the expense of another. Today's consumers choose a church according to the senior pastor and perceive the pastor to be the sole controller of the church. It is common for the churches to be known and recognized in reference to the name of the pastor, such as Dollar's Church. In the past, pastors were revered persons in society and served in guiding the community's decisions.

However, in the present time this view toward pastors has changed. Hybels, Briscoe, and Robinson write that pastors today cannot make it on the basis of their moral standing alone or the dignity of their position.[237] The demands of the people related to church have increased in today's world, unlike the past. Church leaders are expected to be charismatic, have the ability to articulate, and be informed about current affairs. Others demand church leaders to be well-groomed and attractive, just like news anchormen and women in media and network news. The pastors are also expected to relate to the communities' peculiarities. For a number of people, the pastors should act like business CEOs with the ability to attract more people, expand programs to suit the diverse needs of followers, and raise money.[238]

Just like other business organizations, the church is also faced with rampant consumerism, and church leaders have to act organizationally and be fiscally responsible. Since the 1980s, the budgets of mega churches have been increasing and have attained very lofty levels. These levels are on par with and match the budgets of other business corporations. The churches are intensively faced with questions about their financial management. Willow Creek church, with 23,400 attendees, is the third largest mega church in America today, and it was one of the earliest churches that reached a high budget level. Today, Lakewood Church in Houston, Texas, is the largest church. The church has a total of 43,500 attendees, and is led by Joel Osteen. LifeChurch.tv, based in Edmond, Oklahoma, is the second

---

[236] Steve Bruce, *Religion in the Modern World: From Cathedrals to Cults* (Oxford: Oxford University Press USA, 1996), 46.

[237] Hybels, Briscoe and Robinson. *Mastering Contemporary Preaching*. Portland: Multnomah Press, 1989.

[238] L. Anderson, *Dying for Change*, 54.

largest church with 26,776 attendees, and it is led by Craig Groeschel. From 1979 to 1989, the church bank balance of Willow Creek church rose from $1,872,834 to $23,198,725.[239] The growth of the congregation in these churches has resulted in financial growth, as well as the accumulation of power due to the way people view these churches.

Furthermore, churches are embracing the business models of becoming management experts that will assist the leaders in leading their congregations. This is the same way in which businesses conduct their activities, especially in terms of management. In the early 1990s, Bob Buford developed the Leadership Network[240] with the main purpose of examining the changes undergone by the church in the 21st century. The network also aimed to examine the unique emphasis placed by the churches on management skills and entrepreneurial leadership similar to those of large businesses.[241] Buford also collaborated with well-known entrepreneurs Max De Pree,[242] a Fortune 500 executive; Peter Drucker,[243] a management guru; and William Bridges,[244] a consultant in human development who have assisted businesses and churches in developing a proven form of leadership.

The implications of adopting business models are that, there is an increasing dim line that separates the market places and the churches. One dominant aspect that is becoming more conspicuous is the dominant structure of churches that are becoming more business-like, and this implies that the church as a business has to be solvent for it to survive in the coming times. In addition, the wish of the churches to compete in this

[239] James Mellado, *Willow Creek Community Church* (n.p.: Harvard Business School, 1991), 18.

[240] Wikipedia contributors, "Bob Buford," *Wikipedia, The Free Encyclopedia*, accessed October 26, 2013, http://en.wikipedia.org/wiki/Bob_Buford.

[241] Russell Chandler. *Racing Toward 2001: The Forces Shaping America's Religious Future*, (Grand Rapids: Zondervan Publishing House, 1992), 166.

[242] "Max De Pree," Max De Pree Center for Leadership, accessed October 27, 2013, http://depree.org/max-de-pree/.

[243] "Peter Drucker's Life and Legacy," The Drucker Institute, accessed October 27, 2013, http://www.druckerinstitute.com/link/about-peter-drucker/.

[244] William Bridges and Associates, accessed October 27, 2013, http://www.wmbridges.com.

large marketplace of consumer Christians is to align themselves through changing its structure, especially its rhetoric.

Congregational

The dramatic fluctuations in demographics impact the social action and philosophy, thus changes have to be made. The change in population signifies the need to change ideas to those that are credible to people.[245] Barna suggests that it is essential to understand the demographic trends that impact a church in order to increase its ability to respond to the newly emerging expectations and needs of the community that it aims to serve.[246] This is an understanding that enables the church to adapt its message to suit the needs of the potential and current members. The modern church is mainly influenced by various demographic trends that impact leadership of a congregation. These are wealth, educational ethnic diversity, family, and intergenerational breath.

Intergenerational breath is an aspect of the congregation that impacts leadership of churches. The challenge that pastors face is to use the appropriate language that can be well understood by all members of the congregation representing different generations. Barna notes that there are five major generations in the United States today. These generations are the Seniors, Builders, Boomers, Busters, and the Mosaics.[247] Each of these generational groups comprises unique global perspectives and identity factors. Today's aging baby boomers form the largest percentage in the church, and they expect to be addressed directly. The Advanced Management Program by Harvard Business School shows that baby boomers are motivated more through experiences unlike other generations. These experiences include jobs that they enjoy doing, candor and not tact, and change over stability.[248] The baby boomers also have to be drawn to churches with high expectations among the members.[249] Each of the congregational members has a different level of commitment, goals, and

---

[245] Berger, *The Sacred Canopy: Elements of a Sociological Theory of Religion*, 1990, 34

[246] Barna, *The Second Coming*, 52.

[247] Ibid., 77

[248] L. Anderson, *Dying for Change*, 93.

[249] Barna, *The Second Coming*, 214.

different desires to be committed to the traditional structures. The church needs to adapt to each of the congregational segments and at the same time maintain a plausible message. This is a daunting task for most churches in the 21ˢᵗ century.

Another congregational feature is the Family Unit. The family nucleus has dramatically changed, and this can be seen in the current facts such as a high divorce rate in this nation, where 1 in 4 marriages end in divorce. There is also a high number of children out of wedlock, and it is also reported that one-third of married adults do not condone adultery, and instead view it as an acceptable behavior.[250] These facts suggest that major changes have taken place in the prototypical unit in the family. The definition of a family in recent years has shifted from people related by marriages, adoption, and birth to individuals whom we care about deeply and vice versa.[251] Though this definition of the family may sound harmless, the underlying meaning signifies that there is nothing that is constant. Pastors no longer assume that everyone is originating from the same background. Pastors are facing challenges while teaching about the importance of the family in the traditional sense, when most of the constituents may not have been raised in a traditional family unit or are associated with these families. For example, pastors face challenges when preaching on the importance of abstinence to a mother of three children fathered by different men, or when preaching on the concept of fidelity to an adulterer. This means that these pastors have to walk in a much more narrow and delicate rope in ministering to their congregation.

Education is another congregational aspect that church leaders have to deal with in modern day churches. The United States still has a huge number of illiterate individuals despite the efforts of non-profit organizations to promote education among Americans. According to Barna, only half of Americans can read and write at the eight-grade level. This huge number of illiterate people also impact churches because the leaders have to rethink about communication methods with their congregational members. The use of print media and other traditional forms of communication are no longer necessary to facilitate effective means of communication. Barna advocates for the need to adopt new strategies and styles and to use

[250] Ibid., 66.
[251] Ibid.

communication media to help in passing God's message to His people without compromising the Word. These strategies have to be undertaken because of constantly changing context, culture, and technologies.[252]

The use of the Internet in learning institutions has considerably increased in past years. The dramatic use of interactive technology impact the way children and youth interact. At the same time, these technologies have reduced the rate at which students interact in traditional classrooms. This has impacted the development of students' soft skills, such as negotiating, conflict resolution, team building, listening, and creative problem solving as these become underdeveloped. As a result of mass media effects as well as the Internet, the attention span of children is considerably shortened to an average of six to eight minutes.[253] The shortened span of attention also impacts churches. This is because unlike in the past, children now lack full attention and commitment to sit hours listening to lectures and summons. Their learning is mainly through watching what others do. The churches perceive this as a major obstacle, especially in Sunday school classrooms comprising a large number of pupils. This also has an impact on Sunday school teachers as they need to improve their educational strategies so as to capture the attention of children for a longer duration, while at the same time not bore them.

Ethnic diversity is also a congregational aspect that impacts church leaders today. Traditionally, the United States acknowledges that it is a nation that comprises various ethnic groups and supports various ways of expression and thinking. According to Barna, the failure to establish a comfortable blend of behaviors, opportunities, and relationships among different parties and groups has contributed to a high level of dissipation.[254] Many churches abide by the proclamation of Dr. Martin Luther King that Sunday morning is the segregated hour designed to serve God unlike other days of the week. Most Asian, Hispanic, African-American ethnic groups and others are experiencing multiplication in population increases, yet the Caucasian population is constant. Despite the changing population, churches have continued to remain segregated.[255] When these statistics

---

[252] Barna, *The Second Coming*, 57.

[253] Ibid., 56.

[254] Ibid., 51.

[255] Barna, *The Second Coming*, 2.

remain under this level in the coming decades, there will be a significant change in the cultural make-up of the United States in the coming years. This will mean that future congregations will display these changes. The churches in the future will have new audiences, and there is the need for these churches to make necessary changes in order to accommodate the new audience.

It is also important to acknowledge that different ethnic groups have diverse views and backgrounds, and they perceive the world through different lenses. These differences are portrayed in different ways, such as the different forms and styles of worship unlike that used in Christian education. Despite these potential and current changes on ethnic diversity, modern churches are still segregated. This means that, for its success in the future, they should embrace a radical approach in diversifying its constituency.

The constituents of the church have changed with time, and this places huge demands on pastors today. Pastors are no longer perceived to be one-dimensional. They have to deal with various dimensions that directly reflect on the various changes taking place in the United States today. The high rate of illiteracy, the widening affluence gap, disintegration of traditional family values, and the broad spectrum of generations in churches, as well as shifting ethnic trends, all display new dimensions that society has to adopt in this modern day. These changes have to be embraced in modern day churches for them to survive in future.

Materialism

Covetousness is a major problem in modern day churches. The worldly values of possessions, status, and possessions no longer hold as the only worldly things. This is because instead of the churches emphasizing on matters of internal kingdom, Christ followers have instead become jealous of one another and identify themselves through status matters. Some theological authors have published materials on financial authority of a Christian but have failed to mention God's role in the financial aspects of a Christian's life. This is because Christians have forgotten to serve God, and they are serving money instead. In Matt. 6:24, Jesus teaches that it is impossible to serve both God and material wealth because our God is a jealous God. This is a common mistake that is made by many church leaders and the congregation in bringing their worship and love for money to the church. It is common to see Christians living an expensive life, wearing extravagant clothing, and adorned with expensive jewelry. They also drive expensive cars and wish for everyone to see their wealth. In the passing of offering baskets, they take their time to write checks or thumb through their hundred dollar notes in front of others. These are followers who only talk and associate with others of their caliber and standards. They pretend not to notice the homeless and are dubious to individuals sitting at the back corners of the church or to other newcomers. Though they have managed to place small fortunes of their wealth in terms of offering to the church, they have missed the major point of showing their obedience and love to the Lord in helping their neighbors in need.

Wealth is a material aspect that is attributed by the rising stock market. The gap between the poor and the rich is widening, which complicates the public stance of the church. Many people in the United States can be considered wealthy when compared to other nations. One of them is Bill Gates, who has a net worth more than most country's GNP (Gross National Product). A number of studies indicated that many wealthiest people in America have a disproportionate amount of wealth, and yet a significant number of Americans are living in poverty, have to struggles in order to survive, and have to rely on the government to support them[256]. Barna also shows the hardened heart of a large number of Americans toward the plight of unfortunate people.[257] Based on this rhetoric, pastors have to guide their constituents in biblical understanding of their responsibility and stewardship based on the fiscal disparity between the poverty-stricken and the affluent. Therefore, pastors have the responsibility of leading the congregations on practical matters that concern their daily lives such as answering the following questions: How much of an individual's wealth can be given away? How much should an individual invest? How much should be under their stewardship? What does the Christian gospel require of an individual's money and responsibility?

Other materialistic things such as mass media also impact the leadership styles of churches. Unlike past generations, the current globalized world

---

[256] Barna, *The Second Coming*, 54.
[257] Ibid.

has brought instantaneous communication and easy access to information. This is a result of new technologies supported by the Internet. Youths today are more advanced than ever in using computers, the Internet, videogames, mobile devices, videos, laptops, tablets and other emerging media technologies. In his research, Barna found that the average teenager spends seven hours receiving input from various media technologies within seventeen hours of their waking time.[258] This is an aspect that many churches have not yet embraced in integrating technology to their services. The Assembly of God Church in Winston-Salem, NC, one of the mega churches, believe that its main objective is to seek the lost and sinners; the pastors of this church have constantly stressed on the importance of adopting new changes necessary to fit into a media-based society through the use of applying visual Christological representations on the life and work of Christ. These technologies do not in any way water down the Christian message but enhance our understanding.[259]

Due to the impact of modern day technologies on church leadership, pastors have to be aware that the church audience today need to be addressed differently because the media greatly impacts consumer expectations. The mediated mind is that which seeks immediate gratification and one that expects to find results quickly. Therefore, pastors will continue to be faced with the challenge in enabling their stand-alone sermons to be like a sitcom that last for thirty minutes. When this expectation is met, churchgoers will be willing to come back the next Sunday. According to Neil Postman, Christian religion should be made to support the sitcom flavor, so that the religious experience is entertaining. However, he also says that this destroys the authentic characteristic of Christian culture.[260] How to properly mediate the Christian masses, and at the same time ensure that the true Christian calling is maintained, remains the main question facing the next century to come.

---

[258] Ibid., 3.

[259] John Railey, "Images of Religion Tradition: Face of Mainline Churches No Longer Reflects the Faith of the Fathers.," *Winston-Salem Journal*, August 23, 1999.

[260] Neil Postman, *Amusing Ourselves to Death* (London: Methuen Publishing, 1987), 124.

Decline of Religion Thesis

The religion thesis proposes that secularization would lead to the awakening of a progressive decline and shrinkage of religion even to the extent of disappearance. The continuous decline of religion in Europe and the United States, among other nations, is a result of enlightenment that is critiqued by religion. These nations have become the independent carriers of the secularization process so much so that the establishments of churches are viewed as obstacles of the modern differentiation process.

Religion can be defined by its substantive and functional definitions. The functional role of religion means the main purpose of religion and how it is carried out or practiced. One of the purposes of religion is to provide solutions to problems. Religion also acts as a source of guidelines on how to conduct our manners in a way that contributes to the stability and social order of society. The substantive definition of religion means the actual definition of religion and not its functional role. Therefore, religion in its substantive definition can be referred to as the actions and beliefs that involve the supernatural and God. The secularization thesis proponents posit that societal changes have taken place due to modernity and the impact has led to a change of religious aspects resulting from secularization. Religion, mainly Christianity, in the pre-modern era has become a dominant force and cited as a powerful force in society. The knowledge in the world is provided mainly through the religious events that occur on the personable experiences of individuals and from religion. However, with the societal reformations, there have been great changes in the dominance of religious beliefs in the United States and Europe when compared to what was previously accepted and became tradition. These changes had the aim of opening up ways of modernity. Industrialization and science, which are aspects found in modernity, have added to a decline of religion. This is because people establish their values and worldview from their understanding of the world and not from religious aspects. An example is the evolutionary theory by Charles Darwin that explains the evolution of man and not about the creation of man.

Sociological theories have also placed emphasis on the concept of secularization. Durkheim provides the function of religion as being one that promotes social solidarity. Religion, according to Durkheim, also helps to promote social values because society worships the religion. However, industrialization of religion has been perceived as becoming less significant. Other institutions, like the education system, provide social solidarity.[261]

Referring to Michael Haralambos, R.M. Heald, and Martin Holborn highlighted that religion has to be perceived as being eternal.[262] On the other hand, Weber believed that rationalization is the main cause of religion subsidence. Weber foresaw disenchantment of the supernatural with the emergence of rational science. He believes that as societies achieve technological and scientific understanding, the result is that people cease from religious explanations and meanings that help us to understand the world. He postulated that the effects of modernization are inevitable.[263]

Evidence That Shows a Reduced Belief in Religion

Bryan Wilson[264]uses statistics of secularization indicators in a study that he conducted. The statistics are religious ceremonies participation, church membership, and church attendance. The statistics showed that there is a steady decline in these indicators of religious practices such as the rise of civil marriages other than church marriages, reduced church membership, and the decline of other religious practices. These statistics are the evidence that religion is losing its social importance. Furthermore, the forbidding of behaviors such as homosexuality, abortions, divorce, and contraception by the church seem to have no impact on people's lives.

---

[261] Emile Durkheim, *The Elementary Forms of Religious Life*. (New York: Free Press, 1995), 117.

[262] Michael Haralambos, R.M. Heald, and Martin Holborn. *Sociology: Themes and Perspectives*. 7th ed. (London: Collins Educational, 2000), 430.

[263] George, Ritzer. The Weberian Theory of Rationalization and the McDonaldization of Contemporary Society, Chapter 2, The McDonaldization of Society, Pine Forge Press; Revised ed. 1996, http://www.corwin.com/upm-data/16567_Chapter_2.pdf.

[264] Karel Dobbelaere "Bryan Wilson's Contributions to the Study of Secularization", *Social Compass* 53, no. 2 (June 2006): 141–46, accessed October 27, 2013, http://scp.sagepub.com/content/53/2/141.abstract.

Together with the reports given by Morrison (2002)[265] that 4 in 10 marriages are likely to end up in divorce is another indication of declining religion in modern day society. There is also evidence to support the fact that religion by itself is undergoing secularization such as allowing people who had divorced to remarry in the church. The nexus being the much lower standards sets on divorce laws. There is also the ordination of women priests, the abolition of the use of Latin languages in Catholic churches, and abandonment of traditional beliefs—these are all signs of the secularization of churches and religion.

Other evidence seen today that supports the decline of religious institutional influence and power is seen in contemporary times. The union that was there in the past between the church and the state no longer exists. The government does not respect the views of the church. Unlike the relationship between the church and the government, various non-governmental organizations have emerged to take up the role that was previously done by the church. One of the organizations is the welfare state that looks after the disadvantaged in the communities. This clearly indicates that religion has no public influence and has withdrawn from the political and public life. This is the concept referred to as differentiation. Therefore, this means that modern day church leaders have dropped their traditional roles of acting as shepherds for society and ministering to the needy.

Various criticisms have been directed towards the secularization thesis because of many reasons. However, the evidence clearly shows the decline in religious influence because people are not regular attendees of worship places and few religious organization members hold on to and practice religious beliefs.[266] The reason for the decline in church attendance is linked to the inability of the church to exert adequate social pressure for its members to attend. Many critics have viewed the United States as a country that proves the secularization thesis wrong. This is a country that is a highly industrialized and urban society, yet religion plays an

---

[265] Blake, Morrison, "Why do we do it?" The Guardian, October 27, 2002, http://www.theguardian.com/theguardian/2002/oct/14/features11.g2 accessed on November 26, 2013

[266] Michael Haralambos, R.M. Heald, and Martin Holborn. *Sociology: Themes and Perspectives.* 7th ed. (London: Collins Educational, 2000), 434.

integral and influential part in people's lives. This reflects a totally different case from that of Britain. This means that the secularization thesis is a concept that manifests differently for various reasons in specific cases and cannot be generalized because despite the United States' industrialized and technological advancement, its church membership has continued to increase and the influence of the church is still felt in the government and social sectors.

McDonaldization Model and Growth of Churches

In his book, *McDonaldization of Society*, George Ritzer presents the principle of McDonaldization. This is an aspect derived from the fast-food restaurant business and is the most dominant aspect of most business sectors in the United States. McDonaldization of society is obvious in all organizations today. The term was coined by Ritzer to extend the thoughts of Weber's theories.[267] Ritzer shows that the theory by Weber presents the ability of the modern western world to become highly rational and is dominated by calculability, predictability, efficiency, and use of non-human technologies to control human beings.[268] Through efficiency, it is possible to move from one state to another. Predictability guarantees that services and products are identical regardless of the location or time.

McDonaldization in Modern Day Mega Churches

The Protestant American mega church is continuing to grow when the general church attendance has been on the decline. The explanation on the reasons as to why these churches continue to multiply in their membership of over 2,000 at a rapid pace is much needed. The study of various recent periodicals and publications will help to provide answers on the rising rate of mega churches in terms of membership number. The main explanation given is that the mega churches form a new social movement, which is different from early 20th century churches. One main factor that

---

[267] Wikipedia contributors, "Sociology of Religion," *Wikipedia, The Free Encyclopedia*, accessed December 1, 2013, http://en.wikipedia.org/wiki/Sociology_of_religion.

[268] George Ritzer, *The McDonaldization of Society*, New Century ed. (Thousand Oaks: SAGE Publications, 2000), 25.

distinguished the mega churches from churches of the past is that the former operate in the same way as businesses. The churches are involved in competition and adept at applying business principles to develop and deliver a professional worship service product. The mega churches have a business like structure and this enables an effective analysis of the theory of McDonaldization according to Ritzer in areas such as predictability, efficiency, irrationality of rationality, and non-human technology use.

The mega churches are perceived by some people as being the religious phase of the past decade while some view these churches as the modern form of protestant worship. Others view the churches as an everlasting thorn in current churches of the United States. With the profane and dialectical challenges of the sacred ensured, the mega church history has attained minimal competition. Though the characteristics that define mega churches are well known, the basic and standard definitions are that they are churches, which can hold more than 2,000 people on a weekly basis.[269] Some say that the mega churches stand as a symbol of a shift in protestant churches of today, and it is a modern day phenomena. The question is: Will the historical evidence of the mega churches show that this phenomenon is just like any other flow and ebb in the social trend cycle of the United States, or will the evidence show that the trend was in fact a unique set of qualities of the contemporary era?

This question will be addressed in the following section by examining the recent movements of churches, especially in the protestant churches of the United States, which have now adopted business-like structures. Following section will further analyze the way the McDonaldization theory can be applied in the study of mega church structures. Finally, I will examine the resulting struggle that exists between the profane and sacred in postmodern church. The study of these issues is based on various news media surveys, academic sources, web pages, periodicals, and my personal observations to various mega churches.

History of Mega Churches

The establishment of the Willow Creek Community Church in October 12, 1975 in South Barrington, Illinois saw many young Protests

---

[269] Thumma, "The Kingdom, the Power, and the Glory."

American youth joining this church. These young people were mainly from the middle class. This mega church was viewed as the designer church among most middle-class individuals. The founder, Hybels, and the whole of Willow Creek began to accommodate an increasing number of people. This model of the church impacted other areas of Chicago suburbia and also became the prominent model in the Sunbelt states of Florida, Texas, California, and Georgia. Irrespective of the racial and denominational lines, many other churches began to implement various aspects of Hybels' model both in the small towns and large cities. As this model became more dominant, there was also a decline in membership in other churches as more than two million Americans started joining and becoming members of mega churches.

The New Movement of Mega churches

The new trend of mega churches can seem to be a reflection of another religious root in today's American society. For two decades after the start of the 19th century, the same growth of large Protestant churches was witnessed in the United States. Some view this growth as being another development of social trends, as was seen in the early 20th century, while others dismiss these phenomena as being simplistic, saying that the increased number of attendees, the function, and atmosphere provided by the mega churches today are different from the large churches of the past decade.

Comparisons in Numbers

A point of comparison between the past and present large churches is found in numbers. For example, the large churches with notable numbers are the Saddleback Church in Los Angeles with 15,000 members, the Willow Creek Community Church in South Barrington with 17,000 attendees, while the most notable is the Crystal Cathedral in Garden Grove, California, which is the headquarters of Crystal Cathedral ministries. It hosts over 10,000 members, and its services are televised internationally in the *Hour of Power* program.

In the 20th century, there were large Protestant congregations across the United States. Since 1922, for more than a decade, the Paul Rader's

Gospel Tabernacle of Chicago attracted a capacity in the auditorium of more than 5,000 seats. The St. George Episcopal attracted 6,600 people in and outside New York and the Baptist Temple in Philadelphia hosted more than 3,000 members. In addition, the Church of Seattle hosted a congregation comprised of 9,000 people during this period. John D. Rockefeller provided the monetary resources to New York City's The Riverside Church. The church recorded an attendance of 9,000 people. Los Angeles' Angelus Temple was also another famous church during this period with over 5,300 attendees. The sitting capacity of this church was 5,300 seats, and it held full church services on Sundays in the 1920s and 1930s. It was until the period of the Great Depressions and other financial stressors that finally weighed the church down.

Target the Population

In regards to sheer attendance, the mega protestant churches of the 1920s show similarities with today's contemporary mega churches. However, the characteristics of the parishioners in both churches may be different during the two periods. In the early 20th century, approximately one third of the population in the United States was either children of immigrants or immigrants. Though the immigrants were from countries that mainly had Roman Catholic affiliation, they did not maintain their catholic denomination when they immigrated to the United States. The new immigrants took up residence in various downtown districts. With the increase of the population, churches were forced to either reach out to the new immigrants living in the heart of the city or attract older members of the population living in uptown homes. The continuous influx of various types of people led to the growth of the churches that aimed to transform their outreach to fit the needs of the immigrant population.

Large churches in the 1920s appealed mainly to most immigrants; similarly, the mega churches of the 1990s to the 2000s also served a particular segment in the population, which are suburbia families. These types of mega churches provide services as well as a place for its members to worship. The style and services offered in these churches appeal to a wide range of population segments. Therefore, these well-educated, highly mobile, and consumer oriented middle-class families are attracted to contemporary mega churches. This is contrary to the churches of the 1920s and even to those of the 1930s, whose aim was to attract the poor working-class individuals with little or no means of acquiring the services offered by other churches from different sources.

Research studies indicate that churches of different sizes grow at a much faster rate in places with an increasing population when compared to scattered populated areas. At city centers, many people have lost their zeal in attending churches. As a result, church membership has declined in these areas; although, there is growth in these urban areas. The population shift to the suburbs provides an answer to the increased number of mega churches and the drop in city church attendance, which is about 20% during the 1990s. In 1991, church attendance, as part of the weekly activity, was at 40% across the United States, which was a drop from 49%.

Thumma and other religious scholars have defined mega churches as a new phenomenon. In the past, there were only a dozen or so massive congregations. Currently, the number of mega churches has risen to over 700 and is still rising. Others do not support this claim and propose that the population statistics, which has increased in the United States, is the main cause of the rising number of mega churches. However, evidence clearly shows that most major cities of the 1920s and 1930s also had large churches just like the ones we see today.

The explanation given by the Hartford Institute for Religion is that the mega church is a totally new phenomenon that is different from the past, and it goes beyond simply the number explanations. The institute gives evidence to the modern day mega churches' uniqueness, attributing it to the issues of programming.[270] This means that the modern mega churches are programmed in a way that they are able to offer a wide range of worship styles, ministries, music, and other programs that appeal to everyone, and these are all offered in the same church structure.

Staging and Services Productions

The aim of mega churches is not only to seek to grow numerically and to proselytize but also to provide services like counseling, selling books,

---

[270] Megachurches –definition, Hartford Institute for Religion (n.d.), accessed on December 1, 2013, http://hirr.hartsem.edu/megachurch/megachurches.html

and aiding youth and women groups in their projects. These churches also provide awards such as bursaries and scholarship for students, support for teen pregnancy and women faced with pregnancy crisis, as well as ministries for single parents and families faced with divorce issues. This places the churches at a new level of spinning off communities in a new and developed level. On the concept of the need to grow and proselytize, mega churches such as Willow Creek Church provides services meant for different audiences. In this church, more than 17,000 people attend more than six services. Two of these services are specifically meant for Generation X. The services are orchestrated and well-planned productions that incorporate seven rhythm bands, a 75-person choir, 41 actors, a 65-piece orchestra, an arts center, and video production with more than 300 students receiving training to make up worship services. The versatility of classes and programs, as well as worship service styles are the main proponents of today's mega churches that are different from the large churches of the past.

The protestant churches in 1920s-1930s also had programming and accommodated a wide range of immigrants through designing services to meet the needs of the parishioners. The early churches established swimming pools, gymnasiums, employment centers, medical dispensaries, libraries, loan offices, classrooms, and day care centers. These services supported a wide range of languages. The churches taught about the scriptures but mainly emphasized on the use of the English language. The early large churches further provided work skills, home economics skills, and hygiene skills.

The earlier large churches further staged productions that attracted many people to attend the services. The Angelus Temple only had a stage and not a pulpit. This stage supported the use of live ships, camels, sheep, sirens, motorcycles, and proper casting of its founder, Aimee Semple McPherson, also known as Sister Aimee, to be like a casino with searchlights moving up the sky as seen in the Angelus Temple.[271] The Angelus Temple is an example of a typical model of the magi protestant churches of the 1920s and 1930s. Gospel Tabernacles that offered afternoon services to youth groups and had time for choirs, crusades, parades, prayer ministries, adult

---

[271] Thumma, "The Kingdom, the Power, and the Glory."

classes, healing services, choir sessions, magazine fairs, radio broadcasting, and sermons also employed similar techniques.

Differences between Mega Churches of the Past and Present

The churches of the 20th century had the statistics. They also had programming for their churches. However, the large churches of the past and the mega churches of today differ in two aspects.

Mega Churches' Unique Culture

Culture is an aspect that separates the mega churches from the large churches of the past. Culture means the way a congregation develops its own community despite crossing the geographical boundaries. Mega churches have managed to provide a whole new social environment. They have managed to provide a range of services to groups, clubs, and programs, and they have also managed to embark on ministries that are successful and effective in eliminating their members' need for secular programs.

One of the well-known sectors in the mega churches is athletics for both adults and children. The Bellevue Baptists Church is located in the same area of a baseball complex that is used for people of all ages to hold baseball leagues. Furthermore, this church provides a series of practice fields similar to facilities in the city. Other mega churches have also involved themselves in different sports swimming pools, basketball courts, and roller-skating rinks. Other churches provide retirement homes for the old and have movie theaters incorporated into their complexes.

Referring to the article "God on a Grand Scale," written by Lauren Kapp in 2001, Elizabeth Cook in her research highlighted that she liked the wide range of activities offered by mega churches to those of small colleges dealing with liberal arts and Club Med.[272] Many mega churches encourage its members not to engage in worldly activities. However, they have managed to construct a place where members can spend a day in

---

[272] Elizabeth, Cook. "Would You Like Your Jesus Upsized? McDonaldization and the Mega Church" (*University of Tennessee, Knoxville Trace: Tennessee Research and Creative Exchange*, 2002), 16, http://trace.tennessee.edu/utk_interstp2/85

church, and this minimizes the level at which they come into contact with secular organizations. Megachurch is basically a place that juggles athletic events and music lessons for youth, bowling leagues for fathers and aerobics classes for mothers, and they are all facilitated under one umbrella. Therefore, families no longer have to interact with their neighbors. Some mega churches also offer the convenience of auto repair centers. Therefore, the church establishes its community, no matter its physical distance from people.

Poverty and Affluence

Another difference between the mega churches of today and the large churches of the past is the issue of choice. The limited geographic mobility and the financial situation of the immigrants made them rely on the local churches so as to obtain various services they provided. The immigrants lacked a means to obtain services and goods that the large churches offered. This is especially true because most of them were the working classes with minimal wages. However, members of current day mega churches are the affluent individuals in society. Despite their ability to afford a wide range of business services and goods, these affluent members still choose to be involved and be part of the programs offered by the church and not secular ones. In fact, these programs are created by the contributions made by members, which may enable them to feel more at home in these mega churches. Therefore, instead of members going to community centers, commercial gyms, and the YMCA found within their local areas, they are willing to walk or drive to a much distant family life center offered by their mega churches. These churches also offer social events, library books, and counseling services, which members prefer compared to those from other sources.

The population attending a given mega church is not one which reflects the surrounding community situation. The immigrants attended churches that were near their homes, but for the super-sized congregation, people drive to these mega churches. Other families can even drive for one or more hours just to attend a particular church service.

Staff Specialization and Finances

At any given time, large churches have to plan their huge budgets. There is also need to manage the large group of people and numerous programs offered by the church. All these responsibilities call for the need to have qualified staff. A church based in Chicago had at one time a staff of 30 on payroll. Yet another, St. Bartholomew Church, had employed 249 paid workers.[273] The staff members of these churches carry out their tasks through specialization. For example, a church accommodating a moderate 2,700 members also provided various paid positions. According to a church newsletter, these positions included eight pastors, pastor care, executives, senior adults, young adults and family life leader, youth, single adults as well as college and worship leaders[274]. An administrative assistant also supports these pastors. In fact, there is an assistant minister for the tape ministry director, financial director, assistant music trainer, preschool ministry coordinator, children's ministry assistant and coordinator, receptionists, preschools ministry coordinator, facilities director, family life assistants, facilities upkeep coordinators, and kitchen personnel consisting of more than three staff. This accounts to more than 40 paid positions for these mega churches.

The availability of specialized labor division develops bureaucratic limits and barriers to volunteer opportunities and hinders people from contributing on a personal preference basis. *The Onion* once contributed to a satirical message in an article showing that Jesus Christ had appointed an assistant Christ[275]. This article reflects the fun derived from the specialized staff in and outside churches as a source of humor.

The Simpsons, a popular television animated sitcom, further addresses the issues facing the mega churches. In an episode *She of Little Faith*, Bart and Homer constructed a model rocket, and in the process, they lose control and the rocket ended up burning down the whole church. Faced with this challenge, the church had to sell its resources to corporate

---

[273] Michael S. Hamilton, "Willow Creek's Place in History," *Christianity Today*, November13, 2000, 63.

[274] Cook, *Would You Like Your Jesus Upsized?* 16.

[275] "Christ Announces Hiring Of Associate Christ", The Onion, May 6, 1998, Iss. 33:17, accessed December 2, 2013, http://www.theonion.com/issue/3317/

sponsors because the church needed money for the repairs. The main corporate sponsor was Mr. Burns. Lisa became appalled by the billboards were displayed shamelessly and was shocked by the corporate monikers emblazoned on the church walls. She was so upset that she decided to quit the church once and for all.

Unlike the modern mega churches, large churches in earlier times did not specialize in their labor. A few members who served as board members were responsible for making the decisions. There were also paid staff members, who did not carry out specialized services, but were viewed as multi-purpose employees who could carry out any task that required immediate consideration. These employees were had to complete tasks from managing publicity to performing electrical work. Therefore, the administrative structures of the churches were mainly based on unpaid volunteers.[276]

Denominational Ties

The increasing non-denominationalism dominance is another aspect that characterizes modern mega church growth. About 20% of mega churches are affiliated with the Southern Baptists denomination. However, this affiliation is not readily apparent to the uninformed. The mega churches most often down play their denominational ties. Based on an overview, there are no indications from websites, advertisements, or signs that show that a given mega church belongs to a specific denomination. This means that when the church refers to itself or shows signs that it is independent from any denomination, it is likely that it will flourish compared to that which is tied to a specific denomination. This independence also allows the mega churches to assert their autonomy more than before.

The large churches in the 1920s, owned by individuals, were non-denominational while others had established strong ties with a particular denomination and managed to incorporate these denominations in their identities and titles. The Foursquare Gospel was founded by McPherson as a denomination of its own. Similarly, the Willow Creek Community Church, founded by Hybels, established its own model that has significantly impacted the current trend of non-denominational churches.

---

[276] Hamilton, "Willow Creek's Place in History," 62.

In *Inside the Mind of the Untouched Harry and Mary*, the author Lee Strobel discusses the action of Hybels, the founder of the Willow Creek Church, as one who puts off the denominational title because of people's preconceptions held toward these forms of organizations.[277] Hybels also established the Willow Creek Association that helps to train other mega churches on how to deal with and encourage growth. This association similarly avoids being associated with any denomination. The association is a network of resources that is helpful to mega churches and helps them to create symbiotic relationships. In this association, no doctrine is put under debate, no money is exchanged, and no doctrines are shared. However, with the effort of Hybels in providing training to lay personnel and staff of current mega churches, it may imply the non-denominational approach proliferation that he advocates.

Architecture

The architecture of the modern day mega churches is mainly viewed as being innovative. There is a sharp contrast between the older Protestant churches with Gothic style architecture and the sleek boat and other postmodern architectural styles of the new mega churches. A journalist has described the architectural design of the mega church as being much heavily symbolized with the traditional stained glass, Christianity cross, altars, and others which are aspects that were removed from the ultramodern design in the modern auditorium. There is a single cross hanging behind the choir above the baptismal pool. Unlike the mega churches that developed from earlier existing congregations, the building style of the mega churches typically follows this design. The sprawling sleek modern style of the multifunctional buildings and campus is the norm of the postmodern mega church.

The Willow Creek Church is used mainly as the example of a modern day building and not the Crystal Cathedral. The Crystal Cathedral structure was built with all glass, and it first started as a church just like a movie theater, but it is now a massive church that accommodates a congregation including 10,000 members. However, a cathedral with more

---

[277] Lee Strobel. *Inside the Mind of Unchurched Harry and Mary: How to Reach Friends and Family Who Avoid God and the Church*(Grand Rapids: Zondervan), 1993.

than 10,000 windows with silver-colored glass framed with white steel trusses is basically not the preference for most mega churches. Therefore, Robert H. Shuller's model of the church is more likely to be overlooked in favor of the Willow Creek Church model. This is despite the fact that these two churches were built within a year of each other and share similar ministries.

The architectural styles of the large churches of the 1920s were different from the Gothic styles that are now viewed to be traditional or classic. Many of the large churches of the 1920s resembled warehouses. The church leaders did not choose a specific venue to hold their services and conducted services in any building that was available. The contracted places for holding services were nondescript buildings with a warehouse look. The St. Bartholomew Church had a roof-top garden in a nine-story building.[278] Another large church of the 1900s was the Angelus Temple that had no specific uniformity, which was a Coliseum sports arena with an open space. These large churches were in cities, and the high cost of acquiring space made it almost impossible to build a campus like the ones seen in today's suburban mega churches.[279]

Consequences of Size and the Church Decline

This section examines why the large churches in the 1920s and 1930s collapsed despite flourishing. A significant contributing factor to its collapse was that social services, which were used by these churches as an evangelical tool, began to take up all the churches' financial resources. Church attendees placed increased demand on these social services, leading to a decrease of religious services and proselytizing of services. The two roles began to compete to gain more of the available fiscal resources. The decreased emphasis placed on the religious aspects of the church was the main reason that caused the decline in appeal that the church once held. At critical times, the social services created the need for an increasingly larger budget, and the contributions made by the congregation were unable to sustain the increased demand for these services. The great financial strain created the precarious fiscal crisis just before the Great Depression, and

---

[278] Hamilton, "Willow Creek's Place in History," 63.
[279] Ibid., 63.

it marked the final straw. The large churches finally reached bankruptcy, and the Great Depression crippled most of them before they finally faded into obsolescence. Other large churches that survived simply decreased in numbers down to average sized churches and gained the status of a regular church.

After the Depression, a few gospel tabernacles were able to thrive. This can be seen in one located in Indianapolis that continued to provide service to tens of thousands of people all Sunday up to the 1950s. It is possible that the Angelus Temple could have faded, but it brought about a new denomination known as the International Church of the Foursquare Gospel.

Unfortunately, the urban gospel tabernacle popularity lost its status. This was caused by the decreasing population in towns and cities as they moved into the suburbs, as well as and the change in culture to the one based more on consumerism, just like the commercially-driven phenomena seen today. An observer of this trend may say that the root foundation of the current mega church movement is traceable to the churches' situations in the past 30 years. This is a short duration that is filled with new trend, just like the development of non-denominational modern mega churches.

The Decline of Mainstream Federation Churches

With minimal growth of churches and progress in the 20th century, a Methodist minister named Roy Burkhart proposed that there is a need for different denominations to form a united church that reaches the community together and combines resources. An example of this scenario is the United Methodist Church and the Evangelical Unite Brethren. However, despite the combination of churches from different denominations, it had little impact on the growth of churches. The level of attendance at these churches remained at the same level of attendance that each had prior to the newly-combined church. This trend of churches coming together from different denominations was short-lived, and by the 1960s this trend was dead. The social turmoil resulted in every church standing on its own. There was also a shrinking of church attendances, especially in denominations like the United Methodist Church, which had to withdraw from unions of federated churches and started developing its individual approach of dealing with the church attendance decline.[280]

In most instances, the churches do reflect society. The churches are usually not cut off from social trends and are just like teenybopper fashions or various fad diets. Church structure and programming always experience the need to change in order to follow these social trends. The social influences impact programming because they are directly connected to the wants of people. In response to the increasing immigrant population, most gospel tabernacles in the urban sectors managed to provide people with their daily necessities required by communities surrounding the churches. The tabernacles became the source of medical care and food, but they were also opportunities for people to interact. Church-related entertainments, like services, were unique depending on each church.

The development of population centers and the beginning of the Depression meant that people during that period shifted to the suburbs in order to receive other social measures.[281] The federation church failed to attain growth by not drawing new members also fell victim to the social unrest of the 1960s, including the Vietnam War. This social unrest led to more challenges in addition to those already faced by the churches. Today's mega churches are different because they appeal to the uncharted and the disenchanted baby boomers.

The cultural influence on the church and its leadership over the past few decades can be summed up as nothing more than a compromise with the world.

Compromise with the World

2 Chronicles 17–20 shows us how a man's greatest strengths are often also the source of his greatest weaknesses. If a man who has strong convictions and who speaks out boldly for God's truth is not careful, he can become harsh or unkind. On the other hand, a man oozing with love and compassion can err by tolerating everything and everyone, thus compromising God's truth. The latter error seems to me to be the more common danger in the church. Often, in the name of love and out of a

---

[280] Hamilton, "Willow Creek's Place in History," 65.
[281] Hamilton, "Willow Creek's Place in History," 67.

desire to promote unity, Christians have compromised with the world. Scripture is clear: Any compromise with the world, whether in doctrine, morals, or relationships, has disastrous consequences.

The story of Jehoshaphat is about a godly, good king with a major weakness for compromising with the world. Here, we learn that compromise with the world brings disastrous consequences to God's people. The outward damage may not be apparent immediately, but compromising with the world brings inevitable corruption into peoples' lives and into the church. The following four observations from the story of Jehoshaphat can enlighten us on this subject.

Danger for Even the Most Godly of Believers

According to 2 Chron. 17:3–4, 6, Jehoshaphat was a godly man who sought the Lord and walked in His commandments. He took great pride in the ways of the Lord and removed idols from the land. In 2 Chron. 17:7–9, we are told that he sent out teachers to instruct the people in God's law. When a prophet rebuked him for his wrongful alliance with Ahab, as seen in 2 Chron. 16:10, Jehoshaphat accepted it, unlike his father, and went on to institute further religious reforms, as described in 2 Chron. 19:2–11. In 2 Chron. 20, we see his heart as the nation is threatened by a vast army, and he calls the people to prayer and fasting. Jehoshaphat's prayer before the assembly in 2 Chron. 20:6–12 reveals his humble trust in the Lord.

Here, we see that Jehoshaphat was not your average believer. He was a man of strong faith and open godliness who courageously brought reform to the nation. And if he suffered from the danger of compromising with the world, then none of us is exempt. Why did Jehoshaphat and why do we fall into the problem of compromise with the world?

Subtlety

The first instance we read of Jehoshaphat in 2 Chron. 17:1–2 is how he strengthened his position over Israel (Ahab's northern kingdom). Later in 2 Chron. 17:12–19, we read of his valiant army and fortified cities. He was ready for any onslaught. If Ahab had declared war, Jehoshaphat would have won hands down. Instead Ahab was able to get his daughter married to Jehoshaphat's son. The next thing we are told in 2 Chron. 18:3 is Jehoshaphat promising the godless Ahab, "I am as you are, and my people as your people, and we will be with you in the battle." This is not the way God intends for His people. However, this is how Satan works. He does not announce his real intentions up front. He uses trickery, fools you with lies, and before the truth is known, the damage is done.

Why did Jehoshaphat get entangled with Ahab? Jehoshaphat was one of the godliest kings ever to reign in Judah, and Ahab was one of the most despicable kings to ever sit on the throne of Israel. Why did they get together?

As seen in 2 Chron. 18:1, the text does not answer these questions, but given what we do know, we can surmise that due to Jehoshaphat's power, it was to Ahab's advantage to become allies. So, Ahab probably sought the alliance. Remember, Jehoshaphat was a nice man and probably thought it would be good to reunite the southern and northern kingdoms. Thus, he gave his son in marriage to Ahab's daughter for what he thought was for a good cause.

A few years later, Jehoshaphat went down to Ahab's capital, Samaria. Ahab rolled out the red carpet for him. After they dined on Ahab's food, Ahab proposed a "spiritual" project to Jehoshaphat in 2 Chron. 18:3: "Will you go up with me *against* Ramoth-Gilead?" Ramoth-Gilead was one of the cities of refuge ordained by God, and it had fallen into the hands of the king of Syria. What could be more right than to go against this pagan king to recapture this city for the Lord and His people? So, Jehoshaphat pledged his allegiance to Ahab, but it almost got him killed.

That is how Satan ensnares believers. He is not up-front about the disastrous consequences of compromise with the world. He makes it look good and seem wholesome and even right. That is how godly people get lured into compromise with the world—through subtlety. How does it work?

Wrong Relationships

Jehoshaphat got deeply got stuck into wrong relationships. First, he gave his son in marriage, probably for a good cause (to reunite the two kingdoms). Next, he accepted Ahab's hospitality and foolishly gave his word about going into battle. Now, his conscience was bothering him, so he asked for a prophet in order to inquire of the Lord. However, even after the godly Micaiah prophesied against Ahab's expedition, Jehoshaphat felt locked in—he had given his word. Thus, he stood by while the godly prophet was hauled off to jail.

Next, Jehoshaphat naively agreed to Ahab's scheme where Jehoshaphat would wear his kingly robes into battle, while Ahab went incognito. Christians are generally trusting people. When they start running with the world, they get outsmarted really quickly. So, Jehoshaphat went into battle with the godless Ahab against the word of God's prophet. Had it not been for God's grace, Jehoshaphat would have been killed.

We get caught up by the subtlety of the world, and then we get locked in by forming wrong relationships that get us entangled even deeper. Jehoshaphat's experience reveals several areas where we, as believers, must be on guard against forming wrong relationships:

(1) Wrong *social* relationships. We must be very careful in this area. If Jehoshaphat had not been there enjoying Ahab's hospitality, he would not have been so ready to join Ahab on his military expedition. It is not wrong, in fact, it is right to form social relationships with unbelievers for the purpose of leading them to faith in Christ. Jesus was a friend of sinners in that sense. However, we must be clear on our purpose, and we must not compromise our standards as followers of Jesus Christ. "Do not be deceived," Paul warns in 1 Cor. 15:33. "Bad company corrupts good morals."[282] We should not form primary friendships with unbelievers. Our closest friends must be those who share our values and goals in Christ, as is advised in 2 Cor. 6:14: "What fellowship has light with darkness?"

(2) Wrong *spiritual* relationships. Jehoshaphat finds himself lined up with 400 false prophets against the lone prophet of God. How did Jehoshaphat felt as he watched this godly prophet boldly speak for God and then get hit in the face and thrown in prison while Jehoshaphat marched off to battle on Ahab's side?

---

[282] 1 Cor. 15:33, NET Bible.

(3) Wrong *political* relationships. Although our political system is not parallel to the situation in the text, there is a warning here for us as Christian citizens. As soon as Jehoshaphat entered into the military pact with Ahab, he lost his position of strength. Now, he is committed to go into battle with a godless man who operated on different principles than he did. He had to work under Ahab's scheme in the battle. It almost cost him his life.

As believers, we may find it helpful at times to link up politically with unbelievers to achieve some common goal (such as pro-life or pro-family legislation). However, we need to think it through very carefully and keep our goals and methods clearly in view. Some Christians in America are getting carried away with the political process, as if that is the answer to preserving our freedoms. Although not disparaging our political responsibility as Christian citizens, the only hope for the United States and the world is the gospel. We should never forget this. Wrong political relationships can lead us into compromising with the world.

(4) Wrong *business* relationships. Jehoshaphat did not learn his lesson with Ahab, so he entered into a shipbuilding venture with Ahab's son, Ahaziah. The author pointedly states that this was a wicked deed on Jehoshaphat's part. The Lord judged him by destroying all the ships in 2 Chron. 20:35–37.

Many Christians are not adept at applying 2 Cor. 6:14: "Do not be unequally yoked with unbelievers" to business ventures. If we get into a business partnership with unbelievers, their goals are to make money, preferably as easily as possible. A professing Christian's goal is to honor Christ. The Christian should want to be honest and upright whereas the unbeliever will cut corners whenever needed and without conscience. These unholy business relationships never work. Eventually, compromising with the world is inevitable.

We have seen that compromise with the world is a great danger even for the most godly of believers. It is subtle, and it ensnares us through wrong relationships.

Leads to Disastrous Results

It may take time, but sin always has its consequences. Sometimes, the consequences affect future generations more than our own. However, if we compromise with the world, we would not reap God's blessings. If not for God's grace, Jehoshaphat would have lost his life in battle. He later did lose financially in his ungodly business alliance with Ahab's son.

Furthermore, Jehoshaphat's sin affected God's people. In 2 Chron. 18:3, he did not say merely, "I am as you are," but also, "and my people as your people." When Jehoshaphat went into war alongside Ahab, the army of Judah went with him; no doubt, some men in the army lost their lives. Perhaps others in Judah would look at the friendship between the godly Jehoshaphat and the evil Ahab and say, "There must not be much difference between Ahab's religion and ours. Surely, if there was any big difference, such a good man as Jehoshaphat wouldn't be so friendly with him." We never sin alone. Our sin always affects others in the body of Christ, especially the sins of a leader.

In addition, Jehoshaphat's sin helped the enemies of God in their wickedness, as seen in 2 Chron. 19:2. As Christians, we should never help sinners by compromising our standards to help them accomplish their purposes.

The most devastating effect of Jehoshaphat's compromise with the world was the effect it had on his children, grandchildren, great-grandchildren, and on the whole southern kingdom. In 2 Chronicles chapters 21 and 22, we read that after the death of Jehoshaphat, his son Jehoram got married to Athaliah and slaughtered all his brothers, then turned the nation to idolatry, as seen in 2 Chron. 21:6. God struck him with a terrible disease of the bowels, and he died after eight years as king. His son, Ahaziah, became king and lasted one year before he was murdered, according to 2 Chron. 22:3–4. Ahaziah's wicked mother, Athaliah, then slew all his sons (her own grandsons), except for Joash (a one-year-old) who was rescued and hidden from her. The Davidic kingly line from which Christ was descended came that close to being snuffed out. Then, the wicked Athaliah ruled the land for six years. All this was the result of Jehoshaphat's compromise with the wicked Ahab.

Biblical Pastors were not and are not CEOs.

In his book *No Place for Truth, Or Whatever Happened to Evangelical Theology?* David Wells argues convincingly that the church in the United States has lost it's theological foundation and it's God-centeredness. Instead of being "truth brokers" who help their flocks come to know and live in submission to the holy God, pastors have become business managers who market the church and psychologists who help people find personal fulfillment and good feelings. He points out that if the Apostle Paul were looking for a pastorate today, he may be hard pressed because few would warm to his personality and "most pastors stand or fall today by their personalities rather than their character."[283] He argues that the church has blended in with "modernity," promoting God and the gospel as just another self-help method.

Christians must be in complete submission to God who has revealed Himself in His Word in our consciousness, from which all else flows. That is why right theology is so critical in our personal, family, and public lives. This way of being is how God's people relate to this godless culture without being conformed to it, as is described in Rom. 12:1–2.

---

[283] David F. Wells, *No Place for Truth, Or, Whatever Happened to Evangelical Theology?* (Grand Rapids: W.B. Eerdmans Publishing Company 1993), 290.

✠

Chapter 4

Return To The Scriptural Standard

The Servant Shepherd

According to the biblical image, shepherd caring gives the impression that a shepherd has the duty of ensuring safety and leading his flock to clear water and fresh pasture. The shepherd also has the role of healing the wounded and searching for the lost. The Palestinian shepherd image is one that is characterized by tenderness, intimacy, hard work, concern, love, suffering, and skill. In his book, *Skillful Shepherds*, Derek J.Tidball, states that shepherding is characterized by the blend of care, authority, much tenderness, and toughness in the same way as courage and comfort.[284] The establishment of the shepherd-sheep relationship is rich, especially its definition in the Bible showing the relationship between God and His people through love. In the book of Psalms, we see the love of God for David, who was a shepherd and later became a king. In Ps. 23:1, 2, David acknowledges that the Lord is his shepherd who makes him lie in green pastures and beside the quiet waters. In Ezek. 34, there is also the image of a shepherd that is used to describe a person in charge of leading others.

Therefore, when Peter and Paul exhorted the elders to conduct their duties, they both used the imagery of a shepherd. These are the two famous apostles with the task of becoming shepherds to the local churches, not to the congregation but to the elders. Paul reminds the church elders that

---

[284] Derek J. Tidball, *Skillful Shepherds: An Introduction to Pastoral Theology* (Grand Rapids: Zondervan, 1986), 54.

God placed the Holy Spirit in them to help them guide the flock and to be overseers with the role of shepherding the church of God (Acts 20:28). Peter exhorts the church leaders to be shepherds of their flock (1 Pet. 5:2). These statements convey the message that it is not right to view church leaders as CEOs, executives, advisers, or any other title used in corporate businesses.

Therefore, for us to understand the work and the characteristics of Christian leaders, it is essential to understand shepherding as used in biblical imagery. The biblical elders, as shepherds, are expected to feed, protect, care for, and lead their flock through various practical needs. Based on these broad pastoral categories, we shall see in the section that follows how the New Testaments uses examples, teachings, and exhortation to show the work and roles of shepherd elders.

Offering Protection

Major sections of the New Testament illustrate the work of church elders as that of protecting the local church from being swayed by false leaders. When Paul was planning to leave Asia Minor, he called upon the elders of the church in Ephesus. During this gathering, he informs them to guide the flock for the wolves will be coming to shake their salvation. At Miletus, he also advises the Ephesus church elders to guard themselves as well as their flock through the power bestowed upon them by the Holy Spirit to be the overseers and shepherds in the church. Paul further assures the church leaders that they will be attacked by savage wolves coming among them after his departure. Therefore, they had to be alert and not be swayed by the tricks of the wolves.[285]

Paul also shows the qualities and qualifications of servant leaders in the church. He says that a prospective elder is one who acknowledges the Bible and one who uses the Bible to refute false teaching. Paul directs the leaders to appoint elders in every city and to hold fast to the faithful Word of the Lord according to his teaching so that they use their knowledge to refute false and contradictory messages of the doctrine, as described in Titus 1:5, 6, 9. In Acts 15:16, we also see an encounter in which Jerusalem elders met with the apostles to make judgments on doctrinal elders. The Jerusalem

---

[285] Acts 20:17–28.

elders, like the apostles, were supposed to be knowledgeable with the Word of God so that they could guide themselves and their flock from false teachers. The protection of the flock also includes seeking for lost sheep as well as for sheep that had strayed from the flock. This is a critical aspect of shepherding that is neglected by church leaders today. Furthermore, protecting the congregation also means admonishing improper attitudes and disciplining sin, according to 1Thess. 5:12.

The pastor is also required to stop bitter infighting among members of the church. The New Testament though gives advice to the elders on their roles in protecting against errors of sin. They should not forget to correct sinful behaviors among members of the church or seeking lost ones. This means that the protection of the flock is an important role because the members, just like a flock of sheep, are defenseless animals. They are powerless when confronted by wolves, jackals, lions, robbers, and bears.

Through his experiences as an agricultural researcher and experience as a shepherd in Canada and East Africa, Phillip Keller explains in his book, *The Shepherd Trilogy: A Shepherd Looks at the 23rd Psalm*, the vulnerable and unaware state of sheep when in danger or in an unavoidable death.[286] The sheep are animals that stand rooted when face-to-face with bears, cougars, dogs, and wolves. The predator will pounce on the sheep one after another, and the others act like they did not see, hear, or recognize that they are in danger. Therefore, it is the responsibility of church elders to invite God to help them watch over their flock from danger.

The illustrations from the New Testament clearly depict that the role of church leaders as shepherds protecting their sheep from danger is a vital duty. This is exactly how church leaders should perceive their role in providing protection to their flock against false teachers and other false prophecies. Protecting the flock is necessary for their survival. Charles Jefferson, author of *The Minister as a Shepherd* indicates the vital issue of the role of shepherds.[287] He says that the journey of a man's life right

---

[286] Phillip Keller, *The Shepherd Trilogy: A Shepherd Looks at the 23rd Psalm / A Shepherd Looks at the Good Shepherd / A Shepherd Looks at the Lamb of God* (Grand Rapids: Zondervan, 1996), 71. http://books.google.bf/books/about/A_Shepherd_Looks_at_Psalm_23.html?hl=fr&id=QHbTGr3SAIUC

[287] Charles Jefferson, *The Minister as Shepherd* (Fort Washington, PA: Christian Literature Crusade, 1998), 59, 60.

from when he is born to his grave is surrounded by dangers and perils, as though the universe is full of hostile life forces fighting for the human soul. Therefore, the pastor's responsibility should play a critical aspect to watch and ensure that their souls as well as that of their followers do not perish. This, therefore, means that church leaders are expected to be defenders, watchmen, protectors, and guardians for the people of God. The shepherd leaders in their aim to accomplish this goal are expected to be spiritually alert and be men of courage.

Spiritually Alert

Having an alert spirit is a desirable quality of good shepherds. They understand the importance of acting quickly and wisely, and they know and understand the predictor well. Shepherd leaders also have to be highly sensitive and spiritually awake to the dangers and attacks of Satan. This means that the shepherd has to be available and ready to work at any given time. In Acts 20:31, Paul advises the church leaders in Asia Minor to be alert. In his advice to the elders, Paul clearly shows that he was aware of the human tendency in them to be prayerless, undisciplined, lazy, and spiritually weary. This can be proven in the Old Testament where prophets admonished the Israel leaders for their failure to be alert and keep watch in protecting themselves from the wolves. In Isa. 56:9–12, Prophet Isaiah vividly describes the Israel leaders as dumb dogs and blind city watchmen, and that the attackers will find an opportunity to attack Israel leaders when they are the least prepared. Therefore, a good shepherd has to be prayerful, watchful, and aware of the changing issues that impact the church and society as a whole. These leaders also have to equip themselves with education through the help of the Holy Spirit so as to guard their spiritual walk in God and to always pray for the flock and every member of the congregation.[288]

Many churches suffer today because they fail to protect themselves through faithful prayer, by being naïve, and surrounding themselves with inattentive shepherds. Therefore, this is a call for churches to stand firm on Christ's examples and teachings, and to rely on the leading of the Holy

---

[288] Ed. Gerhard Kittel and Gerhard Friedrich, *Theological Dictionary of the New Testament*, (Erdmans Publishing, Michigan, 1968), 492.

Spirit. They should not be like dumb dogs and blind watchmen who are preoccupied by the comforts of life and their own fleshy self-interests. The elders of the churches have to be careful in discerning the spirit of those claiming to be from the Lord because wolves come clothed in sheep's clothing.

Courage

Church leaders and shepherds have to be courageous individuals to fight against predators. King David is one of many persons in the Bible who shows outstanding courage. The book of 1 Samuel presents the experiences of David as a shepherd with the role of protecting his flock from a bear and lion.[289] Courage is an essential leadership quality that church leaders have to possess. Courage is needed in disciplining sin in church, especially among prominent individuals in the church. It is also needed to stand up to the evils committed by theological luminaries and powerful teachers who teach false doctrines. Lack of courage in fighting for the lives of the flock and the Word of God will result in the church of God being washed away by every internal conflict and doctrinal storm that comes its way. There are numerous unstable, weak, and immature believers, and it is important for the elders to establish a safety net around these followers to give them protection from destructive influences and savage wolves, as described in John 10:12b.

Feeding the Flock

The New Testament puts emphasis on the teaching of the Word of God. Jesus, an example of a Good Shepherd, was a teacher who commissioned others to teach on the issues that He teaches, as seen in Matt. 28:20. In John 21:17, Christ instructs Peter to teach or feed His sheep, and Acts 2:42 show that the early Christians and the Apostles were steadfastly committed in teaching the Word of God. Paul was sought by Barnabas to go with him to Antioch to help him in teaching the Word of God.[290] Paul also informed Timothy to pay attention to teaching, exhortation, and public reading of

---

[289] 1 Sam. 17:33–37.
[290] Acts 11:25–26.

the scripture, as seen in 1 Tim. 4:13. According to 1 Cor. 12:28, the third gift that God has given to believers is teaching, which is after the prophet and apostle. Therefore, teaching is among the greatest gifts that have to be desired by the congregation.[291]

In his book, *The Christian View of God and the World,* James Orr (1844–1913), a theologian, states that the Christian religion is the only one that greatly exalts the office of teaching.[292] The New Testament leaders, unlike the modern day board of elders, were expected to be able to teach.[293] In a letter to Titus, Paul shows that the elder has to be someone who has to hold on fast to God's faithful Word according to His teachings so that he may confront and refute those who contradict the message of God. In Titus 1:9, Paul also encourages them to be able to exhort in sound doctrine. This is an important message for the church leaders today. In 1 Tim. 5:17–18, Paul talks about elders who are devoted to teaching and preaching, that they deserve to be supported financially by their local church. The Spirit has assisted the creation of the Christian Community in using his Word.[294] Therefore, this means that it is a spiritual requirement that the church elders are to work against those who refute the teachings of God and those who teach falsehood.[295]

Leading the Flock

According to the Bible, the shepherd is a believer whom God baptizes to guide a group of people to live as God desires.[296] Elder shepherds are in the church of God,[297] and their role is to lead the church. The church elders, therefore, have the responsibility to manage, govern, direct, care, and lead the flock of God.

In Titus 1:7, Paul emphasizes that a prospective leader is one who is spiritually and morally above approach for he is the steward of God

---

[291] 1 Cor. 12:31.

[292] James Orr, *The Christian View of God and the World* (New York: Charles Scribners's Sons, 1908), 29.

[293] 1 Tim. 3:2.

[294] 1 Pet. 1:23; James 1:18.

[295] 1 Tim. 3:2.

[296] Ps. 78:71–72; 2 Sam. 5:2.

[297] 1 Pet. 5.

(Titus 1:7). A steward is associated with a household manager with the responsibility from his master to oversee his property, finances, and servants. Just like them, elders of the church are the stewards of God's household—the local church. Managing and leading the flock is vital because the sheep are naturally born to be followers. This means that the sheep cannot travel by themselves but need a human conductor. They cannot predetermine places to find the best pastures and have no sense of direction. This means that there is no other docile animal like the sheep. Therefore, shepherds must be always available and alert to guide their flock in every direction for them not to perish from hunger or attacked by wolves.

Simone Weil indicates that our attention is formed by culture,[298] when she asks which one of the disciples should be an attentive. The flock has heard the voice of the Master and then follows the world. Church leaders have to shape their attention in determining the culture that will take top priority in their lives. This means that church leaders can form an alternative culture by first knowing Christ. Leaders who are only serving their personal interests are actually not leaders. These people are simply grandiose managers and not shepherd leaders. Leaders guided by the power of Jesus have a larger vision more than themselves, and through this vision they have the ability to make sacrifices. The nature of sacrifice and vision are contagious because they impact the follower. The main goal of leadership is not that of increasing the number of followers as seen in mega and meta churches, but to go beyond the self and to have a transcendent vision. This is a vision that is shaped through the self-revelation of Jesus Christ and the Gospel of the Word of God.

Every Leader is a Servant and Follower

People who are not serving a vision much larger than themselves are not leaders. Leaders guided by Jesus are those who acknowledge that they have a vision much larger than themselves and are ready to make sacrifices. The goal of leadership is one that is driven to a transcendent vision and not to increase the number of followers. This is a vision that is shaped by

---

[298] Wikipedia contributors, "Simone Weil," *Wikipedia, The Free Encyclopedia*, accessed November 9, 2013, http://en.wikipedia.org/wiki/Simone_Weil.

the Gospel of the Kingdom of God and one through which Jesus reveals himself.

Leaders are servants and followers who are ready to listen and be attuned to heaven and not to worldly things. Leaders take resources of the world and provide them to those in need. Their roles are basically poetic, prophetic, and priestly. The priestly role is a stand-in between two worlds but is in the third place. Leaders are not in front of the people they lead or behind them; instead, leaders are among the people. As a prophetic role, leaders stand behind the people and point the way forward, empowering and encouraging them ahead, while at the same time providing them with security and safety.

The prophet role in leadership is to rediscover God and the Word of God. The role of prophets is to call on people to act in accord with God's Word. Their role is to provide an environment where people will become aware of their flawed human nature and rely on God to live a holy life in an evil world. Prophets have to cultivate an environment that enables God's story to be relevant with changing times, where the Gospel is summed up into values and morals, into a spiritual experience. Therefore, the prophet creates a situation in which society trusts that the Bible is reliable and not bound by any period of time.

The first attention that leaders should have is to focus on God and the second is for himself as a person. Leaders have to focus on their own growth as shepherd elders, if they do not, they may fail in their tasks. The resources that help leaders to grow are those which come from within and above. Leaders do not have to rely on their own resources alone because they will find emptiness. Bernard of Clairvaux writes that "a wise man will see life as a water reservoir and not a canal. This is because a canal always pours out all its contents, the water reservoir is one which is always filled and discharges the water yet, retains some in its self. He continues to say that many people in the church act as canals and the reservoirs are rarely found."[299]

The intention of the leaders is always divided between the earth and heaven and between the other and self. The scriptures clearly show that the main intention of God is that the Lord is attentive. Ephesians shows that

---

[299] Bernard of Clairvaux, *Sermons on the Song of Songs* (Kalamazoo: Cistercian Publications, 1984), 27.

the main purpose of God is to build a holy dwelling place. This has to be the same purpose for shepherd leaders by attending to the formation of the holy people to form a center for the redemption work of God.

In developing an alternative culture of God's Kingdom, it is necessary to nurture the faithful community of followers of Jesus. According to Mark 10: 42–43, Jesus called His disciples together and told them that the ones who are regarded as the rulers of the Gentiles lords over the people, for they are under the control of the high officials. The main message that we get from this passage is *diakonos* (servant) and *doulos* (slave). The main statement is that Jesus refers to himself with the title Son of Man, the Messiah, the one who came to serve.

Our response, therefore, is to equate leadership with service. Many have seen few leaders who serve. The main thing that churches need today is servants, who lead according to the examples that Jesus showed us while He was on earth. In his book *Reframing Paul: Conversations in Grace and Community*, Mark Strom shows the need for leaders to follow the examples of Jesus who left His throne in heaven to come down to earth and save man. He writes:

> Evangelism will not change its elitism, idealism, and abstraction until the clergy and theologians are fully prepared to step down to the world. Some may view that because the world has shown concepts to the role of the pastors, this is a step back in professional ministry. It is also a way of ignoring the social realities that are more pertinent. Evangelism is characterized by its own financial security, careers, ranks, rewards and marks of prestige. In this world, professional ministry has status and ranks.[300]

Jesus informs his disciples that they know how things are and have seen them all the time. This is that they live in a world with rulers who impose their authorities over them. This model of ruling in the secular world is referred to in a combination of words such as *kurios* and *kata*. *Kata* is a movement that is above or against. It is an authority that is

---

[300] Mark Strom, *Reframing Paul: Conversations in Grace and Community*. (Downers Grove: IVP Academic, 2000), 17.

used to prod or push. The leaders of this authority are referred to as the benefactors, meaning that they are people's leaders for their benefit, and there is nothing that can be done to these rulers. At the same time, these rulers misuse others by subjecting them to slavery.

Jesus then introduces his followers to a new model, one which is more familiar to them but hardly known to us. He informs His followers that leadership in a new community is one that looks like slavery, which is the most humble service of them all. This is a form of leadership that was only modeled by Jesus Himself. In Phil. 2:5–7, He tells them, "Have this attitude in yourselves which was also in Christ Jesus, who, although He existed in the form of God, did not regard equality with God a thing to be grasped, but emptied Himself, taking the form of a bond-servant, and being made in the likeness of me."

The main word from this passage is *ekenosen* from which the word "kenosis" is derived from. It means the need to remove any form of rank or status that gives prerogatives or privileges associated with rank and status.[301] This passage is similar to one in Mark 10:40–45 that combines the incarnation of God's Word with theological reflection. The author is astonished and amazed by how the High Lord of the whole universe and the King of creation could take up the human body and leave behind all His protection, power, and privilege and become a subject of humiliation, weakness, and even dying at the hands of men. Despite all of the challenges and tribulations on earth, He ascended to his glory in heaven by triumphing over all the earthly powers and death. Therefore, by the name of Jesus every knee shall bow, those in the heavens, on earth and the underworld, and everyone will acknowledge that He is Christ the Lord and God's glory. Mark 10 shows how Jesus calls man to shift away from the *kata-kurios*; this is an authority that is against and above. Instead, He develops the model known as *diakonos*: the sacrificial and humble service of the slave.

In Philippians 2, Paul refers to leaders as the kenotic, a service that is characterized by emptying, humbling, and living for the sake of others. "For the word of the cross is foolishness to those who are perishing, but to us who are being saved it is the power of God. For it is written,

---

[301] Marva J. Dawn and Eugene H. Peterson, *The Unnecessary Pastor: Rediscovering the Call*, ed. Peter Santucci (Vancouver: William B. Eerdmans Publishing Company, 2000), 141.

"I WILL DESTROY THE WISDOM OF THE WISE, AND THE CLEVERNESS OF THE CLEVER I WILL SET ASIDE."[302]

This message implies that the way we think about governance and leadership should not be according to our wisdom. God's perspective about worldly wisdom is that it is foolish. The current preoccupation of churches is the control and competition as seen in various technologies relating to the growth of churches. The churches have significantly grown, but the large numbers of the churches do not have any relation with the fundamental message of God and church formation. The clergy have become professionals with proficiency, but this proficiency is unknown. Is it that of multiplying disciples?[303]According to the Gospel in 1Pet. 5:1–4:

> "Therefore, I exhort the elders among you, as your fellow elder and witness of the sufferings of Christ, and a partaker also of the glory that is to be revealed, shepherd the flock of God among you, exercising oversight not under compulsion, but voluntarily, according to the *will* of God; and not for sordid gain, but with eagerness; nor yet as lording it over those allotted to your charge, but proving to be examples of the flock. And when the Chief Shepherd appears, you will receive the unfading crown of glory."

This is a duty, but it is a duty accomplished out of willingness as expected of shepherd leaders by God. God also expect leaders not to pursue dishonest gains but to be eager to serve and not act like lords to those who have been assigned to care. Shepherd leaders are instead, required to be examples for their flock.

The main words under consideration in this chapter are *poimaino* (shepherd) and presbuteros (elder). The main use of these words in the scriptures is that they do not refer to a specific office but to a function. An elder is a person who carries out a given function in the community, and this is the function of equipping and caring for others. This is a function that is more of a familial task than leadership in a corporation, but one that fits the end goals of maturity and formation of God. Peter calls upon

---

[302] 1 Cor. 1:18–19.

[303] Dawn and Peterson, *The Unnecessary Pastor*, 133.

leaders to act as an example for their flock, and this gives attention to our personal self-governance. Leaders who emphasize more on the task and not on their personal formation will be undermining their fundamental task. This contributes to a tremendous challenge because leaders mainly measure their value according to how busy they are. The use of the word *diakonia* (care or rule) in the New Testament presents the focal point in how the scriptures translate the concepts of care and rule.

The Priesthood of All Believers

The Priesthood of all Believers is a protestant doctrine that places the importance of human individual ability to connect directly with God. This doctrine means that the priest should not be necessarily available in acting as the mediator between an individual and God so that every individual can gain access to God through prayer, faith, and repentance. This is a call to believers that they also have a priestly office in the church by having a direct channel to the grace of God.

The New Testament, unlike the Old Testament, does not use the term priest for any specific ministry among the people of God. The term is, however, reserved for the unique priesthood of all Christians and to the priesthood of Jesus Christ. The Book of Revelation shows the believers as the priests of God, or royal priesthood and kingdom priests.[304] In Exod. 19:6, God sets the people of Israel apart to serve as His priests. Later, in Isa. 61:6, we see that Isaiah mentions they will be recognized as ministers and priests of God and a people who tend and cultivate their flocks and fields.

Peter writes down the specific functions of a priest. These are the Christians who declare the wondrous deeds of God among the nations and have the role of offering spiritual sacrifices. According to the Book of Revelation, the Christian community has been gathered and has been purified by the blood of Christ. They are the individuals who have been made the priest of the Kingdom to rule the earth with Jesus Christ and to serve God.[305]

In the early ages of Christianity, the churches turned to the use of priesthood to provide meditation services as a different unity of the laity.

[304] Rev. 20:6; 5:10: 1:6; 1 Pet. 2:5.
[305] Oden, *Pastoral Theology*, 68.

The Protestant Reformers did not agree with this pattern and aimed to correct it. One of the vocal people in articulating for this change was Martin Luther in his essays, "Treatise on Christian Liberty,""The Babylonian Captivity of the Church," and "An Open Letter to the Christian Nobility of the German Nation,1520."

Luther's argument for the priesthood is that it has social, ecclesiastical, and spiritual implications. He socially accepted the western Christianity context, where temporal rules are meant to be for the Christendom body. According to the Christian special order, God ordains the rulers to protect the good and to punish the wrong doers. Luther is against the medieval division between the church authorities and the temporal and their different jurisdictions on every matter. Since the German nobles had been baptized, they too belonged to the believers' priesthood and had the ability to exercises their vocation in reforming and correcting wrong doing on various practices in the church without respect of priest, bishops and popes.

Ecclesiastically, Luther argues against the monopoly of the clergy in determining the right doctrines, interpretation of the scriptures, exercising discipline, and forgiving sin. This is because all believers are priests and can participate in these functions within the Christian community. Proper understanding of the priest has to be the ministers of the Word, who are supposed to preach the Word to the Congregation and provide sacraments in service and consent of the congregation.

Luther also views the phrase, "kingdom of priests," as one that refers to all believers in the general and spiritual sense. This is because those who believe in Christ are priests and kings who serve Him. All kings through their faith have to work together to protect their salvation. Through faith, all priests are worthy to teach one another about God's purpose and to approach God through prayer.

Menno Simons uses the concept of Christian faith.[306] He states that believers have been made priest and therefore are holy people chosen to serve God. Through this, believers are to live their lives as directed by God and proclaim God's power to the masses. This means that Christians as kings and priest already rein through the sword of the Holy Word of God

---

[306] Menno Simons, "Complete Writings," Menno Simons.net, accessed November 9, 2013, http://www.mennosimons.net/completewritings.html.

and not worldly weapons. The Word of God is more powerful than armies, wealth, prosecution, and the devil.

All believers are referred to as priests because they are sanctified and are called to live like the sanctified people of God. These are individuals who have sacrificed their evil lusts, their unrighteousness, and have admonished others to follow their footsteps. They are not priests whose work is to sacrifice wine and bread for the sin of their followers. Instead, these are individuals who purify their bodies on a daily basis and are willing to make the necessary sacrifice and to suffer on behalf of the truth of God. They are individuals who are ready to forgive and offer thanks joyfully in the Lord's Truth.[307]

In the interpretation offered by Simons concerning the church being the royal priesthood, he places emphasis on the moral and spiritual quality of priesthood. This is a role that every believer has to play guided by self-discipline and multiple disciplines toward other members of the congregation and through missionary witness. It is also a role that believers play through theier dependence on the powerful Word of God and willingness to suffer for the sake of the Gospel. This means that Simons did not interpret priesthood as a temporal authority as seen in the work of Luther. Simons and other Baptists have also not related issues of ordination, appointment, and Christian ministry of the church to the priesthood of every believer.

The concept of priesthood of all believers is a concept that shows the ability of a believer to gain access to God. This is an access that is made possible through the gracious work of the Lord and Savior on the cross. Heb. 10:19 shows that the boldness to enter the holy places is through the blood that Jesus shed on the cross. Our access to the holy places is through the power of the Holy Spirit.[308] This is a direct access that cannot be hindered by anyone. According to 1 Tim. 2:5, this is because there is one mediator between men and God and the mediator is Jesus Christ. Therefore, believers are set aside as the holy priests to provide spiritual sacrifices that are acceptable to God through Jesus Christ,[309] who offered himself in sacrifice for human transgressions. Paul's advice to Roman

---

[307] Ibid.

[308] Eph. 2:18.

[309] 1 Pet. 2:4.

believers in Romans 12:1, was to preserve their bodies as a holy, living sacrifice, and in a form that is acceptable to God.

The Organic Church

The term "organic church" was coined by Austin Sparks to mean a church that gathers and lives as per the spiritual reality of the church.[310] This is a church that acts as a spiritual organism (*Ekklēsia*) and not an institutional organization. Seven different aspects characterize the organic church. First is that the members in the church strive to live according to the life of Jesus and proclaiming His name. This is also a church where the members pursue Jesus as part of their lives and sharing Him in their community life and gatherings. The third characteristic of an organic church is that there is no divide of the clergy and the laity; this is because every member is a participant and has a function in the church. These members have different roles and ministries to accomplish in the church. They contribute in the decision-making process and all contribute to the ministry.

Jesus works as the head and works in a discernible way. The church's foundation is based on Jesus Christ and not a set of methods and practices or a specific theological system. This is also a church that is not determined by any human personality because God makes use of His people to form the root foundation of the church in a continuous relationship with Jesus Christ. Therefore, the people also look up to God and not to one another.

The other characteristic of this church is that the time to worship God is not just on Sunday morning, but these members often meet to give thanks and praise to God any time of the week. Therefore, the members of an organic church live as a face-to-face community. This is also a church that stands firm and always seeks to fulfill the eternal purpose of the church. As such, their meetings are not based on special interests such as social justice, discipleship, evangelism, or church multiplication, but for the sole purpose of being the ultimate intention of God that includes

---

[310] Frank Viola, "Why Organic Church Is Not Exactly a Movement," *Christianity Today*, January 2010, accessed November 9, 2013, http://www.christianitytoday.com/ct/2010/januaryweb-only/12.31.0.html?paging=off.

and surpasses all these aspects.[311] Churches today can learn a lot from the characteristics of an organic church. The concept of an organic church is just like anything else that can be described to be authentic and in its original state. This means that the organic church clearly defines the characteristics of a church that God intended it to be.

In his book *Finding Organic Church*, Frank Viola states that the organic church is not a myth or a theater that follows a script, but it is an authentic journey and a lifestyle with Jesus Christ and His disciples. The organic church, according to Viola, is also one that is born from the spiritual life that is not bond through religious programs or by human intuitions.[312]

Therefore, the organic church is something real that helps us to understand Jesus Christ and not an organization or institution. Viola narrates his personal story of wanting to leave the usual church he attends with his family to look for an organic church. He was surprised to learn that no members of the congregation inquired about his family, sent them notes, or called to ask why they were not attending services anymore. It was only the pastor of their previous church who inquired to know why they had left. Viola told the pastor that they sought a place where they could understand the true meaning of the church and a place to understand God in the true biblical sense. The inquiring pastor also had the intention to leave and join an organic church but felt trapped by the financial benefits he received from his congregation.[313] This is the feeling that most leaders of the church feel today. They are trapped financially and cannot leave their highly-paid positions to form biblical and simplified churches that walk with the Lord. They are swayed away by world materialism and controlled by the intentions of people just like every other organization's CEOs who are driven by customer needs and consumerism. These are pastors who lack the courage to stand firm to the Lord's intention for His church and act and reflect His image to the world.

---

[311] Gene Edwards, *The Organic Church Vs the "New Testament" Church: Issues We Dare Not Face* (Jacksonville: SeedSowers, 2007), 90.

[312] Frank Viola, *Finding Organic Church: A Comprehensive Guide to Starting and Sustaining Authentic Christian Communities* (Colorado Springs: David C. Cook, 2009), 20–21.

[313] Frank Viola, *Reimagining Church: Pursuing the Dream of Organic Christianity* (Colorado Springs: David C. Cook, 2008), 143.

In their book *Pagan Christianity*, Viola and Barna criticizes the Christian lifestyle of today by pointing out that the lifestyle is a pagan culture that practices pagan rituals that developed after the death of the apostles of the New Testament. They opine that this culture and practices violate the biblical principles that have hindered Christian growth in terms of quality but have enhanced church growth in quantity.[314] This is exactly what the United States has witnessed since the late 1990s, whereby there were a fashion of churches just like any otherworldly fad of fashion. Seeker-sensitive mega churches drive this new fashion. Though not all mega churches were into this fashion and not all were seeker-friendly churches, most of the churches' intentions were to become a mega church.

Nonetheless, this has been the notable fashion. The aims of the mega churches were to have large, entertaining, and fun services that they believed were the best ways of spreading the Gospel of Jesus Christ. As a result, they had to model their services to survive in a seeker-friendly environment. Rick Warren is one of the leaders of the concept of mega churches who suggests that the church has to find a way of leading all members to find and utilize their gifts in serving the Lord. This movement has been emphasized through making Christianity fit the attendees' needs by using multimedia entertainment, the latest trends of music, and other relevant suggestions given by the attendees. This is done at the expense of other Christian values deemed negative by the attendees, such as the call for righteous living and repentance. This clearly shows the good intention of this movement to involve the un-churched, but it also leads to disturbing consequences whereby the vital aspects of Christian teachings are left out. The rather obvious picture that we get from the growth of mega churches all across the country is competition among churches. Therefore, the obvious message from this movement is the intention to draw large crowds from other smaller churches. They attract them through entertainment and other attendee friendly activities in the same way a business organization markets its products. As a result, the churches are seen as theatre rooms displaying the "God Show."[315]

---

[314] FrankViola, and George Barna. *Pagan Christianity?* (Carol Stream: Tyndale House Publishers, 2002), 6.

[315] Ibid., 148–52.

The formation of God's future requires conversion—not a conversion in the world system but a transformation of the church system. The formative practices and the structure of the western church is one that is based on a modern dualistic worldview that is philosophical, political, and enlightened according to Christendom. God has given us gifts that help us equip the body for service.[316] The scripture's passages on gifted service are based on the body that is framed by love and one that is designed to show the fullness of God. The passages from Ephesians show critical words such as *katartismos* (equip) *diakonos* (service), *oikodomeo* (build). The word *Oikodomeo*, which is translated to mean build, does not have the mechanical and technological connotation. It means a mysterious organic building. *Oikos* is the root and means "house," and this is likened to the household of God, which is the church. This clearly shows that we were not intended to focus on the leadership part such as designing leadership strategies, holding seminars and conferences for leaders of churches, but to focus on equipping the people of God to reach their maturity. For instance, the question that comes to mind is how the church would be perceived if it develops a leadership culture. The meaning of equip is not specific to an individual; instead, it is something that every one of us has and has a duty to carry out in enhancing the strength of the churches.

Mega Churches as Businesses

Mega churches have become highly mobile, consumer oriented, and comprised of the middle class and educated families. They have also become attractive to a wide range of the American population. Mega churches are young Protestant churches that use approaches that are appealing to various tendencies of consumers. The modern day population is one that is accustomed to marketing promotions and campaigns. Therefore, the mega churches are forced to adopt and align themselves like business organizations with a product to market. The governance of these churches falls into a hierarchy and aim to obtain finances from its members.

Examining the way mega churches make use of its business model to attain solvency is evident. In his book *Exit Interviews*, William Hendricks presents a report from interviews carried out on a large number of baby

---

[316] Eph. 4:11–16.

boomers concerning their disillusionment with current day mega churches. The interviews also aimed to find out from the baby boomers why they were leaving institutional churches. According to Hendricks:

> "The main aspect that distinguishes the contemporary mega churches is not on the size of these churches but on strategy. This confirms the fact that size is always a matter of strategy. This marks a major contrast between the traditional forms of doing church. This is because the mega churches operate based on a marketing mentality by first minding and knowing the customer and how the church is attuned to meet the needs of these customers."[317]

By asking the question and coming up with answers when there is a large population segment is a way of re-examining spiritual issues related to the mega churches. This meant that the issue of worship during the 1990s had to be made relevant to the baby boomer generation culture. This is an aspect that has become rapidly acceptable among executives from different denominations as a way of dealing with declining church membership.

Pastors consider themselves to be like business administrators. In Alice Lukens' article in *The Baltimore Sun*, she quotes Rev. Darrel Baker of Covenant Baptists Church in Maryland: "I have spent more than ten years in Corporate America and when I view the church, it is inevitable for me to look at it as being a business like organization." This shows the mentality that one has concerning how the business world is reflected in every aspect of the church, from the members of the church to its staff members.[318]

Vision Statement

The mega church is modeled to be in the form of a business through its vision statement. The main trend for various mega churches is downplaying

---

[317] William D. Hendricks, *Exit Interviews* (Chicago: Moody Press, 1993), 247.

[318] Alice Lunken, "Church Focus On Land Debate," *Baltimore Sun*, August 5, 1999, accessed October 19, 2013, http://articles.baltimoresun.com/1999-08-05/news/9908050038_1_covenant-baptist-church-develop-the-church-building-a-church.

their denominational commitment. However, this trend has left the individual church's identity in the middle, making it look alike to all its guests, pastorals and members. As a consequence of this trend, the churches have formed a brief declaration of their identity. This not only defines the members of the church but also the churches' character, an epitome that can be viewed by outsiders. This is an aspect that is referred to as the "vision statement." It serves the same purposes just like the vision statement of any other financial company, like a hamburger chain or footwear manufacturer. The mega church vision statement comprises action verbs that denote the vision in the same way as defined in leadership literature. These texts refer to the vision as a reflection of the organization's goals and what it aims to become. The vision statement provides a clear view of the organization's goals to investors and customers, and it also indicates the intention to attain a specific business position.[319]

Sevier Heights Baptist Church in Knoxville, Tennessee can be taken as a very good example of vision statement that can be used for epitomizing the church brand of vision statement. The vision statement of Sevier Heights Baptist Church in Knoxville, Tennessee, states that its aim is to bring people to Christ and His church, to equip and teach them the Gospel in order to gain the kingdom of God and to glorify His name. In comparing this vision statement to that of the General Motors Company (GM), Saturn Division, one can point out some similarities. According to the GM vision statement, the company aims to market vehicles manufactured and developed in the United States and to become leaders in customer satisfaction, cost, and quality production. This is attained through integrations of business systems, technology, and people and to transfer technology, knowledge, and experience throughout GM.[320]

The church vision statement is mainly intended to appeal to people of the suburban middle class, similar to the online, print, or radio advertisements of companies. The church also teaches through repetition, where it repeats its vision in every service program or on its stationery

[319] James M. Kouzes and Barry Z. Posner, *The Leadership Challenge: How to Make Extraordinary Things Happen in Organizations*, 5th ed. (San Francisco: Jossey-Bass, 2012), 167.

[320] Ibid.

and on banners placed around the church grounds. The vision statement becomes their brand name or labels.

The Spiritual Shopping Center Mall

After the church creates the vision statement, it begins targeting its products to a targeted audience. The church administrators and pastors present the product in a masterful way just like as any other product for consumption. The church administrators also consult marketing experts about ways they can apply the same concept in church. Staff members of a mega church are taught that programming marketing is the secret behind a successful mega church.

As a result of the immense variety and number of service outlets, mega churches have to offer other social services like schools, childcare, counseling, and financial support programs, among others. The churches have to offer these services because they are the best tools for competitively vying in the marketplace. In order to market effectively, the churches do not require finances alone, but also need a platform that will enable the church to inform others about the existence of their services. Furthermore, the mega churches have to offer something for every family member, from toddlers to grandparents, so that they become a convenience to the whole family and for them to come back to that specific church.

In one of his studies, Thumma draws his conclusion from different supporting sources and presents a comparison of a wide range of services provided in a shopping world. The mega churches are likened to the mall owner, who provides a building while the core ministries act as the department stores that anchor and welcome customers. These ministries are the choral programs, worship services, children's ministry, and youth ministry. Due to the support of the main ministries, the more diverse and smaller attractive ministries are tailored to fit the specific needs as per fall, rise, fail, and even lack of demand. However, because of the stability of the core ministries, the failings are more or less inconsequential to the overall stability of the church and are considered as a flexibility component.

An example of the setback can be demonstrated through a famous footwear company like Nike, which manufactures a wide range of shoe models. Due to the constant revenue that this company receives from its popular and stable styles, the company can manage to experiment with a wider and more diverse variety of footwear designs that are for a specific targeted audience. This company has the ability to manufacture shoes for tennis's players, runners, and soccer teams and incurs low risk losses due to the fact that revenues are already provided by the already realizable and stable styles.

The Product

Worship is the product that is marketed by a mega church. The mega church is seen as a large corporation or a giant shopping mall, and its main product is worship. The concept of programming is the main tool that is used to draw many church members, and it leads to major financial gain. It is the ticket of appealing to new visitors. So as to keep up with the busy schedule of the large congregation, mega churches have to provide a wide range of services. Apart from the provision of multiple services, it also manages to solve the logistic challenges resulting from huge parking spaces and sanctuary capacities. Churches such as Willow Creek Community Church provide two services during the week and four services during the weekend. This is with the goal of accommodating over 17,000 attendees on weekends and about 7,000 to 8,000 people through the week.

Variety of Worship Styles

The worship content aims at a wide scope of consumers. Mega churches use several approaches in providing the best content in worship. Some mega churches choose a specific segment of consumers, while others provide services aimed for a specific group of individuals. The modern approach to worship service is that which combines the use of drums and guitars, and it is part of the desire of the church to attract the younger generation, including generation X. The church also uses traditional approaches of worship that are attractive to the older generation and the baby boomer generation. This approach involves countless hymns and traditional sermons.

However, most mega churches expand their appeal to attract a number of social groups by use of two main approaches. The first approach is the integration of different forms of services that uses general worships styles, different messages, and music. The Willow Creek Church mainly uses this model. Another approach is a contemporary one that incorporates a combination of traditional and rock in services that are separately offered to meet a wide range of worshipping needs. Through this model, worshipers make use of a product that comes from the same manufacturers, as seen in the program listings of worship services, which resemble movie theaters with multiple genres of movies to present, and with different shows shown at different times.

The popular approach used by mega churches today is the incorporation of different worshiping styles with a wide range of sermons and music genres at different times of the week or month. It is possible to find sermons offered in a chain of four weeks that cover complex theological issues. This is followed by multiple weeks of sermons that are usable for daily living. The sermons are altered as needed on a weekly basis so as to keep all tastes and ages satisfied and engaged. Throughout the services, both the contemporary praise choruses and traditional hymns are interchanged and dispersed with minimal thought to the differences taking place. The musical approach provides members with a minimal satisfaction of their desires and at the same time introduce the congregation to new and alternative forms of worship. These various approaches to worship accommodate the needs of a wide consumer range.

Availability 24/7

Mega churches have in the same way adopted the 24/7 availability that is common to many business-oriented organizations. These services are provided in the early mornings hosting the youth team's prayer and in lock-ins. Some activities are conducted on daily basis.

Professional Worship Services

It is unmistakable to realize the professional quality of services in whichever approach the mega churches use to preach the gospel. The services are mainly characterized by a large infrastructure with order levels and minimal variance in scheduled programs. This high quality level of professionalism is also seen in the televised church services and has to meet the demands of scheduling. Other churches provide complex and full orchestras with beautiful choir performances. Other mega churches have highly talented guitarists, musicals, and drummers. The overall quality is generally at the top level, and there is expert planning of these services. This type of professional approach provides consumers with a top-notch product that is expected from any other profit-making organization.

The musical performers and musicians usually work as volunteers. However, parts of the church services are still done by professionals who work as staff members. The criticism toward this highly coordinated worship is that it provides for little or no personal expression from members of the congregation. This efficiency is achieved through setting of place and time in order to attain a strategic order in worshipping. The enforcement of time limits and control of every aspect of worship service is rooted through a committee or an individual for approval. According to Mark Driscoll and Chris Seay:

> "In the same way, the church as a whole has become a business that exists to attract consumers by marketing a product. So the gospel is no longer something you participate in—it's something you consume. And when it's a business, it has to compete with the church down the street and fight to draw consumers. That's a major reason why we're nowhere near thinking of youth ministry in missiological terms—it's all about goods and services. Profit and loss. Consumption."[321]

The precision planning quality is the aspect that restricts active involvements of parishioners in church services. Because the attendees have little participation, the corporate worship of the mega churches becomes more like a theater or a worship service show. The parishioners play a passive role just like as audiences in a stadium. These kinds of worship

---

[321] Mark Driscoll, and Chris Seay. "A Second Reformation is at Hand," *Youth Specialties*, October 2009, accessed October 19, 2013. http://youthspecialties. com/articles/a-second-reformation-is-at-hand/.

services contrast sharply with the communal worship services described in the New Testament.

The churches' proximity, in terms of location, of one mega church from another is additional evidence that the mega church is a producing organization that calls for marketing of its products. This is the same business principle that large discount stores, grocery stores, merchants, and other businesses employ. They cluster in one location in metro political areas. In the same way, mega churches are now viewed to be located one yard away from each other. Just like businesses that employ the proximity concept, the mega churches will suffer the same consequences of competing for worshippers and have to provide a wider variety of goods and services, in terms of prices and less commitment.

There are streets in Dallas, Texas that are referred to as the mega church row. These streets comprise the Methodist church, the Cathedral of Hope, and the Baptist church, all of which accommodate thousands of worshippers every week even when they are only separated by a few blocks from one another.[322] This set up means that a crowd of people can always come to this area to attend these churches. Families and individuals will try out these churches located in the same area, which is a new exposure. This is not possible if these churches were not in close proximity to one another. However, the proximity of these churches leads to competition—the same plight as those faced by profit-making businesses.

Competition

The business-like model of churches simply places the issue of competition in question. Many churches, both mega and small, continuously compete with one another. In fact, church members are also referred to as customers, and they are found in the same area where competition is high. Nonetheless, the land and space are other aspects of contention in these churches. The competition further implies that there is need for a parking area and space to house more people, as more people means more money is needed to provide them proper services. This means

---

[322] Scott Walter, "The Land of Big Religion," *The American Enterprise* (October 2000): 37–39, accessed October 19, 2013, http://www.unz.org/Pub/AmEnterprise-2000oct-00037?View=PDF.

that the mega churches' aim is attaining profit, and this has to start with the programming of ministries, which in turn means bringing in more people. The churches, like businesses, are centered towards a chain of production, and this trend is anticipated to continue growing.

In the last decade, there was a highly publicized case about a conflict between two competing churches situated near Dallas, Texas. Prestonwood Baptist Church is located close to another church known as the Prince of Peace Lutheran Church. An observer comments: "In appearance, the large mega church is almost gobbling up the other smaller mega church."[323] This conflict is similar to conflicts between business entities. The Prince of Peace Church had more than 2,000 members. At the same time, there was also competition with another nearby church, the First Baptist Church of Hebron, which had more than 800 members. Both churches waited to see what would happen with their membership upon the unveiling of Prestonwood's 7,000 seat auditorium. This clearly shows the fear that many smaller churches feel as they are unequipped to attract a larger audience and are confronted with competition from the larger mega churches. This is the same problem faced by businesses; due to the dynamics of proximity, small businesses on main street are faced with being replaced with strip malls. Wal-Mart, Home Depot and K-Mart have replaced numerous mom and popshops. In this same way, the mega churches draw people away from many smaller and middle-sized churches.[324]

The increase in the number of attendees in mega churches means that the money that the smaller churches receive also decreases. Studies have indicated that church members offer 4% of their overall income to the churches they attend. This percentage is much lower than that of 1980.[325] The act of giving also means the contribution of capital. The smaller churches have little money to establish a financial base that is vital for their expansion. The lack of expansion of these churches means they

---

[323] Jack Cascione, "Dallas Paper Reports as LCMS Mega Church Competes Against New Giant Baptist Mega Church," Luther Quest, accessed October 19, 2013, http://www.lutherquest.org/walther/articles/-400/jmc00040.htm.

[324] Jack Cascione, "'Traditional LCMS Mission Congregation Keeps Growing," Luther Quest, last modified June 12, 2000, accessed October 19, 2013, http://www.lutherquest.org/walther/articles/jmc00157.htm.

[325] J.C. Conklin, "On the Rise," *Dallas Morning News*, May 1, 1999.

cannot afford to offer the services. In Strobel's book *"Inside the Mind of the Uncharted Harry and Mary,"* the author predicted that more than 60% of new members of mega churches have been converted from other churches in the same location. This indicates that the evangelical Christian numbers is not growing in the same rate as the way the churches are exchanging and passing its members. This is because people move to whichever church that offers the most entertaining services in their location.

In this kind of competition, the smaller churches are the ones suffering the most due to their lack of mobility. Jack Marcum, a statistician who attends a small Presbyterian church, says: "We are not like the McDonald's food chain. We don't simply close a store in one spot and open one in another when marketing research tells us that's where the people have gone." By that, Marcum means that when a small church is closes in a specific location, unlike stores, it does not open on other locations where the target market could be found according to marketing research. [326]

With well-created vision statements, the quality of being nondenominational among the mega churches implies that they are nondescript in their theology. This provides the attendees with an opening to decide whether to attend these services or to attend a service with a specific denominational or theological statement of faith. According to Cascione, the crowds going to churches do not seek churches in order to benefit from the theology offered but to gain from the programs, facilities, and for entertainment that suits the needs of all family members. He goes on to say that church attendees are searching for a combination of religious rock concerts and the YMCA services.[327]

Competition with Government and Citizens

The mega churches are not only competing with one another, but also find themselves in odd situations with individuals and the government around them. One of the most publicized controversies was in Seattle, Washington where a Christian Faith Center proposed to become one of

---

[326] "Racial Shift Causes Parish to Disband," *Knoxville News Sentinel*, April 7, 2002.

[327] Jack Cascione, "'Traditional' LCMS Mission Congregation Keeps Growing," June 12, 2000, accessed October 19, 2013, http://www.lutherquest.org/walther/articles/jmc00157.htm.

the largest complexes in the whole of the United States. The proposal was to establish a sanctuary housing and campus. However, this proposal was not acceptable to the residents living in the City of Federal Way, who started to protest. They wanted the church construction to be limited, and the claim made by King County was that such large constructions would tamper with the rural character of the town.[328]

Citizens have also showed their concern that a church infrastructure is not capable of supporting a parking lot for more than 2000 vehicles, a complete K–12 school, classrooms, 1,000 seating capacity, youth center, library, bookstore, and café. The King County land use rules supported the grievances of the citizens. The land intended for the church construction acts as a business park. The citizens' other concern was establishing a precedent that would encourage other churches to also follow the same trend. Furthermore, the surrendering of land that was once zoned for business further implies a decline in the dollars from taxes. The members of the church and the church itself will have to be taxed. There are other pursuits currently calling for rezoning and the sources of these requests are yet to be attained. As a compromise, the planning commission has provided various recommendations and the councils have not implemented them.

Another example of this scenario is the Christian Faith Center located in Timber Lake, Dewey County, South Dakota. In 1996, the church was faced with the same challenge where its members made the proposal to construct a project covering 80,000 square feet. However, the other citizens in this location responded to this project with outrage. The proposal plan ended up in court, and the court only gave the church the decision to only use 48,000 square feet. This decision did not please the church or the citizens. The church members claimed their right to freedom of religion had been violated while the citizens argued that the action of the church was a violation of the Growth Management Act of the country.[329]

---

[328] Eric Pryne, "Church, County Dispute: Large Facility in Rural Area Spurred Move to Limit Sizes," *Seattle Times*, April 22, 2001, accessed November 9, 2013, http://community.seattletimes.nwsource.com/archive/?date=20010422&slug=church22m.

[329] Ibid.

The same conflict is also seen between the church and the government. Mega churches are in competition to gain and control limited land resources and political power. In this retaliation, citizens end up boycotting the organization. However, mega churches have little to lose from the challenges they face at the local outrage, just in the same way as Wal-Mart. As attendees do come from distant locations, upsetting citizens living in the local area has minimal impact because they are not the neighborhood churches.

Advertising

Just like business organizations, mega churches also apply advertising as a means of getting the upper hand on their competition. Mega churches allocate budgets for advertising so as to increase their church attendance rate. The congregations also make use of a wide range of advertising approaches so as to make their services appealing to new consumers. One of the approaches is the traditional method such as conference announcements, printed materials, and audiotapes, including television and radio broadcasts to pass the message.

This phenomenon is now common in the modern day life of churches that is adopted from businesses. With the growing number of mega churches in various strategic locations, billboards are used for advertising and are placed close to the churches.[330]

Apart from the use of these traditional methods of advertisements, the churches have also dominated multimedia. These new forms include web pages, video presentations, and CD/DVD gospel tutorials. These techniques have gone beyond the focus of regional or local advertising to have a national and international impact. Families and individuals who are moving into a new location already have information about a local church in that area. The members of a church can, through these new forms of technology, stay in touch with the latest events taking place in their churches when they are away on vacations or business trips.[331]

---

[330] Diana Ray, "High Tech Enhances Old-Time Religion," *Insight on the News*, July 31, 2000, 26.

[331] David Neff, "Going to the Movies," *Christianity Today*, February 19, 2001, 16.

The least expensive and most effective method used by the mega churches for advertising is the large congregation assisting the church on Sundays. The aspect that the church is able to host a large size audience by itself significantly contributes to a force of pulling other people to join the massive congregation. The size of a church has its own force of pulling interest from passersby and onlookers, who may want to be part of the endless number of people going to church during the week or on Sundays.

The Pastor-CEO

The role of pastors as CEOs in mega churches is an important issue that has promoted the concept that the mega churches have a business-like leadership. The CEOs of these churches are the senior pastors or anyone else with a similar title. This is a position that is held by a middle-aged person to those who are slightly older. These people have great power by means of their charisma, according to Weber's type of authority. Their personality is characterized as being charming and personable. The senior pastors have great influence in decision-making and have the role of directing the church in any ministerial facet. As a result, their personalities are displayed on the vision statement of the church and also in every activity undertaken by the offices within the church.

The demands of organization for these massive churches call for the need to establish a rational bureaucratic operation that has strong business leadership as the top-most priority.[332] These demands require senior pastors to have the responsibilities just as those of the senior executive boards of businesses. The decisions made by the senior pastors are those that are in line with other highly-ranked ministerial staff and pastors. The boards of the mega churches have congregational representatives who have been elected by the congregation or chosen by other board members from other positions such as church elders and deacons.

Church Governance

Just like businesses, the role of the board is to function as a form of check and balance. The main goal of forming these boards is to develop an

---

[332] Thumma, "The Kingdom, the Power, and the Glory," 500.

even distribution of ministerial power. However, the best efforts to attain an equal distribution of power are often a major challenge. The senior pastor plays a major role, especially in choosing members of the board as well as having the power of influencing the people he chooses to join the board. This leads to the formation of a "yes" board comprising persons whose function is to carry out exactly what the pastor says. This board is also responsible for undertaking his plans, protecting him, and functioning as liaisons with the overall church population. In most cases, the senior pastors have been observed to be the ones in control of every affair of the church. This is the same case as with the owner of a business that has the final say of every business endeavor in the company.

Thumma clearly presents these phenomena in a mega church that he was studying, known as the Chapel Hill Harvester. He draws his conclusion from the work of Schaller, who indicated that organizational structures that are successful are based on centralized power and a charismatic leader, and various checks by inadequate leadership enable the possibility of having a full pastoral power and control in one person in a large church. Just like a large corporation when their stock price plunges during the reign of a successful CEO, large churches have the same concern in cases where they have to function with a pastor who is in control.

Leadership

Leadership has become a cultural concept, buzzword, and focus. Leadership as a term is part of cultural expression for those who influence, affect, and change the course of history at the micro and macro levels in cultures. If leadership has had an impact in organizations, then the main question comes as to what impact leadership has on churches? Religious history presents various key individuals such as Mohammed, Jesus, Martin Luther King, and Gandhi, among others. These figures display the importance of leadership as well as the impact they have had among people of different generations after them.

In Joseph Rost's book, *Leadership for the Twenty-First Century*, he presents the point that there are various challenges that have to be solved about leadership.[333] This is a role that needs to be well defined and has to help in the understanding of the gap between the post-industrial age with different other disciplines. However, defining leadership, even up to the modern day has always been elusive. This is a challenge that has to be solved so as to ensure that leaders in the 21st century will understand their leadership responsibilities and be successful. Twenty years after Rost carried out his research, leadership has never been well defined, especially in regard to the various disciplines.

Characteristics of Quality-Oriented NCD

Church development systems have been measured by use of various academic tools such as the Likert scales and questionnaires.[334] These tools have managed to present main characteristics that are seen in Natural Church Development (NCD). NCD is a principle-oriented approach, not a mode-oriented. Models are defined as concepts or examples that have produced positive results for one or sometimes many churches in some part of the world, but it may not be appropriate to imitate these positive experiences for churches in other situations. On the other hand, principles are those elements that have been proven and are standardized to be used by all growing churches across the globe.[335] Based on NCD principles, Christian Schwartz identified eight major components. The components include a gifted-oriented ministry, empowering leadership, functional structures, passionate spirituality, inspiring worship service, need-oriented evangelism, holistic-small groups, and loving relationships. In his booklet "The ABC's of Natural Church Development," Schwarz described the breath and focus of NCD through his intensive research:

---

[333] Joseph Rost, *Leadership for the Twenty-First Century* (New York, NY: Praeger, 1991), 163.

[334] James Carifio and Rocco J. Perla, "Ten Common Misunderstandings, Misconceptions, Persistent Myths and Urban Legends About Likert Scales and Likert Response Formats and Their Antidotes," *Journal of Social Sciences* 3, no. 3 (2007): 106–16.

[335] Christian A Schwarz, *The Abc's of Natural Church Development Booklet* (Carol Stream: Church Smart Resources, 1998), 7.

"For one to create a large database and develop a scientific and significant conclusion, the institution for our research had 1,000 different churches located in five continents. The churches were the declining and growing ones, small and large churches. Churches supported by the state financially and those that are persecuted by their governments, the well-known and prominent church and those which are not known."[336]

In the past two decades, the tools of NCD have been validated. In the initial testing and creation of this tool, Schwarz commented that churches in 32 of the participating countries managed to use this tool. They had to fill in a questionnaire that was translated into eighteen different languages. The researchers then had the task of analyzing the 4.2 million responses they received. In completing the research, Schwarz managed to identify the various aspects he aimed for his study. The research managed to identify the main principles that were meant to prove the universality of God in building His church from the Falkland Islands to Greenland, from Vladivostok to Alaska, and from the Cape of Good Hope to the North Cape.[337]

By 2006, 45,000 churches were taking part in NCD projects. These churches were located in 72 countries around the world with each of them using this tool as a form of evaluation of the eight main qualities expected to be seen in churches and also for the purpose of continuing with the research that started in 1998.

The NCD Tool was created with the purpose of identifying the eight components that define the NCD qualities in churches. These are the components that Schwarz defined as the biotic potential. According to him, the context is within the natural organism and is all around us. This is what the ecologist refers to as the inherent capacity of species and organisms to survive and reproduce.[338] The heart of God, defined as Missio Dei, is the desire to spread God's gospel all around the world and

---

[336] Schwarz, *The Abc's of Natural Church Development Booklet*, 8.
[337] Ibid., 8–9.
[338] Christian A. Schwarz, *Natural Church Development: A Guide to Eight Essential Qualities of Healthy Churches* (St. Charles: ChurchSmart Resources, 1996), 12.

this forms the reconciliation between God and mankind. Schwarz says that the goal of NCD is to enable the growth forces from God to flourish rather than relying on man-made programs in churches. This is with the goal of looking into the specific qualities that define a healthy and religious church. These strategies help the church to undertake strategic steps of improving their final grades. In the effort of churches trying to implement these strategies and changes, they have to assess their growth every year by use of the NCD tool.

The Components of NCD

Schwarz and Christoph Schalk identified the eight qualities of NCD that show the factors that define a healthy church.[339] The NCD tools help to evaluate the eight qualities expected in churches as a means of defining their effectiveness. Through their on-going research, Schwarz and his colleagues were able to note that every church that was willing to grow could not assume or put aside even one single component of the NCD character. Schwarz was also able to point out the aspects that define negative growth of churches, which are mainly the man-made or the technocratic movement. His belief was that by examining the eight characteristics that define the growth of churches, it is possible to find out the signs that depict the underground realities that churches are involved in. These realities are the very principles that contribute to the healthy growth of churches. Schwarz proposes that the traditional and well-known concepts[340] for church evaluation have never had an in-depth look at the root realities that have an influence to the overall growth of churches.

Empowering Leadership

Various studies on the church have shown that leadership forms a vital development aspect of an effective church.[341] Empowering leaders

---

[339] Christian A. Schwarz and Christoph Schalk, *Implementation Guide to Natural Church Development* (Carol Stream: ChurchSmart Resources, 1998), 10.

[340] Schwarz, *Natural Church Development*, 10.

[341] Thom S. Rainer, *The Book of Church Growth* (New York: B&H Academic, 1998), 192.

do not mean individuals, who have all the control in every activity and elements that a church is involved in. Empowering leaders are also not the person with the control and responsibility of the daily activities of the church. On the contrary, this is a leader who invests most of their time in multiplication, delegation, and discipleship. The NCD research indicates that this type of leader does not need to be a person that is burdened down with responsibilities to effectively lead the church.

The NCD definition of such a leader is one whose energy is multiplied.[342] This type of definition is a shift from the commonly known charismatic leadership. The study by Schwarz clearly showed that pastors do not have to be superstars. This is because those pastors who were considered being successful were not well known. These are the pastors who were engaged on leadership principles, yet they were not famous around the world for being spiritual superstars.

The necessary activities to have a healthy congregation involve prayer, bible study, and fellowship among believers. This is in regard to the assumption that proves that churches of excellence are those dealing with biblical teaching and struggles to grow and be effective. In his book *Biblical Church Growth*, McIntosh indicates that there are several factors within the church that have strong biblical teaching, but have to struggle with a lack of effectiveness because of poor leadership.[343] This calls for the need of a person with a vision to enable the church to be effective.

Sometimes, it may look like the matter of leadership is not a spiritual concern. However, this view was challenged by Ed Stetzer and Mike Dodson, who state:

> "The bible clearly presents facts in which God is calling his people to act as his shepherds. These individuals are chosen by God to fulfill His wish. Examples of such leaders in the Bible include David, Nehemiah, Joshua, Moses, Peter, Jesus, Gideon, Pricilla, Debora and Paul among others. Therefore, leadership is actually a spiritual matter and one can be called upon by God to provide

---

[342] Schwarz, *Natural Church Development*, 25.
[343] Gary L. McIntosh, *Biblical Church Growth: How You Can Work with God to Build a Faithful Church* (Grand Rapids: Baker Books, 2003), 11.

servant leadership, help others belief in God's word, and to provide strategic prayer."[344]

For the church to attain its maturity, it is essential to bring a balance between scripture, fellowship and prayer, and leadership.[345]

Although one of the main purposes of the church is growth (making disciples), Hunter opines that churches at times lose focus on their mission and purpose. According to him, the Spirit of God is frustrated, and this hinders the growth of churches because the members are not relying in the help of the Holy Spirit. The Holy Spirit helps leaders and the rest of the congregation to deal with barriers that come their way in the attainment of effective church growth.[346] This makes leadership to be viewed as a vital aspect in the attainment of an effective church since it is the way through which the church can attain its maturity and become mobilized. The person under this kind of leadership is spiritual and practical.

Among the eight key aspects of the markers and characteristics of NCD, Schwarz lists empowering leadership as the top aspect. Leadership plays a vital role in being a component in the development of church leadership. This is because the leader exerts empowerment to the people in growing to attain spiritual maturity, be part of the body of Christ, and to continue working towards the fulfillment of God for His church.[347]

Gift-Oriented Ministry

The second component that forms the development of the church is the ministry that is goal-oriented. This is an element that is linked to the leadership of the church. The main role of leadership in churches is to assist members to know their gifts and to contribute these different gifts in the provision of an appropriate ministry. The main focus of the attainment of this kind of leadership is not based on the technocratic pigeon-hole approach, but it is an approach that forces individuals to take

---

[344] Ed Stetzer and Mike Dodson, *Comeback Churches: How 300 Churches Turned Around and Yours Can Too* (Nashville: B&H Books, 2007), 34, 35.

[345] McIntosh, *Biblical Church Growth*, 154.

[346] Hunter, *Spirit Baptism*, 39.

[347] Schwarz, *Natural Church Development*, 24–25.

up certain roles and fit into different positions of the church. Instead, the approach has to be one that develops a process and system that identifies and develops volunteers' God-given gifts and natural abilities and ensures they are utilized to serve God's purpose. The main correlation of the growth of the church is the ability to train its volunteer layperson in an effective manner. "When Christians serve in their area of giftedness, they generally function less in their own strength and more in the power of the Holy Spirit. Thus ordinary people can accomplish the extraordinary!"[348]

Passionate Spirituality

Passionate spirituality is an element that is supposed to be a genuine overflow of the relationship between man and Jesus Christ. Passionate spirituality is mainly defined as the ability of the Christians of a church to be passionate and to have the fire in their commitment and faith in God. It also means the ability of living in practical ways that are acceptable to God. These individuals are enthusiastic and full of joy for their faith and life. The research conducted by Schwarz indicates that this quality goes beyond the spiritual non-charismatic and charismatic persuasions or spiritual practices. Research shows that the churches that leaned more toward legalism had a below average level of spiritual passions. Schwarz says that the church's disregard of this quality promotes a skewed view of scriptures; therefore, it is almost impossible for it to attain growth, especially when the members are not taught to live by faith and be able to share with others and be enthusiastic about the Word of God.[349]

Passionate spirituality also leads to faith in the faith of Christians. The churches that are noted to grow and are a healthy are able to establish strategic ways to help individuals to mature and grow in their walk with God; as a result, they are able to commit to the church for a long-term period.[350] Therefore, those leaders who have learned and applied the growth principles in discipleship,[351] will be able to reach out to the lost and to

---

[348] Ibid., 26.
[349] Ibid., 29.
[350] Stetzer and Dodson, *Comeback Churches*, 126.
[351] Stetzer and Dodson, *Comeback Churches*, 127

evangelize them. Therefore, if the church cannot mature the ones in the church, church growth will be stagnant.

A congregation that is mature will always strive to attain a balance that is the mission and loving. "People are in search of the servant hood of caring and spirit of love in caring communities and will be able to attain healthy a congregations and loving relationships that are synonymous."[352] According to Bob Whitesel, Acts chapter 2 indicates that the first three stages of church growth and ability to attain maturity are seen in the breaking of bread, in prayer, and studying the Word.[353]

McIntosh outlines the premise of the growth of a church as resulting from the contextual environment, racial factors, general revelation, and the scripture that provides special revelation. These aspects lead to practices and principles that guide the church in their growth. The church growth according to McIntosh is found in biblical moorings and on the passionate pursuance of the beliefs and behaviors of the church. He states that "in effect, the church by its very self depends on the Word of God and is passionate in the articulation of the behaviors and beliefs it uphold. This enables the churches to increase their potential towards biblical growth."[354] The focus on the Bible is mainly based on spiritual maturity as depicted in Acts 2.

The instrument of NCD measures the passionate spirituality of church members. Schwarz defines passionate spirituality as being the development of energy that empowers Christians to carry out the mission of God. This spirituality can only be attained through prayer, studying the Word of God and the genuine fellowship of members.

Functional Structures

The attainment of functional structures as the quality of a mature growth of the church is seen from the ministry multiplication that is ongoing. The main focus of functional structures is to have ministry structures that encourage and train the leaders. It is a structure or process

---

[352] Henry S. Holland, Creed and Character; Sermons, (Read Books, 2008), 32

[353] Bob Whitesel, *Growth by Accident, Death by Planning: How Not to Kill a Growing Congregation* (Nashville: Abingdon Press, 2004), 103.

[354] McIntosh, *Biblical Church Growth*, 45.

through which leaders can continue to develop within the church. This does not mean to say that churches should have similar paradigm and structures. Instead, the churches have to highlight the reality that they have clear and effective structures that enable leadership use and development. The main structural item that crosses the contest and culture of the churches is the concept of the department head. This means that across the board, churches considered as being successful have clear leadership and department heads with assigned duties. The church structures according to the NCD definitions mean the systems through which church growth is accomplished. Functional structures are also affected by the concept of the contemporary versus traditional. Research indicates that a negative relationship can be seen between quality and growth with traditionalism in the church.[355]

Leaders who are effective in churches make the effort of continually evaluating the way the structures are able to hinder or improve the overall mission of the church. This includes the need to provide training in the needed areas in ministry such as developing programs like vocational bible school, Sunday schools, block or time structures for the youth and children, and establishing huge evangelistic events. These structures can be eliminated or changed as needed.

An effective church is defined by its clear structures that enable leadership use and development. Generally, successful churches have a clear leadership style and department heads carry out their assigned duties.

Inspiring Worship Services

When a person has the inspiration to do something, they are more likely to go back for that same event. This is the trick that is also applied in ministries. This is mainly true when referring to matters on internal life, purpose, the plan of God, and the reality of God. The main aspect that defines a growing church, unlike that which is stagnant, is based on its philosophical approach which has not to be one that is sensitive to the seeker, but one that is inspiring to those attending the service. Schwarz showed that services may be intended for non-Christians and Christians, and this makes their style free and liturgical, or their language may be

---

[355] Schwarz, *Natural Church Development*, 13.

secular, which makes no difference to the growth of the church.[356] Despite these different service styles, the strongest one is the church that inspires its attendees.

Worship is on the top of Stetzer's list of church activities. He says that worship is the key element that will make church attendees keep coming back. This is because the attendees are inspired by the mood of worship, especially when it is orderly and celebrative. As a result, there is the need for churches to re-examine their love and passion toward their mission purposes and to God by examining their worship.[357] Therefore, church services should avoid a worship style where the attendees are simply spectators and instead provide a worship environment that enables the congregation to be an experiential inspirational driven society that can promote the actual encounter with God.[358]

The main ingredients that form an effective church, according to Kevin G. Ford, are the ability of an organization to understand their actual DNA and inspiration. This is because the DNA part of the church is the source of a relevant and inspirational worship service.[359] Such a church can talk about their love for God and express this love in the relationships that they form. Inspirational worship is all about the creation of a culture and establishing a genuine encounter with the Church. It is part of the cord of this church that actually defines not just who the people of this church are but what they are becoming.[360]

According to Schwarz, inspiring worship is among the main qualities and markers of a NCD. This is a corporate and personal encounter of living with God.[361] It is a concept that surpasses substance and style and indicates a genuine encounter of working with God in a corporate stetting. The leaders through the forms of service or crafting effort mainly influence such an atmosphere with other teams in the church and allowing freedom of worship.

---

[356] Schwarz, *Natural Church Development*, 32.

[357] Stetzer and Dodson, *Comeback Churches*, 107–108.

[358] Ibid, 197

[359] Kevin G. Ford. *Transforming Church: Bringing Out the Good to Get to Great.* (David C Cook, 2008), 97

[360] Ibid, 83

[361] Schwarz, *Natural Church Development*, 32.

Holistic Small Groups

The importance of multiplications of small group is also another quality characteristic of an effective church, according to Schwarz. He presents the challenge that small groups form the natural environment for Christians to always serve others, both outside and in the group, by use of their spiritual gifts.[362] Quality characteristic is among the most significant aspects of an effective church and even to those that are no growing. The difference is how these churches focus on leadership and holistic aspects of small groups. The focus is the ability to meet the need of evangelism by using the force and impact of small groups. When the groups are not holistic, they fail to satisfy the practical discipleship expected in the life of a Christian. The difference comes on the approach and digestion on the topic under study.

Need Oriented Evangelism

The need-oriented evangelism presents a balanced approach on the topic of gifts of God that causes confusion. This means that walking in God's gifts that he has given to man is different from having the evangelical gift. Every Christian is expected to use his personal gifts in serving Christians and non-Christians around them. They also are responsible for spreading the Gospel and encouraging people to be in contact with the churches at their local communities.[363] The role of the church as designated by Jesus is to take its place in the body of Christ and not to have the professionals in these churches to evangelize on behalf of the churches. The NCD research depicted that Christians are declining, and growing churches had the same number of contacts they made with non-Christians. The main purpose of this contact is to contribute to make a difference. Therefore, the effort is not to establish more bridges to non-Christians but to ensure that there is better use of the relationship that has already been formed.

Part of this purpose is the development of need-oriented evangelism and highlighting the vision of the church. The aim of this characteristic is to provide evangelism that aims to reach out to the lost sheep through

---

[362] Ibid.

[363] Schwarz, *Natural Church Development,* 37.

any means available. Ford says that the main reason for the existence of churches is to reach out as far as they can with the message of Jesus Christ.[364]

Loving Relationships

Finally, loving relationship is the eighth quality aspect that defines the effectiveness of a church. This means the ability of churches to establish loving relationships not only in the church but also with the outsiders. In addition, a church can attain its effectiveness with the unconditional and tenacious love that a leader shows to the people. This is an aspect that will influence people to care and love not just themselves but for others as well. This is the love that Jesus Christ showed the church. Therefore, it is necessary for churches today to continue evaluating and accessing themselves as per the quality characteristics displayed in the NCD Tool.

---

[364] Ford, *Transforming Church: Bringing Out the Good to Get to Great*, 122.

✠

Chapter 5

Conclusion

Protestant churches today have changed in all perspectives. Modern churches are influenced by materialism, consumerism, and wealth among other worldly factors. The leaders of these churches have also shifted away from God's initial intention for them to be shepherds of their flock. The Old and New Testaments clearly show the role of spiritual leaders and church elders. These are the roles that the early churches practiced and are distinct from today's contemporary roles. This paper has shown the various challenges faced by church leaders as they are in the midst of an addictive culture that has captured our attention. The church, therefore, is within the context of an empire that demands allegiance. By looking at the protestant churches in the United States, one will note the frenetic activity in every facet that shows the church of God is immature, that there is a high rate of neglect of justice, self-interest of the pastors, the wish for fame and luxurious lifestyles, a high rate of divorce, addictive behavior, and misuse of power.

These are characteristics that are common in modern day Christianity that has been impregnated by western culture. What is worse is that these tendencies are mainly seen among church leaders, their close aides, and family members. This bad influence starts from the leaders because they have lost the sight of ethics and moral leadership, and therefore, cannot be considered as role models. These church leaders start with great love and enthusiasm that goes beyond all frontiers and eventually end up with a lot of wealth, power, and administration sense. At this level, these leaders have lost their fear of risks, love, and fear of God. These leaders are driven by the need to adapt structures that will enable the growth of individuals and the need to act in conserving tradition. It is an ambition that is built towards the development of prestige and authority.

The modern day culture is what forms us in many different ways through its measures, goals, and ideals. These ideals align with economic, politics, individuality, religion, and philosophy. This means that the western culture has its own definition of the good life and attempts to shape us in all perspectives according to a set of practices and understandings.

On the other hand, the New Testament presents a different perspective of practices and understandings. The ideal shows that leadership is not a measure of success through wealth and position or the growth of the churches by numbers of attendees. The ideal is discipleship, and it is about certain outcomes and practices. Discipleship focuses on the principles of character-based and kingdom-centered Christology. It is oriented toward the cross and incarnation, sacrifice and love, and the formation of a new community as intended by God.

Our culture drives our attention to modern materialism and values that are self-centered. This culture supports an upward journey and sacrifice has no place in it. This is a culture that churches and church leaders are rooted in today and a culture that cultivates force. This is different from the definition given by Jesus Christ on the formation of churches in which is the creation of a new community: A community that is in the world but not of the world. It is a community that has come forth through spiritual formation as purposed by God. This community is the temple of the living God that reflects his loving presence in the world.

God's intention for church leaders is for them to protect and care for the congregation by educating them in the true Word of God and fighting against any behavior that goes out the spiritual context. They were not assigned the role of pastor CEO of managing the church finances and carrying out other investment activities. Church leaders were also not meant to be the mediators between God and man because there is only one mediator who is Jesus Christ. Through the blood of Jesus on the cross, all believers were given the title of priest to directly communicate with God through prayer and to teach others on the goodness and grace of God. There is the need for church leaders to stop focusing on increasing the number of members and instead rely on the effective ways of spreading the Gospel as Jesus and his true disciples did in the New Testament. Churches today need to follow the biblical model for pastoral leadership as intended by God.

The Biblical Model for Pastoral Leadership

A compelling model for pastoral ministry is presented in the Bible that transcends culture, man-made ideas, and history. The Shepherding model is most prominently found in the Bible. Pastor is a commonly used English word, which has made its way through Latin language and is a semantic equivalent to shepherd, term commonly used in the Bible.

Previously, from the ancient times, rulers have been considered as showing their authority to rule based on their ability of pasturing their people. Several rulers from western Asia, such as Hammurabi, were known as shepherds or referred as pasturing their people. [365] Therefore, it has been observed that shepherding leadership model has strong historical and biblical foundations.

Old Testament-God referred as Shepherd

In Old Testament, God has been referred to as the Shepherd of His people. In the Blue Letter Bible, Jehovah is translated as:

> "The Existing One" or "Lord." The chief meaning of Jehovah is derived from the Hebrew word *Havah* meaning "to be" or "to exist." It also suggests "to become" or specifically "to become known"-this denotes a God who reveals Himself unceasingly. Ro'eh from which *Raah* derived, means "shepherd" in Hebrew. A shepherd is one who feeds or leads his flock to pasture (Ezek. 34:1–15). An extended translation of this word, rea', is "friend" or "companion." This indicates the intimacy God desires between Himself and His people. When the two words

---

[365] R. Laird Harris, Gleason Archer Jr. and Bruce K. Waltke, *Theological Wordbook of the Old Testament* (Chicago: Moody, 1980), 853.

are combined—*Jehovah Raah*—it can be translated as "The Lord my Friend."[366]

These terms were used in order to refer to God in Gen. 48:15, 49:24 and Ps. 80:1 and 23:1. In Ezek. 34, Zech. 10:1–5, and Jer. 23:1–4, God has been described as the Shepherd of shepherds. It has been further explained that God appoints shepherds of the flocks and judges their performance highlighting unworthy shepherds who are unfaithful to their responsibilities and duties. God is the ultimate Shepherd as indicated in the Bible.

God cares and is responsible for meeting the needs of His children. The reference of God as Shepherd provides a reflection of His character and His relation with His people. In context of His relation with people as the ultimate Shepherd, God understand His flocks, loves, leads, encourages and provides protection to His sheep. According to Ezek. 34, He binds up the broken and brings back the strays. It was further highlighted in John 1:14 as "I am the good shepherd, and know my [sheep], and am known of mine."

The focus of being a good shepherd is related to flocks, their safety, provision and guidance. Ezekiel 34:16 exposes the essence of bad shepherds, explaining what it looked liked when leaders fail to provide their love and care to their people. It has been explained that these leaders use to slaughter their sheep for their own gains and purposes instead of caring about them and feeding them.

Under-Shepherds described in the Old Testament

The term shepherd is referred in the Old Testament to men who were entrusted with leadership responsibilities and functions. According to Gen. 4:2, Abel has been mentioned in the Old Testament as the first shepherd. In Gen 12:6, Abraham is referred to as shepherd, along with Jacob, Moses, and David being referred to shepherding flocks in Gen. 30:1, Ex. 3:1, and 2 Sam. 5:2, respectively. Each of them was responsible for tending, guiding and guarding their flocks (people). God appointed each of these

---

[366] "Hebrew Lexicon: H3068 (KJV)." *Blue Letter Bible*, accessed 15 Feb, 2014, http://www.blueletterbible.org/lang/lexicon/lexicon.cfm?Strongs=H3068&t=KJV.

men to lead His people using the same guiding principles set by Himself. Furthermore, the Old Testament also highlights the spiritual shepherding responsibilities of prophets and priests.

According to the Old Testament, shepherds were supposed to look up to God as the ultimate Shepherd and were to follow His example of caring for people. God provided them with instructions and expected their faithful obedience to them. The shepherds were held accountable by God for the services they have provided to their flocks. Their main concern was to maintain the spiritual well-being and health of God's flocks.

The most common and well known passage in the Bible is Psalm 23 that was written for David, who was a proven shepherd in terms of sheep and their well-being. In Ps. 78:70-72 it is stated, "He also chose David His servant, And took him from the sheepfolds; From the care of the ewes with suckling lambs He brought him, To shepherd Jacob His people, and Israel His inheritance. So he shepherded them according to the integrity of his heart, And guided them with his skillful hands."

Under-Shepherds described in the New Testament

In the New Testament church, pastors have been given explicit instructions related to their duties and responsibilities towards God's people. In Acts 20:28, the pastor is charged to serve as a "shepherd in the church of God, which He purchased with His own blood." According to Eph. 5:25b–27, Jesus has come to earth for the purpose of saving His church with His own blood. According to Jn. 15:5–11, He has sent the Holy Spirit when He went back to Heaven in order to direct, gift, and empower His church and people. According to Eph. 4:11–12, He entrusted His church men with the leadership; gifted by the Holy Spirit, for equipping the flock to handle the ministry and make its decisions. As indicated in 1Pet. 5:1–4, the shepherds are responsible for providing oversight and guidance to the flocks, leading them according to God's will, becoming an example for the flock, and being self-driven and motivated by God's call. All the while, the shepherd of the flock is held accountable and answerable to the Chief Shepherd. As mentioned in 1Pet. 5:1–4, "Shepherd the flock of God which is among you, serving as overseers, not by compulsion but willingly, not for dishonest gain but eagerly, nor as being lords over those entrusted to you, but by being examples to the flock; and when the Chief Shepherd appears, you will receive the crown of glory that does not fade away." It is further mentioned that God will reward His pastors and shepherds for their faithful services in His realm.

21st Century Shepherds

In today's fast-paced, competitive 21st century environment, the understanding and terminology of shepherding has become foreign to a number of people. The people in ancient time, from the times of the Bible, had a complete comprehensive understanding of the role and responsibilities of shepherd. According to Ted H. Waller,

> "The family often depended upon sheep for survival. A large part of their diet was milk and cheese. Occasionally they ate the meat. Their clothing and tents were made of wool and skins. Their social position often depended upon the well-being of the flock, just as we depend on jobs, businesses, cars and houses. Family honor might depend upon defending the flock."[367]

This image is quite similar to the one's that existed in ancient biblical era. However, people in 21st century are highly disconnected from the agrarian society, due to which most of the people do not understand and some of them are not even aware of shepherding terminology. As result a result they have proposed other principles that are unbiblical in defining the role of pastor as the chief executive officer of an organization.

Richard Kyle, the author of *Evangelism*, claimed that today's churches are depended on the organizational management theories for supporting their bureaucratic challenges of complex and large churches. For example, Fortune 500 churches have potentially employed masses of small armies of volunteers and hundreds of employees. Therefore, in these situations,

---

[367] Ted. H. Waller, *With the Sheep in the Wilderness: Shepherding God's Flock in the World* (Nashville: Twentieth Century Publishers, 1991), 9–10.

the role of pastor is molded to direct and manage entire operations of the church.[368]

The Unbiblical Model of Pastoral Ministry

While discussing about congressional descriptions of what churches require from pastor's of today, Marva Dawn and Eugene Peterson stated, sharing their concern that "With hardly an exception they don't want pastors at all—they want managers of their religious company. They want a pastor they can follow so they won't have to bother with following Jesus anymore."[369] In the modern world, people generally view the role of pastoral from a corporate perspective. The biblical model has been preeminently taken over by the business model of today. John W. Frye stated: "Jesus is shoved into our shadows as we read our management books, do our cultural surveys, attend our leadership seminars, and applaud or criticize one another's endeavors."[370]

Jesus is the Role Model for all Shepherds in 21st Century

We do not need to look anywhere beyond the ministry of Jesus Christ in order to understand the actual and true meaning of shepherd and shepherding. As mentioned in Lk 12:1, Jesus has preached and taught thousands of people. Furthermore, it is mentioned in Mk 3:14 that Jesus focused on developing the twelve disciples and in Lk 10:1 it is mentioned that He sent out 70 people on a special mission. In Acts 1:15, "In those days Peter stood up among the believers (a group numbering about a hundred and twenty)." Peter, James and John have been identified among the few very strong believers in Matt 17, 26:36, 46, and have been identified as loved ones in Jn 13:23.

In the New Testament, the leadership model for the modern church is clearly explained as that of shepherd, which is used as a dominant symbol. Jesus referred Himself as the Good Shepherd in Jn. 10:7–30. As a Good

---

[368] Richard Kyle, *Evangelicalism: An Americanized Christianity* (Edison, NJ: Transaction Publishers, 2006), 227.

[369] Dawn and Peterson, *The Unnecessary Pastor*, 4.

[370] John W. Frye, *Jesus the Pastor* (Grand Rapids: Zondervan, 2000), 18.

Shepherd, He offers salvation to people, gives life to others, sacrifices His own life for His sheep, knows His sheep by their names, and secures His flock till the eternity.[371] In these versus, Jesus describes Good Shepherd in terms of security, intimacy, hope, warmth and strength. In 1Pet 5:4, He describes Himself as the "Chief Shepherd." He also describes Himself as the "Great Shepherd" in Heb 13:20.

Jesus is observed to be a Shepherd full of compassion, devotion, love and care. In Matt 9:36, it is mentioned: "When he saw the multitudes, He was moved with compassion for them, because they were weary and scattered, like sheep having no shepherd." It was due to this compassion of Jesus that people started following Him. Lynn Anderson stated: "Most Christians will want to follow real shepherds who mentor and equip them—shepherds whose lives are credible, whose relationships are authentic and warm, and whose ministry is genuine and helpful."[372] Furthermore, people willingly follow shepherds or pastors who follow the model of compassion set as an example by Jesus.

In Eph 4:11, charging pastors with clear responsibility God stated: "Equip the disciples to do the work of the ministry." He further instructed in 2 Tim 2:2 to commit the truth to "faithful men who will be able to teach others also." The shepherding model of ministry that was demonstrated by Jesus throughout His life consistently focused on these things. According to J. Oswald Sanders, "A leader must be willing to develop himself on many levels and in many capacities, but with a unity of purpose."[373] It is the call to serve the role of a shepherd that provides a unity to the purpose of leadership in church. All the pastoral duties and responsibilities fall under the framework provided by the shepherding model, which covers every aspect of a leaders' responsibility towards the followers.

The shepherd works more under the influence of a role model, rather than using his own power. People, believers and followers, do not just follow shepherds because they are supposed to, but they follow them because them want to, i.e. they follow shepherds willingly rather than forcefully. According

---

[371] Jn. 10: 9, 10, 11, 14 and 29.

[372] Dr. Lynn Anderson, *They Smell Like Sheep: Spiritual Leadership for the 21st Century*, (Howard Books, Louisiana, 1997), 3.

[373] J. Oswald Sanders, *Dynamic Spiritual Leadership* (Grand Rapids: Discovery House Publishers, 1999), 48.

to various examples mentioned in the Bible (the Old Testament and the New Testament), the flocks are supposed to be led not to be driven. This means that shepherds have a duty to lead and guide their followers instead of directing and ruling them. A number of misguided pastors have destroyed this image and ethics of church they serve as they have misused their power and authority and have influenced people to believe and follow their personal agendas, rather than leading them gently to follow the agenda of God for His church. Howard Synder in *Liberating the Church: The Ecology of Church and Kingdom*, explained shepherding in biblical ecology and stated that:

> "In the biblical ecology of the church, pastoring or shepherding is rescued from all triviality and is put at the center of the healthy life of the Christian community. In the community of God's people the pastor is not the head, the pastoral director, the boss or the chief executive officer. Rather, the pastor . . . serves as coordinator, equipper, discipler, overseer and shepherd. This is leadership. But it is leadership for, with and in the body. It is leadership on an organic community model, not on an organizational hierarchy model."[374]

Shepherding has its roots in a genuine and sacrificial love for people, and a pure love and faith for God. This means it is not born out of a desire to acquire authority, power, prestige or prominence over other people. The life of a shepherd-pastor is supposed to be spent in humble service to God with extreme devotion and love for God and His people. In reference to the significance of relationship between believers, Jesus stated in Jn 15:13: "This is my commandment, that you love one another as I have loved you. Greater love has no one than this, than to lay down one's life for his friends." This statement is directly applicable to the shepherd who follows the Good Shepherd (i.e, Jesus) in leading, loving and guiding the sheep of the God.

Indeed, Jesus the Chief Shepherd and the Good Shepherd is the one and only model for pastoral ministry. According to Edward C. Zaragoza:

---

[374] Howard A. Snyder, *Liberating the Church: The Ecology of Church and Kingdom* (Downers Grove, IL: InterVarsity Press, 1983), 246 & 247.

"As servants, pastors are somehow to be like Jesus. Servant leadership is a very attractive image for ministry to other people because it appears to blend what most churches look for in a pastor: a caring person who can also run a church."[375] Most of the current emphasis on the leadership disciple attempts to combine the biblical principles for making them more acceptable to the audience of today. However, there is no need for repackaging the biblical principles concerning pastoral ministry.

The leadership model for the Church given by God is clearly presented and portrayed by Jesus as the Chief Shepherd, the Deacons as servants to the Body, the pastor of the local church as the undershepherd, and the Church Body as performing the works of ministry. This model is timeless and sufficient for the healthy and effective functioning of the Church of God. Nevertheless, it is important for the pastors to carefully study and understand what it means to follow the Chief Shepherd-Jesus in order to guide, lead, and equip people so that they can perform their ministry work properly. It is from this fundamental love and faith and through following the example of Jesus that the pastor can effectively lead others according to the way God wants them to lead.

Primary Qualities of the 21st Century Pastors

After analyzing the biblical model and corporate model of leadership in Church, major competencies were identified for 21st century pastors and were categorized into three sections: pastoral care, church administration and preaching. The basic responsibilities of today's pastor in each disciple are not specific to any particular size of church.

Pastoral Care

Pastoral Care mainly involves servant-shepherd qualities which include: counseling, guiding, loving and guiding the flocks, visiting, crisis ministry, etc. Furthermore, it has been observed that Jesus is the best example found in caring for the flocks, as He has been frequently referred to as Good Shepherd at different places. Frye stated: "Deep felt compassion is one of

---

[375] Edward C. Zaragoza, *No Longer Servants, But Friends: Theology of Ordained Ministry* (Nashville: Abingdon Press, 1999), 10.

the primary and controlling emotions of pastoral ministry. Jesus felt it and, as Chief Shepherd, modeled it for all who would pastor. This emotion is visceral and compels action. It is the heart of God for people."[376] The shepherd must be involved in the lives of his flocks in order to relate to and identify with them and develop relational ministry.

The pastor must have deep affection and love of God flowing throughout his ministry. He plays the role of key leader in the church ministry and is supposed to lead by example, which is the fundamental requirement for pastoral care. In order to become a best example of church leadership in 21st century, the pastor is to love Jesus sincerely and devote his love for Him, as mentioned in Eph 6:18, "He is to surrender himself to being filled with the Spirit of God".

In addition, a faithful pastor is supposed to understand and know how he should relate to his people. According to John R. Bisagno, Pastor Emeritus of The First Baptist Church of Houston, Texas, "Perhaps the best place to start in relating to others is to put yourself in their shoes . . . .Treating others as you want to be treated, caring enough to know where they are coming from, and respecting it, is the heart of getting along with people."[377] In order to develop strong relation with people, the pastor should work in knowing as many people as possible personally so that he is able to understand their tribulations, triumphs, joys and trails. Furthermore, the pastor must also empathize with people so that he is able to deal with their concerns and issues accordingly.

Protecting and guiding the flock were also identified as important responsibilities to be performed by 21st century pastors. The shepherd/pastor should watch over his sheep and work on protecting and leading them away from spiritual dangers. This has been indicated by the image of God as the Great shepherd presented in Psalm 23. It is observed that God being the Great Shepherd provides restoration, food, peace, guidance when approaching danger, guidance in righteousness, fullness, mercy and goodness, comfort, and en eternal dwelling place. Likewise, the undershepherd-pastor, as God's servant, is supposed to lead people

---

[376] C. Sumner Wemp, *The Guide to Practical Pastoring* (Nashville: Thomas Nelson, 1982), 207.

[377] John R. Bisagno, *Letters to Timothy: A Handbook for Pastors*, (B&H Books, 2001), 54.

and guide the way towards the Great Shepherd. God has charged pastors with the responsibility of guiding the sheep, protecting them and leading them away from personal sin. In Ezek 33:7, 9, instructing Ezekiel in his task as watchman, god instructs: "So you, son of man: I have made you a watchman for the house of Israel; therefore you shall hear a word from My mouth and warn them for Me . . . . Nevertheless if you warn the wicked to turn from his way, and he does not turn from his way, that wicked man shall die in his iniquity; but his blood I will require at your hand."

Furthermore, the pastor is responsible for lovingly, yet firmly guiding the sheep regarding the application of the Word of God. In addition, in order to maintain the spiritual wellbeing, purity and health of the body of God's Church, discipline must be practiced and the pastor should be courageous enough to stand for the truth in this 21st century. However, the pastor is not just responsible for maintain church discipline in the church, rather he is also responsible for leading the church to create an environment where the body of Christ responds to people going on the wrong path and to sin in a Godly manner.

Church Administration

The quality of church administration for the pastor includes leadership and oversight in various disciples such as ministries (services and programs), mission (formulation and communication of vision), manpower (volunteer and staff leadership), money (managing finances) and management (managing church facilities). In reference to church administration it is stated in Eph 4:12 that "equipping the saints for the work of the ministry, for the edifying of the body of Christ". If the pastor is not able to effectively equip others, he will have to face lot of severe limitations on his ministry. Effectively equipping the saints results in multiplication of the ministry and followers and increases the degree of faithfulness beyond and within a particular church location. Therefore, it is important for the pastor in 21st century to be a good model in terms of his character, competence and calling because of the principle of multiplication ministry. It is important to understand and pastor must be careful that if he is flawed, then he will multiply others who will also be flawed, thereby damaging the work of the kingdom.

Barna, defining a Christian leader, stated "someone who is called by God to lead, leads with and through Christ-like character, and demonstrates the functional competencies that permit effective leadership to take place."[378] The pastor of 21st century must have the capability of administrating and coordination the work of church in a way that the church maintains its functional viability effectively. Although, the church is purely a spiritual organization; however, there are certain basic business principles that can be applied in all churches in order to maintain and run functions smoothly. Thus, the pastor must have good working and managing knowledge of how to apply basic business principles so that the church can benefit from them.

Moreover, a compelling vision developed for the church ministry sets the direction for everyone across the church ministry. According to James E. Mean, "The art of pastoral guidance requires the ability to interpret the signposts about the future and to influence the church to prepare for it. Just as the historian takes piles of information about the past and constructs an interpretation of what must have happened, so must the leader select, organize, structure, and interpret information about the future in constructing a viable and credible vision."[379] The pastor must know the direction that God wants him to take the ministry and he must be capable of communicating the same to his congregation in a motivating and compelling way in order to become an effective leader.

Preaching

Preaching competency involves a servant-shepherd to feed the flock, teach, exhort, encourage, correct, administer the ordinance, maintain discipline, and evangelize. In his book *The Guide to Practical Pastoring*, C. Sumner Wemp highlighted that "Preaching and teaching the Word of God is a vital part of the ministry. To stand in the pulpit and preach in the power of the Holy Spirit and see God transform lives is just short of tasting heaven itself."[380] In order to faithfully lead the ministry, the pastor must develop an adequate preaching ministry.

---

[378] George Barna, *Leaders on Leadership* (Ventura, CA: Regal Books, 1997), 25.

[379] James, E. Means, *Effective Pastors for a New Century: Helping Leaders Strategize for Success*, (Revell, a division of Baker Publishing Group, 1993), 141.

[380] Wemp, *The Guide to Practical Pastoring*, 207.

In 2 Tim 4:1–2, Paul declared, "I charge you therefore before God and the Lord Jesus Christ, who will judge the living and the dead at His appearing and His kingdom; Preach the Word! Be ready in season and out of season. Convince, rebuke, exhort, with all longsuffering and teaching." Richard Wells and Boyd Luter stated in order to explain this that "Paul seems to be saying, Tim, you have to take responsibility for what the Lord has called you to do and preach. But remember, you are not up there representing yourself, and you are not proclaiming your own message, expecting it to make all the difference in people's lives. You are heralding the God-breathed message, which packs divine authority and has the power to transform your hearers, even as it has you."[381] Preaching is a sacred responsibility as the pastor is suppose to represent God and communicate the Word of God to His people.

Impact and Use of Technology in 21st Century for Preaching Purposes

It has been observed that the listeners of 21st century have a short attention span and they usually get bored easily while listening to a long lecture. Additionally with the technological advancements, it is important for pastors to understand the effectiveness of using technologies in their preaching methods. Our culture has been increasingly dominated by technologies. In argument, David Fisher stated: "The technological age, in particular television, works powerfully against reasoned oral discourse. Images and sound bytes characterize the electronic communication that bombards us day in and day out."[382] In addition to the technology, there is increasingly impact of entertainment in the culture that has ultimately affected the church.

Michael J. Quicke stated that is unfortunate that generally the preachers are perceived as "clueless about popular taste in television, film, video, music, news, and websites."[383] In a survey, 67.8% pastors highlighted that using technology for communicating with the culture is important

---

[381] C. Richard Wells and A. Boyd Luter, *Inspired Preaching: A Survey of Preaching Found in the New Testament* (Nashville: Broadman, 2002), 9.

[382] David Fisher, *The 21st Century Pastor* (Grand Rapids: Zondervan, 1996), 234.

[383] Michael J. Quicke, *360 Degree Preaching* (Grand Rapids: Baker Academic Books, 2003), 66.

in 21st century for preaching effectively. Although, it is highly recognized that message f truth and Word of God cannot be changed over time, but the methodologies for communicating the truth can and must be changed in order to attract the intended audience.

With continuous technological advancements in 21st century, in terms of television as well as the worldwide web, congregants can access to preaching across the globe. People are able to identify good, relevant and effective preaching easily by comparing their preachers to others they see and hear through the Internet. People expect much high from the local preacher, when they compare him to other men who are famous and prominent.

Conclusion

A review of biblical versus and contemporary literature has been conducted in this study, and is reflected in the bibliography, including a wide range of sources. Several resources were included such as journals, magazine articles, newspapers, books and electronic resources. Several works and resources available and in circulation have been used for addressing the individual components of this study.

The conclusion made from the literature have been compared and contrasted with the biblical principles pertaining to the function and role of pastor as a church leader. Analyzing the biblical quotes and existing literature it is concluded that when pastors adopt or imitate their leadership styles based on the corporate model of leadership or model of CEO, the results are a mirror image of worldly practices rather than true biblical conversion, worship and spiritual transformation. The reference and evidences presented in this research should be used for informing, guiding and equipping pastors so that they can become effective church leaders that please God. The main purpose was to assist, enable and challenge pastors to fulfill their actual spiritual calling under the light of biblical ideology and according to the foundation laid by Jesus Christ. By doing so, pastors will be able to demonstrate spiritual faith and trust, and by these efforts God will be glorified.

List Of Figures

Figure 1: Early Church Scriptural Structure. Source:
　　　　　planksandnails.hubpages.com 66

Figure 2: Contemporary Secular Church Structure 67

Bibliography

Books

Amdt, William, and Frederick Danker. *A Greek English Lexicon of Early Christian Literature and New Testament.* Chicago: University of Chicago Press, 2000.

Anderson, Leith. *A Church for the 21st Century.* Minneapolis: Bethany House, 1992.

––. *Dying for Change an Arresting Look at the New Realities Confronting Churches and Para-Church Ministries.* Minneapolis: Bethany House, 1990.

Anderson, James D., and Ezra Earl Jones. *The Management of Ministry.* New York: Discipleship Resources, 1998.

Anderson, Ray S. *The Soul of Ministry: Forming Leaders for God's People.* Louisville: Westminster John Knox Press, 1997.

Anderson, Robert C. *Circles of Influence.* Chicago: Moody Press, 1991.

Banks, Robert, and Bernice M. Ledbetter. *Reviewing Leadership: A Christian Evaluation of Current Approaches.* Grand Rapids: Baker Academic, 2004.

Barna, George. *A Fish Out of Water: 9 Strategies to Maximize Your God-Given Leadership Potential.* New York: Thomas Nelson, 2006.

––. *Leaders on Leadership.* Ventura, CA: Regal Books, 1997.

—. *The Habits of Highly Effective Churches: Being Strategic in Your God-Given Ministry.* Ventura: Regal, 2001.

—. *The Power of Team Leadership: Achieving Success through Shared Responsibility.* Colorado Springs: Water Brook Press, 2001.

—. *The Second Coming of the Church 1998.* Nashville: Word Publishing, 1998.

—. *Today's Pastors: A Revealing Look at What Pastors are Saying About Themselves, Their Peers, and the Pressures They Face.* Ventura: Regal Books, 1993.

—. *Turnaround Churches: How to Overcome Barriers to Growth and Bring New Life to An Established Church.* Ventura: Regal Books, 1993.

—. *User Friendly Churches.* Ventura: Regal Books, 1997.

Barna, George and William Paul Mckay. *Vital Signs—Emerging Social Trends and the Future of American Christianity.* Westchester: Crossway Books, 1985.

Bass, Bernard M. *Bass and Stogdill's Handbook of Leadership: Theory, Research, and Managerial Applications.* 3rd ed. New York: Free Press, 1990.

—. *Leadership and Performance Beyond Expectations.* New York: Free Press, 1985.

—. *Transformational Leadership: Industrial, Military, and Educational Impact.* Mahwah: Psychology Press, 1998.

Baxter, Richard. *The Reformed Pastor: A Pattern for Personal Growth and Ministry.* Portland: Multnomah Press, 1982.

Beebe, Walter S. *The Second Man: All About the Role, the Relationships, and the Responsibilities of a Staff Member in a Local Church.* Murfreesboro: Sword of the Lord Publishers, 1997.

Bellah, Robert. *The Good Society*. New York: Random House, 1991.

Bennis, Warren. *On Becoming a Leader*. Reading: Addison Wesley, 1989.

Berger, Peter L. *A Rumor of Angels: Modern Society and the Rediscovery of the Supernatural*. Garden City: Anchor, 1970.

—-. *The Sacred Canopy: Elements for a Sociological Theory of Religion*. Garden City, NY: Doubleday, 1967

—-. *The Sacred Canopy: Elements of a Sociological Theory of Religion*. New York: Anchor, 1990.

Berger, Peter L., and Thomas Luckmann. *The Social Construction of Reality: A Treatise in the Sociology of Knowledge*. New York: Anchor, 1967.

Berkley, James D., ed. *Leadership Handbooks of Practical Theology*. Grand Rapids: Baker Publishing Group, 1995.

Bisagno, John, R. *Letters to Timothy: A Handbook for Pastors*. B&H Books, 2001.

Blackaby, Henry T., Henry Brandt, and Kerry L. Skinner. *The Power of the Call*. Nashville: B&H Books, 1997.

Blackwood, Andrew Watterson. *Pastoral Leadership*. 1st ed. New York: Abingdon-Cokesbury Press, 1949.

Briskin, Alan. *The Stirring of Soul in the Workplace*. San Francisco: Berrett-Koehler Publishers, 1998.

Borden, William. *Living Like Benjamin: Making Dreams Come True*. Bloomington: Author House, 2007.

Brown, W. Steven *13 Fatal Errors Managers Make and How You Can Avoid Them*. 21st ed. New York: Berkley Books, 1985.

Bruce, Steve. *Religion in the Modern World: From Cathedrals to Cults*. Oxford: Oxford University Press USA, 1996.

Burkett, Larry. *Business by the Book: Complete Guide of Biblical Principles for the Workplace.* Nashville: Thomas Nelson, 2006.

Carroll, Jackson W., and Robert L. Wilson. *Too Many Pastors? The Clergy Job Market.* New York: Pilgrim Press, 1980.

Carson, D.A. *A Call to Spiritual Reformation: Priorities from Paul and His Prayers.* Grand Rapids: Baker Academic, 1992.

—-. *Exegetical Fallacies.* 2nd ed. Carlisle, UK: Baker Academic, 1996.

Callahan, Kennon L. *Twelve Keys to an Effective Church: Strong, Healthy Congregations Living in the Grace of God.* 2nd ed. San Francisco: Jossey-Bass, 2010.

Cedar, Paul, Kent Hughes, and Ben Patterson. *Mastering the Pastoral Role.* Portland: Thomas Nelson, 1993.

Chandler, Russell. *Racing Toward 2001.* Grand Rapids: Zondervan Publishing House, 1992.

Cladis, George. *Leading the Team-Based Church: How Pastors and Church Staffs Can Grow Together Into a Powerful Fellowship of Leaders.* San Francisco: Jossey-Bass, 1999.

Clinton, Bobby. *Spiritual Gifts.* Beaverlodge: Horizon Books Publishers, 1996.

Clinton, Robert. *The Making of a Leader: Recognizing the Lessons and Stages of Leadership Development.* 2nd ed. Colorado Springs: NavPress, 2012.

Collins, Jim, and Jerry I. Porras. *Built to Last: Successful Habits of Visionary Companies.* Harper Business Essentials. 3rd ed. New York: Harper Business, 1994.

Conger, Jay A., Rabindra N. Kanungo, and associates. *Charismatic Leadership: The Elusive Factor in Organizational Effectiveness.* San Francisco: Jossey-Bass, 1988.

Cousins, Don, Leith Anderson, and Arthur DeKruyter. *Mastering Church Management*. Portland: Thomas Nelson, 1993.

Criswell, W. A. *Criswell Guidebook for Pastors*. Nashville: B&H Books, 2000.

Dale, Robert D. *Leadership for a Changing Church: Charting the Shape of the River*. Nashville: Abingdon Press, 1998.

—-. *Pastoral Leadership: A Handbook of Resources for Effective Congregational Leadership*. Nashville: Abingdon Press, 2001.

Dawn, Marva J., and Eugene H. Peterson. *The Unnecessary Pastor: Rediscovering the Call*. Edited by Peter Santucci. Vancouver: William B. Eerdmans Publishing Company, 2000.

Davis, John J. *The Perfect Shepherd: Studies in the Twenty-Third Psalm*. Winona Lake: BMH Books, 1979.

David, Fisher. *The 21st Century Pastor*. Grand Rapids: Zondervan, 1996, 144-240.

Denzin, Norman K., and Yvonna S. Lincoln, eds. *Collecting and Interpreting Qualitative Materials*. 4thed. Thousand Oaks: SAGE Publications, 2012.

Denzin, Norman K., and Yvonna S. Lincoln, eds. *Handbook of Qualitative Research*. Thousand Oaks: SAGE Publications, 1994.

Dibbert, Michael T. *Spiritual Leadership, Responsible Management: A Guide for Leaders of the Church*. Grand Rapids: Zondervan, 1989.

Ditzen, Lowell Russell. *Handbook of Church Administration*. New York: Macmillan, 1962.

Dodd, Brian J. *Empowered Church Leadership: Ministry in the Spirit According to Paul*. Downers Grove: IVP Books, 2003.

Dr. Lynn Anderson, *They Smell Like Sheep: Spiritual Leadership for the 21st Century*. Howard Books, Louisiana, 1997, 1-248.

Durkheim, Emile. *The Elementary Forms of Religious Life*. New York: Free Press, 1995.

Easum, Bill. *Leadership on the Otherside*. Nashville: Abingdon Press, 2000.

Edwards, Gene. *The Organic Church vs the "New Testament" Church: Issues We Dare Not Face*. Jacksonville: Seed Sowers, 2007.

Edward C. Zaragoza. *No Longer Servants, But Friends: Theology of Ordained Ministry*. Nashville: Abingdon Press, 1999.

Engstrom, Ted. *The Making of a Christian Leader: How to Develop Management and Human Relations Skills*. 9th ed. Grand Rapids: Zondervan, 1978.

Eyres, Lawrence. *Elders of the Church*. Phillipsburg: P&R Publishing, 1975.

Finzel, Hans. *The Top Ten Mistakes Leaders Make*. Colorado Springs: David C. Cook, 2007.

Firet, Jacob. *Dynamics in Pastoring*. Grand Rapids: William B. Eerdmans Publishing Company, 1986.

Fitch, David E. *The Great Giveaway: Reclaiming the Mission of the Church from Big Business, Parachurch Organizations, Psychotherapy, Consumer Capitalism, and Other Modern Maladies*. Grand Rapids: Baker Books, 2005.

Flett, John G. *The Witness of God: The Trinity, Missio Dei, Karl Barth, and the Nature of Christian Community*. Grand Rapids: William B. Eerdmans Publishing Company, 2010.

Ford, Kevin G. Transforming Church: Bringing Out the Good to Get to Great. (David C Cook, 2008), 80-130.

Ford, Leighton. *Transforming Leadership: Jesus' Way of Creating Vision, Shaping Values and Empowering Change.* Downers Grove: IVP Books, 1993.

Fulton, Roger. *Common Sense Leadership: a Handbook for Success as a Leader.* Berkeley: Ten Speed Press, 1995.

Frame, John M. *The Doctrine of the Knowledge of God.* Phillipsburg: P&R Publishing, 1987.

Friesen, Garry. *Decision Making and the Will of God.* Portland: Multnomah, 1982.

Frye, John W. *Jesus the Pastor.* Grand Rapids: Zondervan, 2002.

Gangel, Kenneth O. *Team Leadership in Christian Ministry: Using Multiple Gifts to Build a Unified Vision.* Revised ed. Chicago: Moody Publishers, 1997.

Gardner, Howard E. *Leading Minds: An Anatomy of Leadership.* Reprint ed. New York: Basic Books, 2011.

George, Carl F. *Prepare Your Church for the Future.* Tarrytown: Revell, 1991.

Getz, Gene A. *Sharpening the Focus of the Church.* Revisedsubed. Wheaton: Victor Books, 1984.

Gibbs, Eddie. *Church next: Quantum Changes in How We Do Ministry.* Downers Grove: IVP Books, 2000.

Giddens, Anthony *Sociology.* 3rd ed. Cambridge: Polity, 1997.

Greenleaf, Robert K. *Servant Leadership: A Journey Into the Nature of Legitimate Power and Greatness.* New York: Paulist Press, 1977.

Groome, Thomas H. *Sharing Faith: A Comprehensive Approach to Religious Education and Pastoral Ministry: The Way of Shared Praxis*. San Francisco: Harper San Francisco, 1991.

Guinness, Os. *Dining with the Devil: The Mega church Movement Flirts with Modernity*. Grand Rapids: Baker Books, 1993.

Guder, Darrell L., ed. *Missional Church: A Vision for the Sending of the Church in North America*. Grand Rapids: William B. Eerdmans Publishing Company, 1998.

Hambrick, Donald C., David A. Nadler, and Michael L. Tushman, eds. *Navigating Change: How CEOs, Top Teams, and Boards Steer Transformation*. Boston: Harvard Business Press, 1998.

Haralambos, Michael, R.M. Heald, and Martin Holborn. *Sociology: Themes and Perspectives*. 7th ed. London: Collins Educational, 2000.

Heenan, David A., and Warren Bennis.*Co-Leaders: The Power of Great Partnerships*. New York: Wiley, 1999.

Hedahl, Susan K. *Listening Ministry: Rethinking Pastoral Leadership*. Minneapolis: Fortress Press, 2001.

Hendricks, William D. *Exit Interviews*. Chicago: Moody Press, 1993.

Hendrix, Olan. *Three Dimensions of Leadership*. St.Charles: Churchsmart Resources, 2000.

Heuser, Roger, and Norman Shawchuck. *Leading the Congregation: Caring for Yourself While Serving the People*. Revised ed. Nashville: Abingdon Press, 2010.

Hughes, Richard L., Robert C. Ginnett, and Gordon J. Curphy. *Leadership: Enhancing the Lessons of Experience*. 7th ed. New York: McGraw-Hill/Irwin, 2012.

Hull, Bill. *Revival That Reforms: Making It Last*. Grand Rapids: Fleming H. Revell Company, 1998.

Hunter, Harold D. *Spirit Baptism: A Pentecostal Alternative*. Lanham: Wipf and Stock Publishers, 2009.

Hunt, James G. *Leadership: A New Synthesis*. Newbury Park: SAGE Publications, 1991.

Hutcheson, Richard G., and Jr. *Wheel Within the Wheel: Confronting the Management Crisis of the Pluralistic Church*. Atlanta: John Knox Press, 1979.

Hybels, Lynne, and Bill Hybels. *Rediscovering Church*. Grand Rapids: Zondervan, 1997.

Hybels, Bill. *Courageous Leadership: Field-Tested Strategy for the 360° Leader*. Reprint ed. Grand Rapids: Zondervan, 2012.

Hybels, Bill, Stuart Briscoe and Haddon Robinson. *Mastering Contemporary Preaching*. Portland: Multnomah Press, 1989.

Hirsch, Michael Frost & Alan. *The Shaping of Things to Come: Innovation and Mission for the 21st-Century Church*. Peabody: Hendrickson Pub, 2003.

Jackson, John. *Pastorpreneur*. Friendswood: Baxter Press, 2003.

Jefferson, Charles. *The Minister as Shepherd*. Fort Washington: Christian Literature Crusade, 1998.

—-. *The Minister as Shepherd: The Privileges and Responsibilities of Pastoral Leadership*. Fort Washington: Christian Literature Crusade, 2006.

Johnson, Ben Campbell. *Pastoral Spirituality: A Focus for Ministry*. Philadelphia: Westminster John Knox Press, 1988.

Jones, Bruce W. *Ministerial Leadership in a Managerial World*. Wheaton: Tyndale House Publishers, 1988.

Jones, Laurie Beth. *Jesus CEO: Using Ancient Wisdom for Visionary Leadership*. New York: Hyperion Books, 1995.

Jones, Ilion. *Principles and Practice of Preaching*. New York: Abingdon Press, 2001.

Judy, Marvin T. *The Multiple Staff Ministry*. Nashville: Abingdon Press, 1969.

Kanter, Rosabeth Moss. *The Change Masters: Innovations for Productivity in the American Corporation*. New York: Simon & Schuster, 1983.

Katzenbach, Jon R., and Douglas K. Smith. *The Wisdom of Teams: Creating the High-Performance Organization*. New York: Harper Business, 2006.

Keller, W. Phillip. *The Shepherd Trilogy: A Shepherd Looks at the 23rd Psalm / A Shepherd Looks at the Good Shepherd / A Shepherd Looks at the Lamb of God*. Grand Rapids: Zondervan, 1996.

Kilinski, Kenneth K. *Organization and Leadership in the Local Church*. Grand Rapids: Zondervan, 1973.

Kouzes, James M., and Barry Z. Posner. *Credibility: How Leaders Gain and Lose It, Why People Demand It*. San Francisco: Jossey-Bass, 2011.

—-. *The Leadership Challenge: How to Make Extraordinary Things Happen in Organizations*. 5th ed. San Francisco: Jossey-Bass, 2012.

Kyle, Richard. *Evangelicalism: An Americanized Christianity*. Edison, NJ: Transaction Publishers, 2006.

Labovitz, George, and Rosansky, Victor. *The Power of Alignment: How Great Companies Stay Centered and Accomplish Extraordinary Things*. New York: John Wiley & Sons Inc, 1997.

Landy, Frank, and Jeffrey Conte. *Work in the 21ˢᵗ Century—An Introduction to Industrial and Organizational Psychology.* Boston: McGraw-Hill, 2004.

Lencioni, Patrick M. *The Five Dysfunctions of a Team.* San Francisco: John Wiley & Sons, 2002.

Lewis, Phillip V. *Transformational Leadership: A New Model for Total Church Involvement.* Nashville: Broadman & Holman Publishers, 1996.

Longenecker, Harold L. *Growing Leaders by Design: How to Use Biblical Principles for Leadership Development.* Grand Rapids: Kregel Pubns, 1995.

Lovelace, Richard F. *Dynamics of Spiritual Life: An Evangelical Theology of Renewal.* Downers Grove: IVP Academic, 1979.

Malphurs, Aubrey. *Pouring New Wine Into Old Wineskins: How to Change a Church Without Destroying It.* Grand Rapids: Baker Publishing Group, 1993.

—-.*Values-Driven Leadership: Discovering and Developing Your Core Values for Ministry.* 2ⁿᵈ ed. Grand Rapids: Baker Books, 2004.

Manz, Charles C. *The Leadership Wisdom of Jesus: Practical Lessons for Today.* 3ʳᵈ ed. San Francisco: Berrett-Koehler Publishers, 2011.

Martineau, Scott. *The Power of You! How You Can Create Happiness, Balance, and Wealth.* Hoboken: Wiley, 2006.

Maxwell, John C. *Developing the Leader Within You.* Grand Rapids: Thomas Nelson, 2005.

—-. *Developing the Leaders Around You: How to Help Others Reach Their Full Potential.* Nashville: Thomas Nelson, 2005.

—. *Failing Forward: Turning Mistakes Into Stepping Stones for Success.* Reprint ed. Nashville: Thomas Nelson, 2007.

—. *The 21 Irrefutable Laws of Leadership: Follow Them and People Will Follow You.* Nashville: Thomas Nelson, 2007.

McGavran, Donald *Bridges of God: A Study in the Strategy of Missions.* Eugene: Wipf and Stock Publishers, 2005.

McIntosh, Gary L., and Glen Martin. *The Issachar Factor: Understanding Trends That Confront Your Church and Designing a Strategy for Success.* Nashville: B&H Books, 1999.

McIntosh, Gary L. *Biblical Church Growth: How You Can Work with God to Build a Faithful Church.* Grand Rapids: Baker Books, 2003.

—. *Evaluating the Church Growth Movement: 5 Views.* Counterpoints: Church Life. Grand Rapids: Zondervan, 2010.

—. *One Size Doesn't Fit All: Bringing Out the Best in Any Size Church.* Grand Rapids: Revell, 1999.

—. *Staff Your Church for Growth: Building Team Ministry in the 21st Century.* Grand Rapids: Baker Books, 2000.

McNeal, Reggie. *A Work of Heart: Understanding How God Shapes Spiritual Leaders.* Updated ed. San Francisco: Jossey-Bass, 2011.

—. *Revolution in Leadership: Training Apostles for Tomorrow's Church.* Nashville: Abingdon Press, 1998.

—. *The Present Future: Six Tough Questions for the Church.* Jossey-Bass Leadership Network Series. San Francisco: Jossey-Bass, 2009.

Means, James E. *Effective Pastors for a New Century: Helping Leaders Strategize for Success.* Grand Rapids: Baker Publishing Group, 1993.

Mellado, James. *Willow Creek Community Church*. N.p.: Harvard Business School, 1991.

Merkle, Benjamin L. *The Elder and the Overseer*. Studies in Biblical Literature, vol. 57. New York: Peter Lang International Academic Publishers, 2003.

Messer, Donald E. *Contemporary Images of Christian Ministry*. Nashville: Abingdon Press, 1989.

Miller, Calvin. *The Empowered Leader: 10 Keys to Servant Leadership*. Grand Rapids: B&H Academic, 1997.

Mohrman, Susan Albers, Susan G. Cohen, and Allan M. Mohrman, Jr. *Designing Team-Based Organizations: New Forms for Knowledge Work*. San Francisco: Jossey-Bass, 1995.

Mounce, William D. *The Analytical Lexicon to the Greek New Testament*. Grand Rapids: Zondervan Publishing House, 1993

Myra, Harold, ed., *Leaders: Learning Leadership from Some of Christianity's Best*. The Leadership Library. Waco: Word Books, 1987.

Naisbitt, John & Aburdene, Patricia. *Megatrends 2000: Ten New Directions for the 1990's*. Book club ed. New York: William Morrow and Company, Inc., 1990.

Nanus, Burt. *Visionary Leadership, Creating a Compelling Sense of Direction for Your Organization,*. San Francisco: Jossey-Bass, 1992.

Nouwen, Henri J.M. *The Living Reminder: Service and Prayer in Memory of Jesus Christ*. San Francisco: HarperOne, 2009.

Nouwen, Henri J.M. *In the Name of Jesus: Reflections on Christian Leadership with Study Guide for Groups and Individuals*. New York: The Crossroad Publishing Company, 2002. 60

--. *The Way of the Heart*. Reprint ed. New York: Ballantine Books, 2003.

Oakley, Ed. *Enlightened Leadership*. New York: Simon, 1991.

Oates, Wayne E. *The Christian Pastor*. 3rd ed. Philadelphia: Westminster John Knox Press, 1982.

Oden, Thomas C. *Becoming a Minister*. Vol. 1 of the Classical Pastoral Care Series. Grand Rapids: Baker Book House, 2000.

—. *Pastoral Theology: Essentials of Ministry*. San Francisco: HarperOne, 1983.

Ogden, Greg. *The New Reformation*. Grand Rapids: Zondervan Publishing Company, 1991.

Orr, James. *The Christian View of God and the World*. New York: Charles Scribners's Sons, 1908.

Palmieri, Carl Tuchy. *Satisfying Success: And the Ways to Achieve It*. Charleston: BookSurge Publishing, 2009.

Patton, John H. *From Ministry to Theology: Pastoral Action & Reflection*. Eugene: Wipf and Stock Publishers, 2009.

Perry, Lloyd M. *Biblical Preaching for Today's World,*. Chicago: Moody Press, 1973.

Peterson, Eugene H. *Five Smooth Stones for Pastoral Work*. Grand Rapids: William B. Eerdmans Publishing Company, 1992.

—. *The Contemplative Pastor: Returning to the Art of Spiritual Direction*. Grand Rapids: William B. Eerdmans Publishing Company, 1993.

—. *Under the Unpredictable Plant: An Exploration in Vocational Holiness*. Grand Rapids: Eerdmans Publishing Company, 1994.

—. *Working the Angles: The Shape of Pastoral Integrity*. Grand Rapids: William B. Eerdmans Publishing Company, 1989.

Pickett, J. Waskom. *Christian Mass Movements in India*. New York: The Abingdon Press, 1933.

Postman, Neil. *Amusing Ourselves to Death*. New York: Penguin Books, 1985.

—-. *Amusing Ourselves to Death*. London: Methuen Publishing Ltd, 1987.

Prime, Derek J., and Alistair Begg. *On Being a Pastor: Understanding Our Calling and Work*. Chicago: Moody Publishers, 2013.

Quicke, Michael J. *360 Degree Preaching*. Grand Rapids: Baker Academic Books, 2003.

Rainer, Thom S. *The Book of Church Growth*. New York: B&H Academic, 1998.

Renz, David O., ed. *The Jossey-Bass Handbook of Nonprofit Leadership and Management*. 3rd ed. San Francisco: Jossey-Bass, 2010.

Richards, Lawrence O., and Clyde Hoeldtke. *A Theology of Church Leadership*. Grand Rapids: Zondervan, 1980.

Ritzer, George. *The Mcdonaldization of Society*. New Century ed. Thousand Oaks: SAGE Publications, 2000.

—-. *The Weberian Theory of Rationalization and the McDonaldization of Contemporary Society, Chapter 2, The McDonaldization of Society*. Pine Forge Press, Revised ed. 1996, http://www.corwin.com/upm-data/16567_Chapter_2.pdf.

Rost, Joseph. *Leadership for the Twenty-First Century*. New York: Praeger, 1991.

—-. *Leadership for the Twenty-First Century*. New York: Praeger, 1993.

Roxburgh, Alan, and Mike Regele. *Crossing the Bridge: Church Leadership in a Time of Change*. San Diego: Percept Group, 2000.

Sanders, J. Oswald. *Spiritual Leadership*. Chicago: Moody Press, 1974.

Saucy, Robert L. *The Church in God's Program (Handbook of Bible Doctrine)*. Wheaton: Moody Publishers, 1972.

Schaller, Lyle E. *Discontinuity and Hope*. Nashville, TN: Abingdon, 1999.

—. *Effective Church Planning*. Nashville: Abingdon Press, 1979.

—. *The Multiple Staff and the Larger Church*. Nashville: Abingdon Press, 1980.

Schwarz, Christian A. *Natural Church Development: A Guide to Eight Essential Qualities of Healthy Churches*. St. Charles: ChurchSmart Resources, 1996.

—. *The ABC's of Natural Church Development Booklet*. Carol Stream: ChurchSmart Resources, 1998.

Schwarz, Christian A., and Christoph Schalk. *Implementation Guide to Natural Church Development*. Carol Stream: ChurchSmart Resources, 1998.

Sherer, Robert D. *Fear: The Corporate*. Thousand Oaks: Criterion House, 1997.

Shelp, Earl E., and Ronald H. Sunderland. *The Pastor as Servant*. New York: Pilgrim Pr,1986.

Snyder, Howard A. *Liberating the Church: The Ecology of Church and Kingdom*. Downers Grove, IL: InterVarsity Press, 1983, 200-300

—. *The Problem of Wine Skins: Church Structure in a Technological Age*. Downers Grove: Intervarsity Press, 1975.

Luecke, David S., and Samuel Southard. *Pastoral Administration: Integrating Ministry and Management in the Church*. Waco: Word Books, 1986.

Schuller, David S., Merton P. Strommen, and Milo L. Brekke. Ministry in America. San Francisco: Harper & Row Publishers. 1980.

Stetzer, Ed. *Planting Missional Churches*. Nashville: B&H Academic, 2006.

Stetzer, Ed, and Mike Dodson. *Comeback Churches: How 300 Churches Turned Around and Yours Can, Too*. Nashville: B&H Books, 2007.

Stewart, Carlyle Fielding, III. *The Empowerment Church: Speaking a New Language for Church Growth*. Nashville: Abingdon Press, 2001.

Strobel, Lee. *Inside the Mind of Unchurched Harry and Mary: How to Reach Friends and Family Who Avoid God and the Church*. Grand Rapids: Zondervan, 1993.

Stowell, Joseph M. *Shepherding the Church Into the 21st Century*. Wheaton: Victor Books, 1994.

Strang, Stephen E. *Solving the Ministry's Toughest Problems, Volume One*. Alamonte Springs: Strang, 1984.

Strom, Mark. *Reframing Paul: Conversations in Grace and Community*. Downers Grove: IVP Academic, 2000.

Summerton, Neil. *Noble Task: Eldership and Ministry in the Local Church*. Exeter: Paternoster P., 1987.

Sumner C. Wemp. The Guide to Practical Pastoring. Nashville: Thomas Nelson, 1982.

Tichy, Noel, and EliCohen. *The Leadership Engine: How Winning Companies Build Leaders at Every Level*. New York: HarperCollins Publishers, 1997.

Tidball, Derek J. *Skillful Shepherds: An Introduction to Pastoral Theology*. Grand Rapids: Zondervan, 1986.

Towns, Elmer L., Ed Stetzer, and Warren Bird. *11 Innovations in the Local Church*. Ventura: Regal, 2007.

Towns, Elmer L. *An Inside Look at 10 of Today's Most Innovative Churches: What They're Doing, How They're Doing It & How You Can Apply Their Ideas in Your Church*. Ventura: Regal Books, 1991.

Vaughan, John N. *The Large Church: A Twentieth-Century Expression of the First-Century Church*. Grand Rapids: Baker Publishing Group, 1985.

Viola, Frank. *Finding Organic Church: A Comprehensive Guide to Starting and Sustaining Authentic Christian Communities*. Colorado Springs: David C. Cook, 2009.

Viola, Frank, and George Barna. *Pagan Christianity?* Carol Stream: Tyndale House Publishers, 2002.

—-. *Pagan Christianity? Exploring the Roots of Our Church Practices*. Tyndale House Publishers, Inc. 2010.

Viola, Frank. *Reimagining Church: Pursuing the Dream of Organic Christianity*. Colorado Springs: David C. Cook, 2008.

Wagner, E. Glenn. *Escape from Church, Inc*. Grand Rapids: Zondervan, 2001.

Wagner, Peter. *Your Church Can Grow: Seven Vital Signs of a Health Church*. Glendale: Regal Books, 1976.

Waller, Ted. H. *With the Sheep in the Wilderness: Shepherding God's Flock in the World*. Nashville: Twentieth Century Publishers, 1991.

Walton, Steve. *Leadership and Lifestyle: The Portrait of Paul in the Miletus Speech and 1 Thessalonians*. Cambridge: Cambridge University Press, 2000.

Warren, Rick. *The Purpose Driven Church: Growth Without Compromising Your Message & Mission*. Grand Rapids: Zondervan, 1995.

Webber, Robert E. *The Younger Evangelicals: Facing the Challenges of the New World*. Grand Rapids: Baker Books, 2002.

Wells, David F. *No Place for Truth, Or, Whatever Happened to Evangelical Theology?* Grand Rapids: William B. Eerdmans Publishing Company, 1993.

Whitesel, Bob. *Growth by Accident, Death by Planning: How Not to Kill a Growing Congregation*. Nashville: Abingdon Press, 2004.

Whitesel, Bob, and Kent R. Hunter. *A House Divided: Bridging the Generation Gaps in Your Church*. Nashville: Abingdon Press, 2001.

Wilkes, C. Gene. *Jesus On Leadership*. Wheaton: Tyndale House Publishers, Inc., 1998.

Wilkins, Michael J. *Following the Master: Discipleship in the Steps of Jesus*. Grand Rapids: Zondervan, 1992.

Willimon, William H. *Pastor: The Theology and Practice of Ordained Ministry*. Nashville: Abingdon Press, 2002.

Wofford, Jerry C. *Transforming Christian Leadership: 10 Exemplary Church Leaders*. Grand Rapids: Baker Publishing Group, 1999.

Wren, J. Thomas. *The Leader's Companion: Insights On Leadership through the Ages*. New York: Free Press, 1995.

Wright, Walter C. *Relational Leadership*. Waynesboro: Paternoster, 2002.

Young, David S. *Servant Leadership for Church Renewal: Shepherds by the Living Springs*. Scottdale: Herald Pr, 1999.

Yukl, Gary. *Leadership in Organizations*. 8th ed. Upper Saddle River: Prentice Hall, 2013.

Dissertations and Unpublished Works

Anthony P. Celelli. "The Just Pastor: An Ethical Hermeneutic Of Biblical Justice, Positional Power Theory, And The Theology And Practice Of Pastoral Leadership." ProQuest, 2012

Dunahoo, Charles. "Team Building Key to Church Growth." PhD diss., Westminster Theological Seminary, 1999.

Fidati, David. "Building a Unified Leadership Team." PhD diss., Covenant Theological Seminary, 1998.

Fletcher, David. "Case-Studies of Policy and Vision Implementation by the Executive Pastor." PhD diss., Dallas Theological Seminary, 2004.

Hip, Guy. "A Strategy for Building a Large Staff in a Large Church." PhD diss., Southwestern Baptist Theological Seminary, 1993.

Pritchard, G. "The Strategy of Willow Creek Community Church: A Study in the Sociology of Religion." PhD diss., Northwestern University, 1994.

Taylor, Richard. "Team Leadership." PhD diss., Westminster Theological Seminary, 1994.

Thumma, Scott. "The Kingdom, the Power, and the Glory: The Mega Church in Modern American Society." diss., Emory University, 1996.

Turner, Wendy. "Team and Hierarchical Leadership in Multiple Staff Churches." Master's thesis, Trinity Evangelical Divinity School, 1992.

Woodruff, Timothy. "Executive Pastor's Perceptions of Leadership and Management Competencies Needed for Local Church Administration." PhD diss., Southern Baptist Theological Seminary, 2004.

Articles

Bargiol, William "Role Change from Single Staff to Multistaff Church." *Church Administration* 39, no. 4 (January 1997): 33–35.

Butler, Martin, and Robert C. Herman. "Effective Ministerial Leadership." *Non-Profit Management and Leadership* 9, no. 3 (Spring1999): 229–39.

Carifio, James, and Rocco J. Perla. "Ten Common Misunderstandings, Misconceptions, Persistent Myths and Urban Legends About Likert Scales and Likert Response Formats and Their Antidotes." *Journal of Social Sciences* 3, no. 3 (2007): 106–16.

Chandler, Russell. Racing Toward 2001: The Forces Shaping America's Religious Future. Grand Rapids: Zondervan Publishing House, 1992.

Ciampa, Dan, and Michael Watkins. "The Successor's Dilemma." *Harvard Business Review* 77, no. 4 (November–December 1999): 161–68.

Cook, Elizabeth, "Would You Like Your Jesus Upsized? McDonaldization and the Mega Church." *University of Tennessee, Knoxville Trace: Tennessee Research and Creative Exchange.* 2002. 10-36 http://trace.tennessee.edu/utk_interstp2/85

Dobson, Ed, and Jim Buick. "Two-Part Harmony." *Leadership* 16, no. 1 (1995): 18–24.

Dobbelaere, Karel. "Secularization: A Multi-Dimensional Concept." *Current Sociology* 29, no. 2 (1981): 1–213.

Drucker, Peter. "The Shape of Things to Come." *Leader to Leader*, no. 1 (Summer 1996): 12–18.

Foote, Nelson N. "Parsonian Theory of Family Process: Family, Socialization and Interaction Process." *Sociometry* 19, no. 1 (1956): 40–46. http://www.jstor.org/stable/2786102.

Gopez-Sindac, Rez. "The CE Interview Dr. David Fletcher." *Church Executive Magazine*, July 2004. http://www.churchexecutive.com.

Gronn, Peter. "Substituting for Leadership the Neglected Role of the Leadership Couple." *Leadership Quarterly* 10, no. 1 (Spring1999): 41–62.

Hamilton, Michael S. "Willow Creek's Place in History." *Christianity Today*, November 13, 2000, 62–68.

Hinson, Glenn. "The Spiritual Formation of the Minister." *Review and Expositor* 83, (Fall 1986): 587–95.

Holland, Henry S. Creed and Character; Sermons. Read Books, 2008.

Jackson, John. "How to Be a Pastor and Manager." *The Christian Ministry* 20, 1989.

Kalmijn, Matthijs. "Shifting Boundaries: Trends in Religious and Educational Homogamy." *American Sociological Review* 56, no. 6 (Dec, 1991): 786–800. Accessed September 29, 2013.http://www.jstor.org/stable/2096256.

Kennedy, Diane. "A Contextual Theology of Leadership." *Theological Education* 37, no. 1, 2000, 67

Koenig, John. "Hierarchy Transfigured Perspectives On Leadership in the New Testament." *Word and World XIII*, (Winter 1993): 26–33.

Kolden, Marc. "A Lutheran Understanding of Pastoral Ministry Implications for Pastors and Congregations." *Word and World XIII*, (Winter 1993): 6–12.

Kotter, John. "What Leaders Really Do." *Harvard Business Review* 68, no. 3 (1990):103–111.

Litfin, Duane. "The Nature of the Pastoral Role: The Leader as Completer." *Bibliotheca Sacra* 139 (January–March 1982): 57–66.

McDonald, John. "Teaching Pastors to Lead." *Christianity Today*, 5 February 2001. Accessed September 15, 2013. http://seminarygradschool.com/article/Teaching-Pastors-to-Lead.

McDowell, Clyde. "Ten Ways to Support Your Staff." *Vital Ministries* 1, no. 3 (January–February 1998): 38–41.

Mitchell, Preston. "The CE Interview Preston Mitchell." *Church Executive Magazine* 3, no. 9 (September 2004): 10–13.

Morrison, Gregg. "Being a Pastor Today." *Christianity Today*, 5 February 2001. Accessed September 15, 2013. http://seminarygradschool.com/article/The-Changing-Landscape-of-Pastoral-Leadership.

Neff, David. "Going to the Movies." *Christianity Today*, February 19, 2001.

Nelson, Alan. "Home Grown Staff." *Vital Ministries* 1, no. 3 (January–February 1998): 26–29.

—-. *Leading Your Ministry: A Moment of Insight is Worth a Lifetime of Experience.* Leadership Insight Series. Edited by Herb Miller. Nashville: Abingdon Press, 1996.

Ray, Diana. "High Tech Enhances Old-Time Religion." *Insight on the News*, July 31, 2000.

Reid, Topper. "Building Teamship in the Church Staff." *Growing Churches* 7, no. 1 (Fall 1996): 32–34.

Schaller, Lyle E. "A New Day Calls for New Initiatives." *The Clergy Journal* 70, no. 7 (May–June 1994): 11–12.

Siler, Mahan. "Leaves from a Pastoral Notebook." *Review and Expositor* 83 (Fall 1986): 521–33.

Simmons, Paul. "Priorities in Christian Ministry." *Review and Expositor* 83 (Fall 1986): 535–43.

Spicer, Gearl. "Church Staff Team Building." *Growing Churches* 7, no. 2 (Winter 1997): 34–35.

Stafford, Tim. "The Third Coming of George Barna." *Christianity Today*,5 August 2002,34.

Story, Jeff. "Team Building and Lay Leadership." *Church Administration* 39, no. 4 (January 1997): 30–33.

Sull, Donald. "Why Good Companies Go Bad." *Harvard Business Review* 77, no. 4 (July–August 1999): 34–41.

Thompson, Mervin E. "Leadership for Growth." *Word & World*13 (Winter 1993): 25.

White, Ernest "The Crisis of Christian Leadership." *Review and Expositor* 83 (1989): 545–57.

Wheeler, Barbara "What Kind of Leadership for Tomorrow's Churches?" *Word and World XIII*, (Winter 1993): 34–41.

Cassette Recordings

Hybels, Bill. *Creating a Volunteer Intensive Organization.* 1997.Willow Creek Association DF9704. Audiocassette.

Internet/Online

Blake, Morrison, "Why do we do it?" The Guardian, October 14, 2002, accessed on September 26, 2013 http://www.theguardian.com/theguardian/2002/oct/14/features11.g2

Brentm Riggs, Godly Leadership – Character Traits 1 – Part 2, BrentRiggs (blog), accessed on September 16, 2013 http://www.brentriggsblog.com/2009/08/godly-leadership-character-traits-1-part-2/

William Bridges and Associates. Accessed October 27, 2013. http://www.wmbridges.com.

Cascione, Jack. "Dallas Paper Reports as LCMS Mega Church Competes Against New Giant Baptist Mega Church." Luther Quest. Accessed October 19, 2013. http://www.lutherquest.org/walther/articles/-400/jmc00040.htm.

—. "Traditional LCMS Mission Congregation Keeps Growing." Luther Quest. Last modified June 12, 2000.http://www.lutherquest.org/walther/articles/jmc00157.htm.

Dobbelaere, Karel. "Bryan Wilson's Contributions to the Study of Secularization." *Social Compass* 53, no. 2 (June 2006): 141–46. Accessed October 27, 2013. http://scp.sagepub.com/content/53/2/141.abstract.

Driscoll, Mark, and Chris Seay. "A Second Reformation is at Hand." *Youth Specialties*, October 2009. Accessed October 19, 2013. http://youthspecialties.com/articles/a-second-reformation-is-at-hand/.

"Peter Drucker's Life and Legacy." The Drucker Institute. Accessed October 27, 2013. http://www.druckerinstitute.com/link/about-peter-drucker/.

Kaleem, Jaweed. "Best Paid Pastors Make Hundreds Of Thousands To Millions Of Dollars Annually." *Huffington Post*, January 19, 2012. Accessed June 23, 2013. http://www.huffingtonpost.com/2012/01/19/best-paid-pastors_n_1214043.html.

Kapp, Lauren. "God on a Grand Scale," *abcnews.com*, December 3, 2001.

"Max De Pree." Max De Pree Center for Leadership. Last modified November 1, 1976, Accessed October 27, 2013. http://depree.org/max-de-pree/.

Piper, John. "Christian Elders in the New Testament." Desiring God. Accessed October 12, 2013. http://www.desiringgod.org/articles/christian-elders-in-the-new-testament.

Schooley, Keith "What is a Pastor?" *Quodlibet Journal* 2, no. 2 (Spring 2000): add page number. http://www.quodlibet.net/articles/schooley-pastor.shtml.

Simons, Menno. "Complete Writings." Menno Simons.net. Accessed November 9, 2013. http://www.mennosimons.net/completewritings.html.

—-. "True Christian Faith." Menno Simons.net. Accessed November 9, 2013. http://www.mennosimons.net/ft022-truechristianfaith.html.

"Steven A. Lineberger." *Bloomberg Businessweek*, n.d. Accessed June 23, 2013. http://investing.businessweek.com/research/stocks/people/person.asp?personId=24001424&ticker=KKD.

The Pastoral Office of the Modern Church is not Biblical. Hub pages, 2014, accessed on September 24, 2013, http://planksandnails.hubpages.com/hub/The-Pastoral-Office-is-not-Biblical

Viola, Frank. "Why Organic Church Is Not Exactly a Movement." *Christianity Today*, January 2010. Accessed November 9, 2013. http://www.christianitytoday.com/ct/2010/januaryweb-only/12.31.0.html?paging=off.

Walter, Scott. "The Land of Big Religion." *The American Enterprise* (October 2000): 37–39. Accessed October 19, 2013. http://www.unz.org/Pub/AmEnterprise-2000oct-00037?View=PDF.

Wikipedia contributors. "Bob Buford." *Wikipedia, The Free Encyclopedia*. Accessed October 26, 2013. http://en.wikipedia.org/wiki/Bob_Buford.

Wikipedia contributors. "Differentiation (sociology)." *Wikipedia, The Free Encyclopedia*. July 2, 2013. http://en.wikipedia.org/wiki/Differentiation_(sociology).

Wikipedia contributors. "J. Waskom Pickett." *Wikipedia, The Free Encyclopedia*. June 30, 2013. http://en.wikipedia.org/wiki/J._Waskom_Pickett.

Wikipedia contributors. "James Orr (theologian)." *Wikipedia, The Free Encyclopedia*. Accessed November 24, 2013. http://en.wikipedia.org/wiki/James_Orr_(theologian).

Wikipedia contributors. "Max Weber." *Wikipedia, The Free Encyclopedia*. Accessed October 27, 2013. http://en.wikipedia.org/wiki/Max_Weber.

Wikipedia contributors. "Seventy (LDS Church)." *Wikipedia, The Free Encyclopedia*. Accessed June 30, 2013. http://en.wikipedia.org/wiki/Quorums_of_the_Seventy.

Wikipedia contributors. "Simone Weil." *Wikipedia, The Free Encyclopedia*. Accessed November 9, 2013. http://en.wikipedia.org/wiki/Simone_Weil.

Wikipedia contributors. "Sociology of Religion." *Wikipedia, The Free Encyclopedia*. Accessed December 1, 2013. http://en.wikipedia.org/wiki/Sociology_of_religion.

Wikipedia contributors. "Word of Wisdom." *Wikipedia, The Free Encyclopedia*. Accessed June 30, 2013. http://en.wikipedia.org/wiki/Word_of_Wisdom.

Wikipedia contributors. "Young Men (organization)." *Wikipedia, The Free Encyclopedia*. Accessed June 30, 2013. http://en.wikipedia.org/wiki/Young_Men_(organization).

Printed in the United States
By Bookmasters